Unite

Peter Ridsdale, a renowned businessman, is one of football's most colourful and controversial characters. Born and bred in Yorkshire, he was the ardent Leeds United supporter who was a non-executive director at the club from 1992 to 1997, when he took the helm as chairman; a tenure that lasted five years until his resignation in 2003.

In those five unforgettable years under his stewardship, Leeds reached the semi-finals of the UEFA Cup in 1999–2000, and then the Champion's League in 2000–1, and never finished lower than fifth in the FA Premiership League.

Peter is currently the chairman of Championship side Cardiff City, but still lives in northern England with his family.

Peter Ridsdale

UNITED WE FALL

BOARDROOM TRUTHS ABOUT THE BEAUTIFUL GAME

PAN BOOKS

First published 2007 by Macmillan

First published in paperback 2008 with a new chapter by Pan Books
an imprint of Pan Macmillan Ltd
Pan Macmillan, 20 New Wharf Road, London N1 9RR
Basingstoke and Oxford
Associated companies throughout the world
www.panmacmillan.com

ISBN 978-0-330-46130-6

1 3 5 7 9 8 6 4 2

A CIP catalogue record for this book is available from
the British Library.

Typeset by SetSystems Ltd, Saffron Walden, Essex
Printed in the UK by CPI Mackays, Chatham, ME5 8TD

Visit **www.panmacmillan.com** to read more about all our books
and to buy them. You will also find features, author interviews and
news of any author events, and you can sign up for e-newsletters
so that you're always first to hear about our new releases.

Contents

Preface

My wife, Sophie, recently bought me a cushion, embroidered with the words: 'Life is a game. Football is more serious.'

It's not quite Shankley-esque with its matters of life and death. But the reality for anyone involved in the game is just as profound. And you don't have to be a player, manager or chairman to be 'involved'. I can think of no greater involvement than being a fan; involved *without* the messy politics or business of football, and merely consumed by its highs and lows and end-of-season run-ins. Sophie has learned to understand just how important football is to me, whether as a fan or chairman, and she's like millions of other long-suffering football widows, vicariously eating, sleeping and breathing the game because of the world and man she married. Her cushion could easily fit in at millions of homes around Britain. You, of course, might simply see me as just another corporate suit in football and maybe that's one reason why I'm writing this book: because my story, for a long time, was no different than anyone else's on the terraces and in the main stands. I was the ordinary fan who found himself in an extraordinary position – handed an opportunity on a plate to get truly involved with my club at board level.

I'm not sure it matters, anyway, whether you wear a suit or jeans. It's not status or attire that marks out the true football fanatics: it's our universal behaviour, habits and passion. It doesn't matter which club you support, or what division you're in, we're all the same. Football is the one God, and the clubs are the varying churches of our different religions. And we all pray like mad when the weekend comes.

My clock-watching world has revolved around – and some would say is ruled by – 3 p.m. on a Saturday, 4 p.m. on a Sunday, or 8 p.m. on a Monday; not forgetting the rush home from dinner, or the halting of social activities, on a weekend night, to watch, uninterrupted, *Match of the Day*. And, like anyone else, if we can't watch – because there's a family wedding, an anniversary or it's Valentine's Day or something else equally inconvenient yet unavoidable – we make damn sure it's videoed so we can watch it as soon as we get in, or first thing in the morning before the kids get up. It's been like that for millions of us since the 1980s.

We're all the same. We sit there with our glossy programmes, on the train, in the car or back at home, working out how the latest results have altered the tables. We flick on Teletext when we get home, or maybe the internet, to confirm our calculations on points and positions; how many points needed to make Europe, or the play-offs, or to avoid relegation?

Then, in the morning papers, we'll double-check it all, note the match attendances, read what the manager has to say and scrutinize next week's games, already forecasting the scores in our heads, giving ourselves three points and our nearest rivals a shock defeat, thus sending us back to the tables to work out the points we'd completely invented, and where that would then leave us in the league.

The eternal optimists among us won't let a mid-table position ruin our dreamy equations because we'll convince ourselves that one good run of six or seven back-to-back wins, with other results going our way, and miracles happening, could mean sneaking qualification, or reaching safety. Only for April to come along with all its mathematical realities to burst our over-inflated bubble.

Football fans: creatures of annoying habit or superstition, students of statistics and match facts, and sufferers of obsessive compulsive disorder, week in, week out.

If you're like me, you'll gladly sit back in the armchair, flick on Sky Sports, and watch either Manchester United v Chelsea, or Wrexham v Barnet. Football is mesmerizing whatever the game. I can associate with the fervour and passion that sustain the game on any level, having been there and done that – from my days playing in goal for Adel Memorial Hall FC in a Yorkshire Sunday league through to supporting Leeds United in the FA Premiership. I know what it is to get the bug with home games, then evolve into a home-and-away supporter, and then become an obsessive, determined not to miss a single game; to out-attend the biggest anorak on the supporters' coach; to develop an encyclopaedic statistical knowledge that leaves others gasping.

Yet we remain the same: *real* fans; those hard-core followers who belong to the non-exclusive, fully paid-up, fully dedicated band of men, women and children who make up the army of British football supporters; fans who know what it is to go hoarse from chanting, to burn the roof of your mouth on a half-time meat pie, to have collected the match programmes, and stacked them in prized collectable piles, as tokens of loyalty; those people who have travelled the football specials – the trains and the coaches – to follow teams on the road, knowing that to survive a bitter winter's day in the open end at Oldham Athletic's Boundary Park was to survive the coldest place on earth; knowing the true definition of perseverance and endurance upon reaching East Anglia and the worst grounds to reach: Carrow Road and Portman Road; knowing that there is no better feeling than turning over Manchester United at Old Trafford.

We know what it is to get drenched by the downpours that were never forecast, to almost lose our toes to frostbite on Boxing Day – but still find the spirit to sing and laugh – and then bask in the sunshine, wearing our team strips, on those warm days that typically herald the start and end of each season.

We accept there is no calm, no sense of peace; there is only ever soul-soaring joy or soul-crushing despair; the ecstasy of a last-minute winner or the agony of a last-minute defeat; or the blind referee or cheating linesman that robbed us of a winner in a tedious nil-nil draw. There is no in-between state in football, only extremes. Football is not a sport – it's a bloody fantastic, nerve-racking adventure that makes the heart race with its beautiful anticipation, its ninety minutes of adrenalin, its irrationality, its heroes and villains, its joy and heartbreak.

At one time or another, we've all visited our clubs on an open day, a supporters' special or corporate visit, and walked the corridors of football power, and felt momentarily special for the privileged access that, for one glorious moment, has led us away from the seats where we normally sit.

Yet perhaps, as fans, we should never get too close; we should always maintain the mystique because the idolatry of the players and the glamour of the club tend to diminish when we learn more about the politics and personalities that prop up our dreams. As Walter Bagehot said, 'We must not let daylight in upon magic,' and perhaps he was right.

Maybe those that give standing ovations should never tread back-stage, but should leave with nothing more than the memories of a performance, and promise to return. Blind loyalty, they call it.

Well, I suppose I was the fan who got too close, and became intoxicated by the magic, on and off the pitch. Because I became chairman of the club I'd loved since being a boy; consciously blessed, subconsciously cursed.

We've all been there in our imaginations – that person who gets lost in the daydream of 'What if . . .'

'What if I got the chance to play for my club?'

'What if I was the manager – what team would I pick?'

'What if I was the chairman – what would I do?'

I was the car showroom employee turned businessman who found himself in charge; a supporter who always found it strange to be referred to as 'Mr Chairman' at a club which had been my life. I wasn't the archetypal self-made millionaire who wanted a club as my next empire, my latest plaything. My values as chairman matched the values I'd obsessed about as a fan: being the best, winning matches, chasing trophies.

•

So the story you are about to read revolves around Leeds United, and may well be set in and around Elland Road because that's where the dream started – and where it all went so wrong. But I suppose it could be any fan at any club. It just happened to be me.

Regardless of allegiances, regardless of titles and trappings of office, this is the story of what happened when that fan found himself in the chairman's seat; his 'what ifs' coming true. And, for many who judged my tenure as chairman, I'm sure the 'what ifs' will continue: 'What if Peter Ridsdale had never been chairman? What would the rewritten history look like then?' Because, in many eyes, I became the man responsible for the 'Meltdown of Leeds United', and a financial implosion that ultimately caught the eye of the Department of Trade and Industry, which investigated me, and the transfers I'd overseen, with an exhaustive inquiry conducted between 2004 and 2006. It has since cleared me of any wrong-doing.

It is that finding that has now freed me to write my version of events for the first time.

I don't intend to launch a defence because many fans and many quarters of the media have already reached their damning verdict. I will be guilty forever more for the demise of Leeds United.

Instead it is my intention to show fans what really happens behind the scenes of a Premiership club chasing the dream. By inviting fans into the chairman's office, I want to shed some light not only on Leeds United, but football itself.

It's an explanation that is open to varying judgements. God knows I've learned some valuable lessons along the way, and spent hours, if not days, sat in judgement on myself. But I will say this from the outset: every decision I took – in conjunction with the board – was made in good faith, with the interests of Leeds United at heart, and without the benefit of hindsight. Looking back, we made errors. We messed up. We gambled. We won. Then we lost. Big-time. Yet we were striving to achieve the status and recognition such a legendary club deserved: best in the Premiership, best in Europe; 'the finest football team the world has ever seen'.

I was first a fan of Leeds United, who happened to become a director, then chairman. I played a small part in creating the dream, which then became a very personal nightmare. For that nightmare, I hold up my hands and say sorry, now, taking my share of responsibility.

But what follows is that story. And it was the journey we *all* marched on, together . . .

Peter Ridsdale
August 2007

PROLOGUE

I knew, of course, why they all hated me. But that didn't make it any easier to accept, especially when I'd once enjoyed their admiration; all of them – all thirty thousand of them – singing my name, applauding me, and appreciating one simple fact: first and foremost I was one of them, a Leeds United supporter, in my bones, in my blood.

But, as winter turned to spring in 2003, and the fond memories turned to resentment, and triumphs turned to disaster, I soon morphed from short-term hero into long-term villain. The writing seemed to be on every wall and unfurled banner throughout the city.

I was Peter Ridsdale: traitor, Judas, disgrace, club-wrecker, the enemy within. It's why they chanted 'Ridsdale out' week in, week out; why home-daubed slogans, held aloft behind each goal, screamed, 'Ridsdale is full of shit' or 'Go now Ridsdale' or 'Lies United', and why pockets of mobs hung around outside the Elland Road stadium, as if waiting for the accused to be smuggled from a court house on bail.

It hurt. It hurt like hell.

It was a steep fall from the days when a Leeds fans' website described me as 'Peter Ridsdale, chairman, friend of the fans, and now super-hero' on 12 March 2000. So much had changed in three years.

I'd always said it would be the fans, not the board, who would sack me as chairman of this great institution, and there they were, tossing my P45 in the air from the stands, like pre-match tickertape. A magical period – one that included a European odyssey – had run aground on the pitch, managers had failed to get the required results and we consequently buckled under the weight of debts of £78.9million. Our dreams had gone bust.

For someone once so proud and privileged to hold the chairman's office, I struggled to keep my head held high. It's hard when you're jostled, reviled, spat at and threatened each time you exit your beloved ground.

No longer the dream-maker. Just the kamikaze pilot. I felt shot to pieces, stripped of self-confidence and self-belief.

'I can't see you take much more of this,' said my wife, Sophie, one night, starting to question what had once been a strong sense of self-respect. No matter how desperate I was to revive the dream, and to be given time to put everything right, the decision to step down became inevitable.

As a family, we fled to my sister-in-law's house in Suffolk. It was a world away from the city of Leeds, and a place of refuge, if only for a few days.

In the reflection that distance allowed, I didn't feel the shame others expected of me, that others wanted me to feel. That's not because I'm shameless or, as some argued, too arrogant to care. Far from it. It was because if there was any shame to feel, it was swamped by a more profound sense of bewilderment. I simply could not comprehend why it had all gone so wrong so quickly. But the self-analysis would have to come later, along with the internal audits and DTI investigations.

I was angry, too, that my wife and two young children, who had nothing to do with football and the decisions taken, were made to feel the same intimidation and fear. Why is it right that my daughters, Charlotte and Olivia, then aged seven and six, cried themselves to sleep because fans had pinned notes to my front gate saying, 'We know where you live'? Why should Sophie be kept awake, wondering if 'they' would attack the house? Not that anyone cared whether I was a husband and father first. It doesn't matter that you're human or fallible. All that counted was that I was the face of Leeds United; the buck rested with me. I was behind the wheel when the club lost control.

The fans and media had found me instantly guilty on *prima facie* evidence of 'financial incompetence' and 'gross mismanagement'. That was the hardest thing to swallow – being blamed for ruining the club I loved, which had been my life as much as that of any other diehard supporter within that stadium. Yet I was cast as the outsider who had betrayed them all.

'We thought you were Leeds . . . we were wrong . . . we thought you were Leeds . . . we were wrong . . .' they sang on the Kop.

It hurt. It continued to hurt like hell.

I was reduced to a trembling wreck whenever I contemplated the hatred vented towards me; reduced to being ushered into grounds by security guards for my own safety, ducking to avoid the darts of spit that came like showers; reduced to opening mail and reading menacing death threats; reduced to having security guards patrol the grounds of my home.

Don't let anyone tell you that football is *just* a game.

Had people needed passports to cross the borders of Yorkshire, I'm convinced mine would have been revoked to ensure I never walked the streets of Leeds again.

There might be some people reading this who think I'm exaggerating emotions of the time. Should that be the case, just read what that paragon of virtue, David Mellor, had to say in his *Evening Standard* column, recommending all my answers could be found by looking down the barrel of a gun.

He wrote: 'A man half as decent as Pious Pete always claimed to be wouldn't have asked for money, just a glass of whisky, a revolver and the loan of a lockable room . . . Ridsdale is utterly unfit to be put in charge of a tiddlywinks club.'

Sophie was so sickened that she wrote him a letter, but received no reply. Then Jimmy Greaves waded in with his thoughts in the *Sun*, saying I'd 'committed a terrible crime against football'.

I didn't need the likes of David Mellor or Jimmy Greaves to remind me how bad things were. I was already hurting to the core. There was also guilt; weeks filled with guilt, and nights of not much sleep spent calculating income streams and cashflow, trying to conjure financial miracles, wondering if selling player A and player B would help, or just turn more fans against me. It was no longer the football mind that spent its time working out how many points were needed to qualify for Europe; it became the mind that worked out how millions could be clawed back.

This huge pressure culminated in an overriding need to run away and escape all the noise in my head. Hence the journey 260 miles south to Sophie's sister's Suffolk house.

So it was ironic that, as I deluded myself into thinking I'd found a place of anonymity, I discovered my lowest moment in those final eight months of hell as chairman. If I needed reminding of how vitriolic and personal the attacks had become, then the stinging reminder was duly delivered on the Saturday morning of 29 March 2003 during a casual walk to the shops in High Street, Halstead, across the border into north-east Essex.

Mothering Sunday was the next day, and I'd just nipped out of the house on the pretext of buying the morning newspapers when, in fact, I was going to the shops to buy Sophie a Mother's Day card from our girls. My mind was elsewhere as I stood on the pavement, looking at a gift shop's display, when I suddenly noticed the reflection of someone coming up behind me.

I didn't see the hand that darted for my throat, spun me round and pushed me against the window with a thud. I was eyeball-to-eyeball with a scruffy young man, hair all over the place, his mouth and nose and cheeks all twisted and snarling.

'You're that fucking Ridsdale!' he spat, his grip clamped around my throat.

Suddenly, the fear within me that had been braced for a random mugging was ratcheted up a notch or two.

This was anything but random.

It's amazing what the mind computes in slow motion while

the event itself happens so quickly. *Has he followed me? Watch his other hand . . . keep watching his hand. Has he got a knife?* All those thoughts, plus the kind of fear that stings your veins, ran through me. If he were recounting this episode, I'm sure he'd boast of the blazing panic in my eyes. Even if he hadn't been holding me by the throat, the crippling fear within me would have pinned me against that shop window.

My focus was solely on him, trying to take all of him in despite him being so close; his nose almost touching mine, his beer-breath steaming into my face. I can't even remember saying a word.

There were shouts of intended intervention from do-gooders in the street but, wisely, they were too afraid to actually step in, and someone started banging on the window behind me.

'Ridsdale!' this thug went on, 'you've fucked up *my* football team. Now, you better sort *your* mess out – or else!' he threatened. His hand dropped from my throat, he phlegmed up, spat at my feet and was gone as quickly as he'd arrived. I sat on the perch of the window sill, steadying myself, gathering my breath, sensing my legs turn to jelly. I watched him leg it down the street. I composed myself, then went into the shop, made my apologies, bought the girls' card and returned to the house, without letting on about the incident. My wife and daughters were worried enough without adding to their anxiety.

I should have known there was no hiding place. Leeds United have a legendary following of support up and down the country and around the world. But how ironic that the physical attack that I had long feared had actually happened so far from home.

I'd been chairman for almost six years from 1997, and a director since September 1987. In my tenure as chairman, we'd finished fifth, fourth, third, fourth and fifth. Every single season, we had qualified for Europe, four times in the UEFA Cup and once in the Champions League. We'd even reached the semi-final of the latter in the quest to become champions of the champions. Everything the club had set out to do, we'd achieved.

But beyond all that, what mattered most was that I had been a true supporter since the age of eight. Yet there I was, aged fifty-one, held to account against a shop window. I'm not even sure I'm right in calling him a thug, even though he acted like one. He was an enraged fan who came to symbolize, and then act out, the hatred and anger felt for me both inside and outside Elland Road. The same fans who had demanded the dream, and banked the memories, were suddenly asking why we had ever gambled in a game that no longer seemed so beautiful.

There was an irony to the episode in Essex because what that fan could never have known, along with everyone else, was that he'd already got his way. I'd handed in my resignation just twenty-four hours earlier. But if I thought the hostilities and controversy would end just because I'd stuck my hands in the air and surrendered, I couldn't have been more mistaken.

TERRACE TALK

My heart sank when I saw the length of the queue snaking around Elland Road. I'm *never* going to get a ticket, I thought, and slouched all the way to the back of the line.

Looking back, getting my hands on a 1965 Leeds–Liverpool FA Cup final ticket was the equivalent of Charlie Bucket dreaming about a golden ticket to Willy Wonka's chocolate factory. Only mine was for Wembley, that faraway place that had seemed as reachable as another planet for First Division Leeds United, a club described as 'a molehill-high monument to mediocrity' by football writer Frank McGhee.

Just three seasons earlier, they had narrowly escaped relegation to the Third Division. But Don Revie, the player turned manager, had changed all that, and his revolution transformed Leeds.

'WEMBLEY AT LAST' said a souvenir special in the *Yorkshire Evening Post*. The club even bought the players brand new white socks – nylon, not wool – to mark the occasion. I was thirteen, it was Leeds' first-ever FA Cup final, and I wasn't going to miss it for the world. I'd religiously saved the weekly match programmes and cut out the special tokens needed to buy a ticket. We'd knocked Manchester United out in a replayed semi-final at Nottingham Forest's City Ground, and tickets went on sale a couple of weeks later, immediately after a home game.

The moment the ref blew the whistle at that match, I was ducking and weaving out of the old 'Scratching Shed' (now the South Stand) to rush to the ticket office, thinking I'd be among the first supporters to claim a spot, sleep overnight and be in prime position for the next day. But others had been wiser, missing the league game for the sake of guaranteeing themselves a Cup final ticket. I couldn't believe it when my eyes followed the queue away from the ticket office, passed the main stand, round the car park and out through the main gates before turning right into the busy Elland Road.

When my dad, Arthur, showed up at the pre-arranged time of 6.30 p.m., he'd walked the line to find me sat, looking glum, against the wall outside Jackson Boilers, adjacent to the wooden hut that housed the supporters' club.

'Why are you so down in the mouth?' he asked.

'You seen the queue, Dad? I'm never going to get a ticket!' I sulked.

It took him to point out that, since I'd arrived, there were hundreds more behind me. 'Do you think they're all queuing for nothing? Stop fretting – you'll get a ticket,' he assured me, and laughed as he handed over a bottle-green sleeping bag, an extra blanket, a flask of coffee, and some sandwiches Mum had made. It seems odd in today's age that parents would allow a thirteen-year-old boy to sleep in the street overnight, all alone. But it was a different world then. Besides, when you're surrounded by the family of other supporters, you're hardly alone. As darkness fell and the traffic died away, I tucked both arms into the zipped-up sleeping bag, and nodded off with the match tokens in my hand, clutched tight because I was so scared of someone stealing them during the night. I wouldn't rest until that ticket was in my hand.

Dad was back in the morning with a fresh supply of sand-wiches and a fresh Thermos of soup. He said how much he admired my determination; that meant a lot coming from him, someone who'd always worked hard to get what he wanted, to provide for us and make us comfortable in the working-class life that we had.

It took five hours for me to shuffle to the ticket office window. A stern lady at the kiosk took my sheet of match tokens, counted them one by one, and then handed over the Wembley match ticket, for the terrace behind the goal. I kissed it the moment it was in my hands.

That story is the abiding memory of a childhood rich with Leeds United flashbacks. No one will forget the actual game, of course, which went into extra-time after a goalless ninety minutes between two sides who had never won the Cup. Liverpool's Gerry Byrne, who played on with a broken collar-bone (there were no such thing as substitutes in those days) set up Roger Hunt's goal before Billy Bremner equalized, only for Ian St John to break our hearts with a winner nine minutes before time.

'Eee-Aye-Addio, we've won the Cup!' sang the red half of Wembley while I stood in the silence of the white half, spellbound by the noise. I couldn't get upset because it had been such an unforgettable day: from the atmosphere on the supporters' special train to the excitement that crackled around the stadium, crammed with 100,000 people who witnessed 120 minutes of edgy football.

Dad was waiting for me at Leeds station that night, and was surprised to find me bounding forward, all smiles, still clutching my one-shilling programme. I must have relived every minute on the short car journey home. The entire experience bound me to Leeds United for evermore.

•

No one would have imagined such ties when I was born on 11 March 1952, the son of Arthur, who worked in a factory making hospital equipment, and Audrey, a part-time Comptometer operator, recording a company's wages on a portable machine that resembled an old shopping till. I can still see her now, her fingers flashing and punching away on the numbers.

The media were to christen me 'Publicity Pete' sometime in the years ahead. But my parents christened me Robert Peter Ridsdale; born and bred in Leeds, if not quite a born and bred United fan. Football didn't register on our family radar. Dad, like the rest of our terraced back-to-back street, was into rugby league. Everyone talked about Hunslet and then, in the summer, Yorkshire cricket. People only ever discussed one United foot-baller, John Charles, and floodlights hadn't even been installed. Leeds was a club struggling in the dark, and its finances were crippled after fire destroyed the West Stand in 1956.

With a dad indifferent to football, it took a Middlesbrough supporter, a man called John Young, to introduce me to Elland Road in the 1960–61 season, when the floodlights had arrived but the crowds hadn't – games pulled in attendances of around 8,000. Boro were playing us in a league match and John, who lived round the corner from our house in West Park, dragged my dad along and said: 'Why don't you bring young Peter with us for a treat?' I was eight years old. Dad was bored by half-time. I was hooked by the excitement of a 4–4 draw.

My cousin Paul Johnson and I saved our pocket money and went to a match once a month, standing in the boys' pen at the Kop, with my blue-and-yellow scarf wrapped around my neck, and a rattle that I spun above my head. Paul, more interested in cricket than football, soon dropped away as my match buddy. By the age of eleven, I went to every game alone.

Leeds were finally promoted into the top flight from the Second Division in the 1963–64 season. Don Revie had been in charge for about eighteen months, and he'd dropped the blue-and-yellow team colours in favour of the all-white strip to mimic the famous Real Madrid; the Mighty Whites had been born. Newly installed chairman Harry Reynolds had given Revie £100,000 for team-building; new talent afforded by this cash injection was to kick-start a famous renaissance.

Mum and Dad bought me a season ticket for the terraced West Stand Paddock, and I paid them back in instalments from my pocket money and paper round. Every other Saturday, I'd get to the ground for 1 p.m. and hog the exact same spot – a concrete block in which one of the crush barriers was set; the extra few inches that one block allowed me gave me a perfect view over the cloth-capped heads and Brylcreemed hair of adults. I stood to the left of the players' tunnel, next to the same couple – Mr and Mrs Beesting. They took me, this lone boy, under their wing, and I got to know them so well that Dad dropped me off at their house and together we'd walk the one mile to the ground.

I also went to every away game, travelling alone on the Wallace Arnold supporters' coaches. But nothing beat the sight of Elland Road coming into view on the walk down from Beeston Hill, especially for evening kick-offs: seeing the white haze of the floodlights always made me want to walk that little bit quicker, eager to get there. In later years, the club installed two monster floodlights on one side of the ground. At 260ft high, they were the tallest in Europe; stilted monsters in the distance, like something striding out of *War of the Worlds*, fifty-five eyes on full beam on each pylon. Nowadays, many Leeds fans still recall that sight on the horizon, and how much they miss seeing such a landmark.

That next season, 1964–65, was an unforgettable one as the stadium witnessed the Revie Revolution in full flow. The 'Father of Elland Road' transformed us from a promoted side to near world-beaters, matching Liverpool, Manchester United and Chelsea. Billy Bremner, his legs whiter than his strip and hair redder than Jack Charlton in a sweat, was a hero of mine, as was keeper Gary Sprake. We finished second in the First Division, agonizingly pipped by champions Manchester United. Then came that FA Cup final. The Revie era was reaching a sustainable peak. It was the beginning of the most memorable chapters in the club's history, spanning ten great years from 1964 to '74.

●

'If you don't do your homework, you'll end up working at Burton's for a living!' Mum used to warn me.

She wasn't the only parent who brought out that whip when schoolwork lagged behind, and many kids grew up in Leeds with an instilled dread of ending up on the machines making suits at the Hudson Road factory, a mere two miles from our house. Burton's was one of the largest employees in the city, and its dragnet was vast. If you looked across the hilltops from the local churchyard, you could see the factory on the horizon – a bleak and ugly reminder of what our futures could hold, as if to illustrate Mum's point.

She only wanted the best for me. That's why she ensured I became a choirboy at St Mark's Church, and why she arranged for a rather stern lady to come to our house once a week for elocution lessons in which she made me repeat, over and over, things like, 'My Far-ther's car's a Jag-u-ar which travels very far-st.' It must have worked because my broad Yorkshire accent was soon drummed out of me. According to other boys at school, I started talking 'all fancy'.

I think this drive towards being 'all fancy' had a lot to do with Dad working as a volunteer for the Conservative MP and minister Keith Joseph, whose Leeds North-East constituency included the affluent area of Alwoodley. Once a month, as a family, we also went for 'posh' Sunday lunch at the Astoria in Leeds. Having moved from Hyde Park to West Park, it was as if my parents were aspiring for better things, and wanting to provide a better life for me and my sister Judith, five years older. She was – and still is – an exceptionally talented artist and dress designer who shone far brighter than me. I didn't really know what I wanted to do. I flirted with the idea of being a journalist but didn't think I'd be hard-nosed or ruthless enough.

I remember my childhood as a happy one, dominated by sport and the collection of Leeds United match programmes that grew in neat piles in the corner of my bedroom. I never went short of anything. Mum and Dad often bought me new goalkeeping gloves. I'd rush home from school, dump my tan-coloured satchel in the hallway, and be out in the street with my mates Chris Haynes and Paul Smith. I pretended to be a Gary Sprake or David Harvey, using one lamp-post and a bundle of coats for 'the sticks'.

'One day, I'll play in goal for Leeds United!' I'd say at the dinner table, afterwards, convinced the dream was possible.

'And I keep telling you, never mind football. If you don't do your homework, you'll end up working at Burton's!' said Mum. In the end, the best I achieved was to turn out for Adel Memorial Hall FC.

Judith had the benefit of a private education whereas I went to the state Leeds Modern School (now known as Lawnswood). I'd been desperate to go to that school and, unlike most kids, couldn't wait to get into the school uniform. For me, putting on that black and red striped blazer with matching cap was my coming of age. Even though I was only eleven, I felt like one of the big lads. That was until I walked into the playground, all pristine and proud in my shorts, blazer and cap, and some sixth formers whipped off my cap, chucked it in a puddle and stamped on it. I was distraught.

Uniforms meant status to me. I remember being given a policeman's uniform, and walking up and down Woodhouse Street pretending to be on the beat. Then I saw a car crash, and ran all the way home. Mum reckoned I'd apply to join the police force but I never did. 'A position of authority is always respected in society,' she said. In those days, policemen were respected but their role was no more than a childhood fascination for me.

I was also mesmerized by the man who, each night, came to light the gas lamps in our street when we lived in Hyde Park. I'd watch him from the window, and couldn't understand how someone with such a boring job could be so meticulous about his task. He stood there with his long-reaching lighter, flicked open a pane of glass and lit the gas mantle. 'If a job's worth doing, it's worth doing well,' Mum said, when she caught me agog at the window, puzzled by the perfectionist outside. All on his own, this silent figure created a dim line of light all down our street with one single touch. At least, that's what it seemed like to me. I called him 'the man who brought power to our streets'.

I was very much my own person as a child. I had friends – a few – but in the summer I'd go off and do my own thing. I was mad about buses for some reason and spent entire days travelling different bus routes, endlessly boarding the green double-decker buses of Leeds; leaving at nine in the morning and not returning till four o'clock in the afternoon.

I was a team player as regards football, cricket and rugby but, away from sport, I preferred my own company. I suppose I was a loner, not because I was sad or lonely or anything like that. But from an early age I became used to being by myself, and was happy with it.

It's funny looking back but Mum and Dad, while they were loving, never came to watch me play sport. Not even when I was representing the school or the community. Not even when I became the youngest pupil of Leeds Modern to play for the cricket first XI. At summer scout camp, on visitors' day, I'd be the only boy whose parents didn't show; at church, the only boy whose parents didn't come to watch him sing.

I suppose it only struck me as odd in later life when, at Elland Road, I'd meet goalkeeper Paul Robinson's mum and dad who went to every single game to watch him play, and I remember thinking how nice that was.

Dad ran me here, there and everywhere and made sure I got to all the Leeds United games. But there was never any parent–son participation; it seemed more like a paternal duty. Don't get me wrong, I wasn't unhappy because that's the way it was; what you grow up with becomes the norm. But maybe that made me fiercely independent and self-sufficient, and subconsciously instilled within me a work ethic to succeed on my own. I'd like to think that's the good thing to take away from it.

Dad was an exceptionally hard worker, and that's how he supported us; that's how he showed his love. He was the factory man who worked his way up to become sales manager at the hospital equipment manufacturer Charles F. Thackray, making things like patient trolleys and operating tables. Mum and Dad never had savings. I can't say that times were tough but we were certainly not well off. Dad ran a tight ship, obsessing about the family budget. What my parents earned, they pumped back into the home. What they didn't have, they worked to obtain (even if Mum gave me 'treat' hand-outs when Dad wasn't looking). But they were always pushing themselves, wanting to move up to the next level. It's why Mum took the part-time job as a compto-meter operator. And when Dad's day's work was done, he wasn't finished. He'd have tea with us at six o'clock and then be out again on three nights of the week, doing charitable work with The Lions; raising money for the local community was just as important as earning for himself, he used to say.

On Saturday mornings, he often took me into his office. I'd swivel in one of the chairs as he finished his week's paperwork. My abiding memory is of this bedraggled man sat at a desk in chaos, smothered in papers and files; and the place stank of smoke. He'd sit there under a thin, swirling cloud generated by the forty to fifty cigarettes he smoked every day. His fingers yellowed with nicotine as the years went on, and I can visualize him, sat in the armchair at home, unbothered by the ash that fell into his trousers. Dad wasn't what you'd call image-conscious. He was a grafter but there seemed no cleanliness or order in his world.

That's probably what turned me into a meticulous, anti-smoking teenager, spurred on by Mum's incentive that if I reached twenty-one years old without having ever smoked, she'd give me a pound for each year. She was as good as her word.

I insisted that everything around me had to be neat and tidy; that my school uniform was pristine, and my tie perfect. I kept my bedroom with equal fastidiousness. It was, as my Auntie Evie often said, 'immaculate': nothing out of place, and the bed military-made. Books were stacked flush in towers, and I wrapped each cover in brown paper to stop them being thumbed or marked. I've kept such order to this day. People laugh about my cars. You climb in as a passenger and you'd think it gets valeted every day. I don't know what it is, or what it says about me, but everything in my life needs to be kept in order, from files to cars to books.

Mum's warning about working at Burton's haunted me when I left school with just one O-level, achieved in English. Dad said I needed better qualifications, and made me attend Park Lane College to resit my exams, but I failed them all again. I'd got distracted by the freedom that a Lambretta scooter allowed me, I became a Parker-wearing Mod and formed a pop group called Midnight Orange.

I steered clear of the Hudson Road factory by landing a job at Bryan's fish and chip shop in Headingley. At first, anything seemed better than Burton's. My job was to fillet around sixty fish a day, from 8 a.m. till 1 p.m., for £7 a week. After a few weeks of such tedious work I was stinking of fish, no matter how hard I scrubbed in the bath. I started to wonder if life at Burton's would be so harsh, after all. It was a horrible job at Bryan's but it made me determined to make something of myself, and I scoured the classified ads in the newspapers and started viewing a career more seriously.

In 1969, as Allan Clarke joined Leeds United, I joined the car distributor Appleyards as a clerical assistant. It occupied one of the largest showroom sites in Europe, off North Street, and showcased British Leyland, Jaguars and Daimlers. I'll never forget the time when my hero Gary Sprake drove on to the forecourt, and stepped out of his MG sports car. He'd brought it in for a service. I'd never before seen a player away from the context of a football stadium. I might as well have been a boy seeing Superman in the flesh. I stood glued to the spot as he walked in, dropped off the keys and walked out. I was surrounded by cars, no longer stank of fish and worked in a place where Leeds players had their cars serviced. I loved it.

There was a downside to working at Appleyards, as I discovered when the Morris Marina was launched on 26 April 1971.

I'd never missed a single game at Elland Road. But personnel director Jack Harrison, a fellow fan, said the launch of this 'exciting new car' meant we all had to muck in at the evening launch – which coincided with the top of the table clash between Leeds and Arsenal, the penultimate game of that 1970–71 season when the title chase went to the wire between us and the Gunners. We needed a victory to stay in the running. Gutted at missing such a crucial match, I spent the entire evening ducking out of the launch with local dignitaries, and kept rushing to the office phone, unable to rest, unable to get excited about this bloody Morris Marina, and spent all my time ringing the club results service.

Elland Road went crazy when a Jack Charlton goal sealed the match, 1–0. I bolted downstairs to the showroom to tell Mr Harrison. For a minute, we managed to forget the Morris Marina and celebrated the engine that was Jack Charlton instead. Ultimately, Arsenal pipped us to the title by one point the following week, a dismal repeat of our narrow second to Everton the previous year, and we'd be condemned to second place in the 1971–72 season, too, finishing one point behind Derby; 'the agony of last-fence failures,' as Charlton described it.

I owed a lot to Jack Harrison, despite the fact he made me work that evening, because it was he who persuaded me to take a correspondence course in business and economics from the Institute of Personnel Management – and the businessman in me was born. I started the course in 1970 when Leeds drew 2–2 with Chelsea in the FA Cup final, then lost the replay. And I'd qualified by 1972 when we became FA Cup winners with that single Allan Clarke diving header against Arsenal.

In between those two footballing milestones, I met my first wife, Shirley Evans, a student of history at Leeds University. Her dad, Roy, was regional sales manager for Esso and, after leaving Shirley and her mum in the kitchen, I walked into the lounge to formally ask for his daughter's hand in marriage. His response was to ask me a question: how much did I think I'd need to earn to obtain a mortgage and provide a good home for a family? My answer can't have been impressive: he refused me permission and added: 'I do not think you're yet in a position to give my daughter a lifestyle that she should expect.' In books on etiquette, they don't teach you the proper exit after that kind of setback. So I left him in his armchair, and walked back into the kitchen to find a smiling daughter and mother, hanging expectantly on my every word.

'He said no – he doesn't think I'm good enough for you.' They were more upset than me.

Three months later, in the December of 1972, I landed a job at a subsidiary of Baker Perkins in Leeds. With my self-worth inflated a little more, I returned to the living room of Mr Evans, asked again for his daughter's hand in marriage and this time he agreed, grudgingly. As he shook my hand, he told me, 'For what it's worth, I don't think you'll ever make anything of your life.'

The smug-looking manager of the Burnley Building Society didn't help matters when he refused me a mortgage for our first home, a three-bedroomed house in Garforth, Leeds. 'In my opinion, you're never going to have enough earning potential to pay back the £5,500,' he sneered.

There I was, a twenty-one-year-old trying to stand-up in the adult world, and I had a future father-in-law and one building society manager branding me a failure before I'd managed to get up from my knees.

I'll show you . . . I'll show you both, I thought.

Thank heavens for the Leeds & Holbeck Building Society, which granted me the loan. We bought the house, and I married Shirley in 1973. She knew she'd married both me and Leeds United. Despite my new responsibilities in the world, I still went to every match, home and away. Even when the new job meant moving to Lincolnshire to be at the company's Peterborough HQ – responsible for identifying the high-fliers and selecting them for senior management training – I never missed a fixture.

At that time, Leeds were reigning supreme in the First Division, and the team was at its strongest with the likes of Harvey in goal, Jack Charlton, Norman Hunter, Paul Reaney and Trevor Cherry at the back; Peter Lorimer, Billy Bremner, Johnny Giles and Eddie Gray in midfield; Allan Clarke and Mick Jones up front – 'The Untouchables', said the *Daily Mirror*, 'years ahead of even their most advanced contemporaries in development and application'.

The club had become a giant, and success on the pitch had led to the development of Elland Road in 1974. The old 'Scratching Shed' made way for a new £500,000 South Stand, and they had to move the pitch down a few feet to accommodate its structure, which is why the players' tunnel is nowadays not on the halfway line, and is slightly offset. The pinnacle of the Revie Revolution came when we clinched the league title that same year. No more second places. Revie was the maestro of his day. It's why inevitably he moved on to become the England manager, bringing to an end his twelve-year reign as Leeds boss that summer.

•

I knew that Mum was seriously ill and bedridden come the autumn of 1974 but no one told me it was cancer, or that she was dying – probably because I was worried sick enough without having to know the worst. I kept visiting her. She didn't want me to know she was dying, and I didn't want her to know that I was worried about her dying from whatever it was. So the irony was that, while she hid from me the devastating truth, I hid from her the motives for visiting every Saturday evening.

'I've been to Elland Road and thought I'd pop in,' I'd say, knowing she'd never know whether we'd played home or away. I'd sit on the edge of her bed, and tell her all about the match.

'Just like you used to do as a child, Peter,' she smiled. I should have known by how weak she looked that her life was drawing to its end. She lay there, looking old and fragile, and the times we reminisced about were the reflections of someone who could no longer look forward.

It was the spring of 1975 when I was doing my usual Friday afternoon journey from Peterborough to home when she died. As I arrived at the gates of my parents' house, Judith ran out crying. 'It's too late, Peter – it's too late!' After all those weeks of being there, in my vigils to the unknown, I'd missed the chance to say goodbye.

Mum died one week before she and Dad were due to move into a flat; one year before my first son, Simon, was born.

Soon afterwards, Dad's best friend, John Young – the Boro fan – died following a heart transplant operation. His widow, Vera, found solace in sharing her grief with Dad and, in clinging on to one another during that time, they grew inseparable. In 1977, they married; fate had it that my stepmother was the widow of the man who had first introduced me to Leeds United.

Sometime between Mum's passing and the funeral, and before Vera arrived on the scene, I was walking with Dad past Leeds Modern. He seemed lost in his grief and shock, and had wanted us to walk-and-talk. Then he aired one of the things that had been bothering him: 'Now your mum has died, will you still come and see me?'

I was stunned. 'Why wouldn't I, Dad?'

'Because I know how close you were to your mum,' he said, at the same time acknowledging some form of guilt that he'd spent too much time at work, or with The Lions.

If we hadn't been as close as most fathers and sons up until that point, we became closer after that. It was the first time I'd ever seen him express emotion, and show how much he needed me. Maybe he recognized what I later understood – that we hadn't shared much as father and son. But he was a massive influence on my life, and I didn't want him beating himself up over the past. He'd done everything he possibly could to make our lives better, and we were indebted to him for that.

It was sad then that when Mum died, I couldn't be with her at the end. But when Dad slipped away, nine years later, I sat with him and held his hand. As he died, we couldn't have been closer, and that comforted me in the intervening years.

•

At Elland Road, they mourned the days of Don Revie, especially when Brian Clough was appointed as his successor, arriving from Brighton & Hove Albion. I was stunned because he'd always slagged us off, and no one imagined he'd have a true Leeds United heart in him. As it turned out, he was the worst and most unpopular appointment in the club's history. His forty-four-day reign said it all. A famous players' revolt in the dressing room had made his position untenable. 'Player power' – even though it wasn't rooted in finances and agents' fees – was a force to be reckoned with even back then. It said much about Clough's reign that the only thing people now remember about one of his signings, Duncan McKenzie, was his pre-match party trick for the crowd: performing a running jump over a Mini in the centre of the pitch, or throwing a golf ball from one end of the stadium to the other. Can you imagine the stars of today being allowed to limber up like that for a big match!

Jimmy Armfield, one of the game's true gentlemen, stepped into the breach in October 1974 and pulled off what Revie never achieved – taking us to a European Cup final, in Paris. We lost 2–0 to Bayern Munich but defeat on the pitch was not the shame of that night – it was the thuggish behaviour of the Leeds hooligans who ripped out seats and hurled them on the pitch, leading to a three-year European ban. The Leeds hooligan element would become notorious and cause great damage to the club's image.

On the pitch, a worrying decline in performances set in and the Don Revie team began to break up. In my view, the board made a mistake in getting rid of Jimmy Armfield because he'd proved more than capable of steadying the ship through an inevitable transitional period. Jock Stein took over in 1978 and it was downhill all the way from there. It would take until 1988, and the reign of Howard Wilkinson, before the glory days were restored to Elland Road.

•

'Mr Ridsdale, if you don't agree to the following amendments to our working hours, we'll take our men out on strike,' said the forthright shop steward from the Transport and General Worker's Union.

Five minutes into a new job and the union pistol was being held to my head. It was 1978, and I'd moved on to computer company ICL, hired as regional personnel manager for the north-west, based in Duckenfield, Cheshire. It's not funny on your first day in a new job suddenly to be faced with your whole plant shutting down. I'd not even had a chance to sort out my desk when the brusque union man came marching in around eleven o'clock, made his demands, said they needed answers by four o'clock, and then walked out.

I flew into instant panic mode, and rang head office in Putney, desperate to speak to the head of industrial relations, Pat Barraclough; it was a call to be made way above my newly recruited head.

'Mrs Barraclough is in meetings all day. Can I take a message?' asked her secretary.

'Just tell her it's very, very urgent and I really must talk to her soon,' I said, and then waited. The phone rang within half an hour.

'I'm sorry but Mrs Barraclough is in meetings all day and cannot be disturbed. She'll be available at five o'clock or tomorrow morning.'

That was far too late. But, without wanting to sound like some hysterical new boy who couldn't cope under pressure, I hung up, paced my office for the rest of the afternoon and rehearsed ways of pleading with the union man to delay any decision until that evening, or the following morning.

Not that he was in the mood for waiting. He knocked on my door on the dot of four o'clock.

'Well, have you agreed to our terms, then?' he asked, eye-balling me.

'No, I haven't, and I can't. I haven't got the authority to do so,' I told him, eyeballing him back. He shook his head disapprovingly, and stared at me for what seemed like an eternity. Then his face cracked into the widest smile.

'You'll do for us, Mr Ridsdale!' he said, bursting into laughter and reaching out his hand to shake mine. 'Put it there! You've got balls of steel. We were just testing the new man out!'

He laughed. I laughed – more out of relief than anything else – and it was all very jovial. The moment he left the office, chuckling away to himself, I slumped back in my chair, utterly drained and relieved, knowing how ludicrous his 'balls of steel' comment really was. I was learning all about confidence and the performance of ruthlessness in the business world. In my mind, I was starting to be somebody; starting to make something of myself – even if the recognition was only from the TGWU.

I worked all the hours God sent to better myself, Dad's influence making its mark. Our second son, Paul, was born in 1979 but the new job meant I had to live in a hotel in the north while Shirley and the kids remained in Peterborough. Then, just when we'd found a new home in Congleton, Cheshire, the bosses at HQ offered me a promotion in Putney. For the next seven months I was destined to live out of a suitcase again, and apart from my family.

That distance contributed heavily to the breakdown of my marriage to Shirley. We'd been apart almost continuously for fourteen months, save for the odd weekend, and we were more like strangers than husband and wife. And like a typical male coward, I found intimacy with someone at work, instead of making the effort with my wife. In growing apart, I pulled away, and became blasé about my marriage. With that attitude, it was not surprising that I found interest – or was it an escape route? – with someone else, and fell for a secretary at ICL, called Jackie. It's not something I'm proud about and I know that I let my family down. I can't make excuses, even with the benefit of hindsight. I had an affair. It happened. And what pained me most was the fact Shirley's dad was proved right – I wasn't good enough for his daughter.

Our marriage ended in 1981, and that was also the year I left ICL to join Scholl, the London-based footwear company, as personnel manager for the UK. I married Jackie in 1982, the year I then became personnel director for Europe, the Middle East and Africa for the parent company, Schering-Plough. In what seemed like fast-track career advancement, I was then promoted to vice-president of human resources for its international division, with responsibility for business in twenty-eight countries. By 1984, my third son, Matthew, was on the way, and I'd moved companies to join Del Monte because Schering-Plough had moved my job to America but I couldn't leave my boys behind. So I found myself back in charge of Europe, the Middle East and Africa.

My life was spent travelling, but no matter where the different jobs took me – to America throughout Europe or the Middle East – I ensured that I was back in Leeds every Friday night, every other week, to take my regular seat at Elland Road. No job, no amount of promotion, was going to deprive me of seeing Leeds United at home. And there are thousands of fans just like that who continue to fill that stadium, with that same dedication and loyalty, to this day.

In 1985 I received a phone call to ask if I'd be interested in the post of personnel director – at Burton. Only this wasn't employment at the Hudson Road factory, this was in Oxford Street, London, with responsibility for the menswear divisions: Burton, Top Man, John Collier and Principles for Men. An interview was arranged to meet the chairman, Sir Ralph Halpern, and I was told the interview would be a formality.

'I bet they told you this interview with me was just a rubber-stamp exercise?' he said the moment I walked in to his office, tucked behind his famous TopShop branch in Oxford Circus. My broad grin confirmed it all.

'Well, let me tell you,' he said, 'my rubber-stamp has got ink on it!' and, with that remark, he was telling me that *he* decided whether I got the job, no one else. My interview was conducted with me sat down in a chair while he was stood up, being measured for a suit, arms outstretched. But he clearly felt I measured up nicely for the job. After half an hour, he shook my hand and said: 'You'd best go away and sort out your employment terms. And I'd like to take this opportunity to wish you the very best of luck, Peter.'

I could hardly contain my excitement at the prospect of working for this true legend of the retail world. As I walked down Oxford Street with a skip in my step, I felt completely elated. I had a quiet word with Mum in my head, knowing she'd be laughing at the fact I'd ended up working at Burtons.

ON THE INSIDE

We were a curious sight at Elland Road – me, Jackie and our baby son Matthew. It's not often you go to football stadiums on a match day to find a man and wife, cradling a baby, feeding him warm milk, hoping he'll fall asleep in time for three o'clock. With average attendances of around 12,000 in the old Second Division, we tended to stand out when we took our seats in the West Stand Paddock, beside the players' tunnel. We knew that Matthew – only a few months old – was going to be a placid child when he slept through the roar that greeted kick-off, and didn't even stir when the Kop burst into 'Marching On Together', the Leeds anthem. It was the mid-eighties, and Jackie and I drove north from London every other week, arriving in Leeds in time to eat at the Goal-Line Restaurant, at the rear of the South Stand, before settling down for the match.

The sight of this couple with babe-in-arms clearly caught the attention of club director Bill Fotherby. He came to our table one afternoon and remarked on how strange it was to see a baby at a match. Bill, with his large, wise-owl spectacles, always dressed in a pinstripe suit with a folded handkerchief poking out of his breast pocket. He had all the patter of a salesman but was as down to earth as you like.

He wanted to know all about us, how long we'd been Leeds fans, and where we were from. When he realized we made a 500-mile round trip every other weekend, he was amazed. 'That's dedication!' he laughed loudly before looking down at Matthew, 'and this young man will grow up supporting the right team.'

But it was when I told him that I worked for the Burton Group that his eyes really lit up. Unbeknown to me, the club was actively seeking bigger sponsorship and, from that moment, this one director always made a beeline for our table. Sponsorship was almost embryonic in those days. It was the era when the fan on the street had more of a presence than the corporate supporter; the days when BBC *Match of the Day* cameras arrived at two or three main games, not at every fixture; and when live televised football was restricted to internationals and FA Cup finals. But Bill Fotherby was a forward-thinking man and, because I'd moved from a career in personnel to become managing director of Top Man, he'd detected my passion for the club, and spotted a commercial opportunity.

Within a matter of weeks, he raised the possibility of Burton sponsoring Leeds United, and his contagious energy and drive made it sound like it would be the best union in commercial history.

I almost ran back to London with the proposal to put it before the next executive meeting of the menswear sector. Not that convincing my colleagues was plain sailing. There was real concern that, as a national brand, if the company backed one club, supporters in other cities would turn against Top Man, especially with a club that was currently in the Second Division doldrums, seemingly going nowhere.

But a vote was taken, the company made the leap and, in the summer of 1986, a twelve-month deal, worth around £50,000, was agreed. As the club's main sponsor, I became a welcome guest in the boardroom at all home and away fixtures. When the team ran out with 'BURTON' on the shirts for the first game of the 1986–87 season against Blackburn Rovers, I felt as proud as punch that I'd achieved something for club and company. Up until then, the best I'd been able to do was sponsor the match ball for £50 three or four times a season.

The club's chief executive, Terry Nash, said he 'was always intrigued to know who this Peter Ridsdale is' – he'd only ever

known companies sponsor match balls with that regularity. He
didn't realize an underlying motive was to bring my wife and
baby boy in from the cold because match ball sponsors were
allowed to sit in the warmth of an executive box!

'Wasn't one autographed ball enough?' he used to tease.

If *only* he knew the significance of an autographed ball to
me. As a kid, I remember hearing on the grapevine that a signed
Leeds United ball was being raffled at the youth club at Busling-
thorpe Hall, several miles from home. In those days, it was
impossible to get your hands on such gold. So I saved a month's
worth of pocket money, got the bus to the event and spent all
my money on raffle tickets. I was gutted when I saw a young
boy racing away with his prize after his number came up. Mr
Nash needed to understand that a fan can never have enough
autographed balls. Or shirts. Or programmes. Or other memora-
bilia.

What was great about that first year of sponsorship for the
1986–87 season was that Leeds had one of their best runs in
years, led by manager Billy Bremner and his five-man defences.
We reached the FA Cup semi-final and lost 3–2 to eventual
winners Coventry in that unforgettable thriller at Hillsborough,
and then we came within ten minutes of promotion to the top
flight after reaching the Second Division play-off finals, losing
out to Charlton, sunk by two late goals. In terms of brand
recognition for Burton, the exposure couldn't have been better.

•

In the summer of 1987, QPR's flamboyant chairman, David
Bulstrode, unwittingly had a hand in my being appointed as
director at Leeds United. He'd approached me, looking for a
sponsor to replace Guinness, and said if I manoeuvred the
menswear group to Loftus Road, I'd be offered a seat on the
board. When Bill Fotherby got wind of the approach, he negotiated direct with my football heart.

We were playing snooker one evening at the Alwoodley

home of Geoffrey Richmond, a regular corporate fan at Elland Road, wealthy owner of Ronson lighters, and someone else with aspirations to be a powerful figure in the game (as his later acquistions of Scarborough and then Bradford City proved). At the time, though, his daughter was married to the Leeds chairman's son, Mark Silver. So Bill's offer to me, under Geoffrey's roof and around his green baize, was a little cheeky in the circumstances, but he made the quietly spoken offer anyway: 'Don't do QPR – I can also offer you a seat on the board, you know,' he said.

At first, I wasn't sure whether it was a clever manoeuvre to make me miss one of the reds. But he went on to explain that he could persuade chairman Leslie Silver to offer me the one vacant seat on the Leeds board – with the proviso that sponsorship was continued. I didn't allow myself to dream but the thought alone was enough to make me forget about winning the frame that evening. Bill was a consummate salesman and could pitch an idea, or convince someone to do something *his* way, with a polished, persuasive argument – whether he meant it or not. He was flattering me, I thought, to ensure I turned down QPR. Then I'd be fobbed off with the excuse that Leslie Silver hadn't agreed to my appointment as a non-executive director. At least, that's what I told myself as Bill went on to sink the rest of the colours on the table.

In the days that followed, he proved as good as his word. I was appointed as a director in time for the Second Division home game of 30 September against Stoke City, which finished goalless. I walked into the stadium that evening feeling elation and pride. I grabbed the match programme, flicked to manager Billy Bremner's notes for the game and there, under his editorial and the Leeds United AFC emblem, was a list of the president, chairman, vice-chairman and directors. There was my name, plus a write-up of my appointment on the club news page. My passion and enthusiasm for everything that was Leeds United could now be pumped into the club from the *inside*. I was a fan transported from the West Stand paddock into the boardroom. I actually had a voice at my own club, and I can't begin to explain how fulfilling that felt.

These were some of the most exciting times in British retailing, and with the combination of working for the most talked-about retail giant, sponsoring and then becoming director of my hometown club, I had to ask myself: could life get any better?

Not that everyone was happy about a man living in Cobham, Surrey, being appointed director of a West Yorkshire club. A number of well-heeled contenders thought they deserved the vacant seat, not me. In my joy, I was blind to the politics and jealousies that raged, and there were whispered accusations that I'd 'queue-jumped'.

Such politics was rooted in 1956, when the Leeds stand burned down, and the club turned to the city's leading businessmen to help finance the rebuilding programme, and that created the tradition of the '100 Club' – the most influential businessmen in Leeds forging loyal ties with the city's club. Businessmen from *Leeds*, not London, as someone pointedly said. It didn't seem to matter that I'd been an avid and loyal supporter since 1960.

Obviously, I'd previously had access to the directors' box and boardroom at half-time as representative of the main sponsor. But even then, Bill had to approach the visiting club's chairman and ask, as a matter of etiquette, for permission for me to join them. Suddenly, I had a right to be there. Unlike my wife Jackie. We discovered that the wives of directors were barred from the tiny boardroom – big enough for around twenty people. A separate room was designated for the women. I wasn't going to make a stand and cause trouble at my first match but it was remarkably chauvinistic for a club that was big on promoting a family image to the fans. In the end we didn't protest too much because Jackie wouldn't be making too many matches that winter and following spring because she was pregnant with my fourth son, Joe, born later in May 1988.

Aged thirty-five, I was Leeds' youngest director. Sitting

around the oak table at my first board meeting, I was in awe of the debonair, millionaire chairman, Leslie Silver, and, to my left, the ex-chairman, Manny Cussins, who remained a director and a legend at the club.

'You could be the future for this club,' he said, tapping me on the knee; the wise owl to the green apprentice. He'd heard how I'd brought in the sponsorship deal, and how I'd drive from London to Leeds for those 4 p.m. board meetings every Monday, stay to hear the business in hand, then drive back south. 'Young blood', he called me.

I settled into the position, observing the characters, and grasping the club politics, increasingly fascinated by manoeuvres off the pitch. I was also getting to understand how the ambitious Bill Fotherby worked; he'd come up with some outlandish ideas, or spin the wildest of headlines (off the record, of course). His philosophy was that boundaries were there to be pushed, and if you didn't try or test something out then how would you ever know if it could work, or was a live possibility?

And that was his thinking behind the most ridiculous, audacious plan of them all – to bring Argentine legend Diego Maradona to Leeds United for the 1986–87 season just months after the 'Hand of God' had punched the ball over the head of Peter Shilton in Mexico and knocked England out of the World Cup.

'Do you know Jon Smith of First Artists?' Bill had rung to ask me and, yes, I knew the football agent well. 'Good, because me and you are having lunch with him at Elland Road,' he added.

So the three of us sat down in one of the executive boxes to a pleasant lunch where it emerged that Jon was Diego's English agent. There was a lot of banter about *that* goal cheating our nation but, after lunch, I didn't think any more about Maradona. Bill hadn't mentioned a word, at that point, about his ambitious idea. But later that afternoon, I received a frantic phone call from Mike Wood, the finance director of Burton.

'The Stock Exchange has asked me to make a statement

about Leeds United being in secret talks with Diego Maradona!
What's going on?' he said.

That evening's edition of the *Yorkshire Evening Post* had
gone to town with Maradona speculation, saying a deal was on
and his agent had already held discussions at a business lunch
and also present was a representative of the club sponsors.

In what was our first year of sponsorship, upsetting the
markets was the last thing I needed, and everyone wanted to
know how the club was going to fund such a transfer. I rang
Bill, suspecting his hand was behind it all.

'What?' he protested.

'Bill, people can't go dropping in announcements like that
when you're dealing with a public company, especially when
there's no truth in it! Do you realize the impact of this story?' I
said.

There was no prospect of Diego joining Leeds. Not in the
player's mind. Not in Jon Smith's mind. Not in my mind. But I
suspect Bill was off and running and dreaming, testing out an
idea by dropping it into the public domain. If his hand was
behind it, it certainly illustrates his ambition for the club.

'You never know where such speculation might lead to,' he
argued, in defiance of logic and then added the story wasn't
entirely untruthful: 'Look, Peter, all I said was that we had been
in discussions with his agent. *True*. Because we were. And that
you were present. *True*. Because you were. I really can't help
what the press make of that . . .'

Forever the salesman trying it on, forever insisting he was
right – you couldn't help but admire the man's chutzpah at
times. I'm not even sure he'd discussed the Maradona dream
with the manager but that was another side to Bill's character:
he was a frustrated football manager. He believed that he could
play a crucial part in creating the Leeds United dream team.
Apparently, he'd always been one to make 'helpful suggestions'
to managers about players they should sign, and he wasn't

always thanked for it! But Bill only ever had the interests of Leeds at heart, and his intentions were in the right place.

In the summer of 1988, the board had more serious matters to debate: the future of Billy Bremner. We'd convened at the grand home of the chairman where a few of us voiced concerns that the manager had taken the team as far as he could, and it would be far better to cut him loose in the summer than halfway through the season. The vote was split down the middle, so Mr Silver used his casting vote to save Bremner. The harsh truth was that he'd had one good season since 1985. It was also a surreal truth for me to confront because there I was, voting to dismiss one of my schoolboy heroes, the man who'd rendered me speechless through nerves when I was first introduced to him as the new sponsor. I remember him calling me 'Mr Ridsdale' and I cringed inside. 'No, Mr Bremner, please call me Peter,' I insisted. The reverence was all mine.

So the child within me hid in shame as Ridsdale the director ultimately dared to say out loud, 'I don't think Billy Bremner is good enough.'

As much as I admired the man and the player, he wasn't cutting it as manager. But he was blindly retained and the chairman kept his head in the sand for the first nine matches of the 1988–89 season. Then he was made to confront reality with our fifth defeat of the new season, at home to Watford, 1–0. The boardroom was subdued afterwards, filled with awkward chuntering and muttering because none of us could ignore the deafening chants from outside, from the car park below, beneath the boardroom window.

'*Bremner out! . . . Bremner out! . . . Bremner out!*' screamed a mob.

I didn't see the brick that smashed into the window. I just remember ducking at the sound of shattering glass. Bremner was sacked the next day.

The inevitable outcome hit the chairman hard because Bremner had been personally recommended by Don Revie who, from his sickbed, had phoned Mr Silver, pleading with him to give his old player the chance to prove himself. Revie was convinced Bremner deserved bigger and better than the hot seat at Doncaster Rovers. So Mr Silver, who revered Revie and was perhaps swayed by sentiment, made the bold move. But when it failed to pay off, it was as if he couldn't accept that Bremner's management hadn't worked out because that would have meant Revie was wrong. It took that one incident after the Watford game to shock him to his senses.

What struck me about the board, which comprised eight directors and four city council members, was how little influence the directors actually had. The power lay with the inner-circle of the chairman, Leslie Silver, vice-chairman Peter Gilman, commercial director Bill Fotherby and director Maxwell Holmes. Those four men made the key decisions; the rest of the board appeared to be 'involved' but, in reality, were just rubber-stamping, or checking and signing off expenses. So I learned to make it my business to know what was going on and, because of my close association with Bill, which led to a trusting relationship with the chairman, I was fortunate to have the ear of that inner circle. I quickly found out that the real business took place *outside* the boardroom.

One day, I arrived in the car park for a board meeting and saw Bill Fotherby and Bremner's successor, Howard Wilkinson, who introduced me to the man stood between them – Mickey Thomas.

'We've just signed Mickey from Shrewsbury,' Howard said as we all shook hands.

About half an hour later, the board meeting started with all the directors and the manager present. The agenda turned to the transfer market and possible new signings. All eyes turned to Howard.

He said nothing.

I looked at him. He winked at me. The meeting moved on to other business.

Outside, I asked Howard if Mickey Thomas had been a figment of my imagination. Howard laughed. After all, there was nothing 'possible' about this signing, because it was already a done deal. I later learned that had the board known that evening, the signing would have made the *Yorkshire Post*. And that could never have been allowed to happen because the club had an arrangement with its sister paper, the *Yorkshire Evening Post*, that all new transfers must be exclusive to them first.

Howard succeeded Bremner in October 1988 with Leeds languishing in twenty-first position in the Second Division. Howard Kendall and Arthur Cox had also been interviewed but the chairman decided the man for the job was the no-nonsense manager at Sheffield Wednesday. He'd taken the Owls to the First Division in his first season in charge and Mr Silver wanted him to work the same magic at Elland Road. Howard wouldn't be interviewed by the board, only by the chairman. He wasn't 'offered the job by the board' as newspaper reports suggested. All the board did was nod like donkeys. But we knew we had a man who had taken a risk in stepping down a division, clearly believing that he could awaken Leeds United from its slumber.

I met him at his first game, home to Peterborough United in the League Cup. I welcomed him aboard and wished him luck. In truth, though he smiled and was polite, he didn't appear to have much time for directors like me. Besides, all he wanted to do was focus on the pending kick-off.

Over time, because I stayed at the team hotels for away games, I would forge a good relationship with the dour, know-ledgeable, strict but fair disciplinarian, the man they nicknamed 'Sgt Wilko' – and he could spot a good wine as much as he could spot a good footballer.

Howard knew his own mind, and had a very black-and-white, focused approach to the game. But it was on those Friday evenings in the team hotels, sat with him and Bill Fotherby, sharing a bottle of red, that he enthused me with a fervent belief that Leeds United would return to the First Division.

Here was a man who had total self-belief in his own skills and ability to win things. I'd not seen such self-confidence in anyone before, and haven't seen it in many managers since. You can learn from people like Howard Wilkinson, learn all about drive, focus, belief and determination. Players who had previously been under his charge – Nigel Worthington, Lee Chapman, Imre Varadi and Mel Sterland – wanted to play for him again, and that says everything about the respect players had for the man. With a team unity that he bred, and the talent he amassed, he would lead Leeds United out of the wilderness.

It was sometime into Howard's first few months in charge that I was first allowed into the dressing room, the one place I'd always wondered about as a teenager. In those days, once the players had disappeared down the tunnel and out of sight, I'd imagined in my own head what the likes of Giles, Lorimer and Hunter did next, and what *really* happened in the dressing room.

So when the time came, as a director, to visit the dressing room two hours before kick-off one match day, I *had* to walk off the pitch and do it properly, just to flatter that same imagination: looking up at the West Stand, down the tunnel which didn't slope or rise, it just stayed flat before turning right through two swing doors and into a corridor; ref's room on the right and then, another twenty-five yards further down on the right, the words 'Home Dressing Room' on a wooden blue door with yellow handle. I entered and walked down a short hallway before the dressing room opened into a square, and the shirts that hung off the pegs denoted where each player sat.

Those shirts now bore the name Top Man, not Burton because, by the time of Howard's appointment, the menswear group had decided to switch the club sponsorship to a different division of the company. It was a smart move because, in the following 1989–90 season – his first full season in charge –

Howard returned us to the top flight, answering the demands on the T-shirts that Leeds fans started to wear, saying 'Shit or Bust – Promotion's a Must'. It wouldn't be the last time the fans would cry out 'Shit or Bust', as I would discover much, much later on.

It was a memorable season becoming Second Division champions. My son Matthew, no longer the babe in arms, ran out as a mascot for the 2 December 1989 home game versus Newcastle United, wearing the No.9 shirt of Ian Baird. And on that day it was Baird who scored our only goal in a 1–0 win. In my superstitious mind, that made the No.9 shirt the lucky number to wear that season.

I'd been superstitious since being a teenager when, on a youth club trip to Whitby, I'd bought a little glass 'Lucky Duck' and, since that day, I'd always carried it around in my wallet, and became convinced it was why my career was going from strength to strength. And if Leeds won a match, I'd have to wear the same suit, shirt and socks for the next game.

So when it came to the last game of the season, which would decide the championship away at Bournemouth, my superstitions kicked in. We needed to win in our neck-and-neck race to the top with Sheffield United. I insisted Matthew ran out with the team as mascot again, wearing No.9.

Sure enough, history repeated itself when Lee Chapman, the new occupant of the No.9 shirt after a £600,000 transfer from Nottingham Forest, met a Chris Kamara cross and scored the winner with a bullet header in a 1–0 win on the south coast. We were back in the big time, nicking the title on goal difference from the Blades, and with a club-record 85 points.

In the steam-filled dressing room afterwards, and with the championship trophy misting up on a table, champagne was on everyone's lips and in everyone's eyes as Magnums exploded like party-poppers. The team celebrated long after the final whistle, splashing about in the baths, and singing 'Marching On Together' as loud as they could. Then, for variation, Chris

Kamara led the beat with 'Champ-eee-oney . . . Champ-eeee-oney.'

Bill Fotherby, Peter Gilman and Mr Silver and I walked towards the baths, and were ambushed with a fresh shower of bubbly that came from all directions, drenching us from head to toe in our suits and club ties. I'd never been so happy at being so uncomfortably wet.

In the old days, I'd have been left to hang around on the terraces, savouring the moment, wanting to make it last. But, for my first taste of triumph as a director, I was at the heart of the club's private celebrations.

For me, being a director felt a bit like being a superfan – tremendous, privileged involvement but without the pressure or huge responsibilities. Once inside that dressing room, I breathed in the atmosphere of raw football; animated scenes from *Roy of the Rovers* comics brought to life. No longer was I on the periphery of the action with thousands of other fans, getting a waft of the drug that is football. I was at the heart of everything, swallowing it whole. All of us – fans, players, staff and directors – had waited eight years to be back in the top flight, and I jumped around, sang the songs and downed the champagne with the best of them.

The sad tinge in the air was that some players celebrated knowing they wouldn't be back the next season.

'I brought in players who aspired to be in the First Division. And others who were only meant to get us there,' Howard had said privately. He needed to be brutal if the club was to strengthen for the top flight, and certain players would be dispensed with. He had no emotion when it came to breaking up the squad. One team was designed for promotion. One team would be designed for life in the First Division.

Goalkeeper Mervyn Day knew he'd be one of those to go, having read strong newspaper speculation that linked Arsenal keeper John Lukic with a move to Yorkshire. When the cheering had died down in the dressing room, and as certain players got dried and changed, Mervyn was still in the bath when he caught the attention of Mr Silver, standing nearby.

With an air of resignation, he turned to the chairman and said in a calm voice, 'I've got what matters. I've got my Second Division championship medal. Now you can go and get John Lukic.'

And that's exactly what the club did.

Even more sadly, around 3,000 ticketless hooligans who couldn't get to see the bank holiday match at Dean Court marred the occasion by rioting on Bournemouth beach, staining our triumph by fighting running battles with Dorset Police. It was those shameful front-page headlines – with these hooligans rioting and wearing Top Man-sponsored Leeds shirts – that led to my being summoned to see company chairman Sir Ralph Halpern at his London offices. He wasn't a happy man.

'Can you explain all this negative publicity?' he frowned; his desk covered with all the newspapers.

I decided to adopt a fire-meets-fire policy. 'What do you mean, negative publicity, Sir Ralph? We've just sponsored the Second Division champions,' I protested.

'Peter, just think of all those little old ladies looking at the newspaper and seeing the Top Man shirts.'

'But little old ladies aren't Top Man's customers and this doesn't affect our brand, it affects Leeds United. As far as we're concerned, we've got a widespread brand. The association people make will not be Top Man and Riots but Top Man and Leeds United,' I argued. I opened the sports pages and showed him a photo of the team celebrating in a squad line-up. Top Man was emblazoned across twenty-two shirts. 'That's the images we should be concentrating on. That's what people will remember,' I said.

Sir Ralph partly accepted the argument and he allowed the continuance of sponsorship to continue – but only for the duration of the contract, which had one more season to run. 'Then I think we should call it quits,' he said.

•

Jackie pretty much said the same thing about our marriage.

The curse of being a workaholic had always been my Achilles heel in relationships and things were difficult at home mainly because of my own selfishness; working away in London, being involved in an exciting industry when fashion retail was at its height, working hard and playing hard, and travelling to Leeds United games became my life. Leaving home at 6 a.m. and not getting in till past 9 p.m. was never going to be conducive to marital happiness. Home life seemed like an afterthought; a duty. I found my joys elsewhere; like an idiot I felt I could ride the crest of the wave on my own.

Life for me couldn't have felt much better. But Jackie couldn't have felt more miserable. She also suspected I'd been playing away, and she was right; typical of a man who tastes success and thinks that, somehow, that gives him three dicks, and that he can achieve anything, and anyone, he wants. It's nonsense, of course, but it's a truth about the delusions within the male mind. Just as in football, success leads to confidence which leads to a belief of invincibility. And then comes the fall.

One night, as Jackie and I were preparing for bed, everything came to a head.

She couldn't have been calmer with her opening salvo: 'Are you seeing someone else?'

'Don't be daft. When do I have time to meet someone else?'

She looked at me, nonchalance written all over her face. 'I know you have,' she said, 'and I don't care. Things have been bad between us anyway so you can just tell me. I'm not bothered.'

There it was, a new lesson to learn – the not-bothered attitude that lulls so many men into a false sense of security, manipulated to foster a confession that will then unleash holy Armageddon.

And so I confessed to seeing someone but it not meaning anything.

Jackie came at me harder than Norman Hunter taking his man out, and she wanted to do a lot more than just bite my legs off. She went from calm to berserk in a matter of seconds, leaving me running down the stairs, out the front door and down the street in my sweater and jeans. I ignominiously slept that night in the car, my black 735 BMW, parked in the driveway.

The next morning, Jackie wouldn't let me back in the house, and I ended up shouting through the letterbox, telling her I needed my suit, ties and shirts for an important meeting with Sir Ralph that day. About five minutes later, the bedroom window opened and a suit, a pair of shoes and a collection of shirts landed on the lawn. I gathered them into a bundle, ducking from the abuse that rained down from the bedroom, and retreated to the car to get dressed. It was then I saw that she'd cut the arms off all the shirts. It was a hot day, and one I'd have to spend in a stifling jacket to hide my wife's new fashion trend for summer.

I walked into the meeting to find Sir Ralph and five other men sat around a table with their jackets off, and shirt sleeves rolled-up. The Burton Group was not one to stand on ceremony in its meetings, and how I cursed such informality on that day.

'Peter!' said the welcoming voice of Sir Ralph. I sat down as beads of sweat rolled from beneath my fringe, and undid my collar and took off my tie. Sir Ralph looked at me quizzically as I sat there in my jacket, bare arms cool against the inner lining.

'You not going to take off your jacket?' he asked.

'No, I'm fine . . . much prefer to sit here with my jacket on,' I blustered.

'But you look hot,' he said, not letting it go.

'I'm not well, Sir Ralph. Got the fever, got the shivers. Best keep the jacket on,' I lied again.

I must have lost several pounds in weight through sweat during that meeting. But everyone was informed that the Leeds United sponsorship would cease after a further year, and I was thanked for making it happen. And then I drove back home to attempt to rescue my marriage.

•

On the pitch, Howard Wilkinson was beginning to rescue Leeds with his vision for the future. He didn't just believe Leeds belonged in the First Division. He believed they could get there and conquer it. To this end he transformed the Leeds squad, and made big-money transfers.

In came Gordon Strachan (£300,000 from Manchester United), Chris Fairclough (£500,000 from Spurs), Vinnie Jones (£600,000 from Wimbledon), John Hendrie (£600,000 from Newcastle United), Mel Sterland (£650,000 from Rangers) and John McClelland (£150,000 from Watford). Later on in the new season, he added Lee Chapman (£600,000 from Forest).

I'll never forget his attitude to new signings: 'If you get three out of every five signings right, you've done a good job,' he said. It was an interesting observation from a manager but an honest truism. Fortunately for him, most of his signings proved effective.

What I learned from him was that whatever you spent, there was always a purpose to it. For example, bringing in Lee Chapman made all the difference even though we sat atop the Second Division come Christmas. Howard never sat on his laurels, and never stopped trying to improve the team. It reinforced what Brian Clough used to say: that you should never stop acquiring players, and every club should be a buying and selling club; the day you're satisfied with the team you've got, you'll start going backwards.

Everyone talked of Gordon Strachan being one of his best signings but, for me, Vinnie Jones from Wimbledon was equally impressive. He proved to be an inspirational signing, a true motivator. He fitted into the direct style of play perfectly, and his hard-man reputation belied the truth that he was one of the nicest guys you could ever wish to meet. When he signed, he put pen to paper in my offices in London, also witnessed by Bill Fotherby, while Howard was on holiday. We cracked open a bottle of champagne to welcome him to the club.

The following week, there was an interview with him in *Match* magazine. I couldn't stop giggling as I read how Vinnie was reported to have said he was sold on the move by Howard, and how impressed he was at the stature, surroundings and sights of Elland Road when he visited the stadium. There was only one drawback to that great insight – Vinnie hadn't even been to Leeds let alone the stadium; the deal was clinched by Bill ringing Sam Hamman at Wimbledon after Howard had made his wish-list clear. I started to realize how the PR was spun for the sake of the fans.

When he eventually did drive up the M1, Vinnie was a superb ambassador for the club, and he became a cult figure with the fans. He gave 100 per cent week in, week out, and his spirit encapsulated the work rate and belief that sent Leeds United romping towards promotion. In the space of a year, Howard and his team had taken Leeds from twenty-first to league champions – and they were ready to return to the land of the giants.

MARCHING ON TOGETHER

Elland Road was the only place for me. When that packed stadium found its voice, there was no better sound. I'd stand in the directors' box, look to my left and marvel at the sight of the terraced Kop, a compact mass of white ever so slightly surging and swaying; passion on the boil. And then, two minutes before kick-off, every man, woman and child would sing their hearts out, as fiercely as a staunch patriot would burst his lungs for the National Anthem.

> Marrrrrr-ching Onnnn Tog-ether . . .
> We're gonna see you win . . .
> Nah-nah-nah-nah-nah-na . . .
> Coz we are so proud . . .
> We shout it out loud . . .
> We love you, *Leeds, Leeds, Leeds!*

I couldn't help but join in as that chant reverberated around the Kop, through the West Stand and bounced across the pitch to the old, rickety-looking Lowfields Road Stand. I didn't care that the manager and fellow directors were around me. I bellowed as loud and proud as the next man.

I remember Howard's face when he first became manager and he heard me singing, and he swivelled in his seat on the row in front of me to find out where such a noise was coming from. For such a phlegmatic man, it must have seemed odd to have this director acting so animated, like a supporter. He never said anything, and maybe it showed him that I wasn't just some corporate suit, indifferent to the outcome on the pitch.

They always said that roar was worth a goal start, and I was aware that the opposing sides, and fans, must have felt the edge in such an atmosphere; that pre-match fervour was almost tangible. I was certain this stadium and this atmosphere belonged in the top flight.

Life did feel great in the Barclays First Division. For many of us, it was like a nonstop party from August 1990 to May 1991, starting the moment the whistle was blown for our first match, away at Everton when Speed, Varadi and Fairclough ensured there was no anticlimax with goals that sealed a pulsating 3–2 win.

But Elland Road had long been hungry to taste the big-match vibe again, and so it seemed apt that we lifted the roof to herald our first home match, versus Manchester United. The likes of Denis Irwin, Steve Bruce, Paul Ince, Brian McClair and Mark Hughes trotted out in front of almost 30,000 fans. We'd last seen their like at home in the 1981–82 season, the year we fell through the trapdoor into the Second Division.

At the start of the nineties, Manchester United had not yet found their full stride under Alex Ferguson; they were still striving to clinch their first league title since 1967. But he was still diligently building his empire with a board that took a long-term view, affording him the luxury of time that the myopic boards of today would find hard to understand.

Sat in the West Stand high above the players' tunnel, perched on the left shoulder of Howard as he used a phone line to ring the dug-out, and overhearing some of his instructions, it was surreal to be back in the big time, having the inside track on the game.

'This is what it's all about!' I said to a beaming Bill Fotherby, sat to my right.

That season, every match was a huge one as a newly promoted side, and we held Manchester United to a goalless draw. As the months went on, the more we realized we were holding our own, coping admirably with the leading teams of Arsenal,

Liverpool, Manchester City and Crystal Palace; Chapman, Speed, Strachan and Carl Shutt were regularly finding the back of the net. Howard had bolstered the squad with Chris Whyte (£400,000 from West Brom), John Lukic (£1 million from Arsenal) and Gary McAllister (£1 million from Leicester City). John Hendrie, Mickey Thomas and Vinnie Jones were let go for the sake of a stronger future.

Bill Fotherby ensured I wouldn't forget Vinnie's £700,000 transfer to Sheffield United in a hurry. Out of the blue, I received a call from the commercial manager at Bramall Lane, asking to send him Vinnie's logbook for his BMW three series.

In those days, I'd persuaded Burton to buy two cars, sponsoring them for individual players. One went to Mark Aizlewood, the other to Vinnie. But it always remained a Burton car, owned by the company. So why Sheffield United wanted the logbook was beyond me.

'Well, it's his car now,' said the matter-of-fact voice on the other end of the phone, 'he's been given it by Leeds United as part of the deal.'

And so it transpired that the player was still owed signing-on fees by Leeds and Bill, without realizing who owned it, had waived those fees in exchange for the £17,000 car instead.

'Bill, you can't just go giving Burton's cars away!' I protested, having spelt out the facts.

'Well, it *was* second-hand, Peter!' he laughed, and we both saw the funny side. It had all been signed, sealed and delivered, minus the logbook.

After the Maradona share-price scare, I found myself handling another hot potato back at Burton, explaining why we had no choice but to write off the car as an asset. 'Why don't we have a choice?' someone asked.

'Because the car's been sold to Vinnie Jones,' I said.

That December, with us riding a surprise fifth in the table, I received a phone call from a sports reporter on the *Daily Mail* called David Walker. He'd been given permission to talk to me, he said, by Bill Fotherby, and was seeking my comments on the club's new initiative to have directors stand with supporters on the terraces at away games because of complaints about fans' treatment at other grounds.

'I'm not sure I understand why you're coming to me for a comment.' I said.

'Because you're the first director to be chosen to stand with the fans versus Manchester United this Saturday,' he explained.

I had no idea what he was talking about but had to pretend to the contrary otherwise I'd have revealed one truth about life at Leeds United – that most directors were kept in the dark about the decisions being taken. When I rang Bill, he enthusiastically confirmed the 'initiative', raved about the *Daily Mail*'s interest and thanked me for being the first director to step forward.

Three days later, as a snowstorm lashed the Pennines, I flew from Heathrow to Manchester while the travelling Leeds support fought through the blizzards on the M62. As the teams ran out at Old Trafford, I wore two coats but still had never felt so cold in my life. It was the kind of cold that ached the bones. The kind of cold I'm sure the other directors were not experiencing.

''Ere, aren't you that geezer from Top Man?' asked one fan, recognizing me from the many pre-match Player-of-the-Month presentations at home which saw a £50 voucher gifted to star players.

'The Geezer from Top Man' – that's all I was known as back then.

'Is that coat from Top Man then!' another one laughed. There was plenty of good-hearted banter with the fans, and how everyone laughed about the director that was freezing his nuts off. But the cold was all we had to complain about; there was no bad treatment from stewards or police. And the *Daily Mail* photographer got his picture of the director stood behind the goal as Mel Sterland equalized in a 1–1 draw. I actually enjoyed being back on the terraces. It took me back to the last time I'd been stood at Old Trafford in the 1964–65 season when we beat them 1–0 in dense fog, only for them to pinch the title from us on goal average.

At the next home game, Bill was still applauding his initiative, the ensuing article and my feedback.

'So who's the next lucky director in line then?' I asked.

Bill looked almost apologetic before launching into another one of his convincing explanations. The man's got more nerve, more patter and more excuses up his sleeve than Del Boy on a good day.

'Well, Peter, we actually thought that you gave us such an in-depth insight into what it's like to be a travelling fan that we don't really think we need to do it again . . .'

Bill had got his headline. Job done.

The one good thing to come out of that episode was meeting David Walker because it was the start of not just a professional relationship but a long-standing friendship. He's an honest gent in the world of sports journalism; someone who works only with facts and couldn't be fairer. Sports journalism needs more people like him. And football would be dull without characters like Bill.

In that first season back in the top flight, we pulled off a remarkable feat, finishing fourth behind champions Arsenal, Liverpool and Crystal Palace. It surpassed all our expectations. But Howard wasn't satisfied. He was determined to keep team-building, determined to push for title in 1991–92, the final season of the First Division before the creation of the Premiership.

More money was made available and more players released as the financial gamble refused to let up. In came Tony Dorigo (£1.3 million from Chelsea), Steve Hodge (£900,000 from Nottingham Forest), David Weatherall (£125,000 from Sheffield Wednesday) and twins Rod and Ray Wallace (£1.6 million and £100,000 respectively, from Southampton). We signed the twins because it was felt Rod would be happier and settle better if we kept his twin with him. The funniest moment came when Bill

Fotherby weighed up the prospects of the new signings from The Dell.

'I think Rod's got an exciting future ahead of him because he's only twenty-one,' he said earnestly. 'As for Ray, I don't know how old he is so I really couldn't say . . .'

Bill had bigger sums to concern himself with in the transfer market. If you take football in general, the teams that have made it have always pursued the path of spending big, as Blackburn Rovers, Manchester United and Chelsea would prove in later years. And that season we would follow that path. In that era football clubs depended on money from ITV's live matches – First Division sides were earning around £2 million in television rights, giving them the chance to fund their ambitions. Howard was backed by the board to spend big, and it achieved success.

In those pre-Sky TV bounty-money days, Howard's spending was relatively heavy as a proportion of the club's income, but the consequences of failure were potentially less catastrophic than today. Nevertheless, the fans never complain when the financial gambles are taken, the board provides the resources, and the manager delivers success. As I would discover much later, when the managers do fail, it's a completely different story. Under Howard, everything gelled: a policy of attacking football reaped rewards and the crowds came flooding back.

By the winter of 1991, I left Burton to become managing director of Alexon plc, switching from menswear to womenswear, and Burton stopped sponsoring Leeds United. The *Yorkshire Evening Post* stepped into the breach – and no doubt guaranteed more transfer exclusives! It was good timing for the new sponsors because everyone was talking about Leeds again, and average home attendances soared to almost 30,000. In our second season in the top flight, we were breathing down Manchester United's neck, vying for top spot. The sense of revivalism of the glory years was in full swing.

•

On the advice of Michel Platini, a mercurial Frenchman by the name of Eric Cantona arrived on our shores, initially to have trials with Sheffield Wednesday. He arrived with very little English, and a bad-boy temperament that, sadly, went before him and did little justice to his brilliance with a ball. He'd received a one-year ban from the French team for calling the coach, Henri Michel, 'one of the world's most incompetent trainers'. Then he was suspended by Marseille for throwing his shirt at a ref when substituted. And he was banned for ten days at Montpellier, where he was on loan, after smashing his boot into the face of team-mate Jean-Claude Lemoult.

I found out from the newspapers that Leeds had signed him from Nîmes for a reputed £900,000 in February 1992. It was a significant signing in our race to the title with Manchester United, and it was one fraught with risks if reports of his volatility were believed.

He played wide-right despite not being a natural winger, and brought a fascinating unpredictability and flair to our game. Whenever he came off the bench – he was predominantly used as a supersub in his first season – he lifted the crowd just by running on to the pitch.

His relationship with fellow striker Lee Chapman was fractious to say the least. There was talk that Eric didn't rate his counterpart, and that it rankled with him that the team's style of play was built around Lee. Eric wanted to be the team's tactical linchpin, and never understood the reliance on Chapman.

Either way, their contributions, in very different ways and styles, were equally vital as the club defied everyone who doubted our stamina for the championship run-in. We were the club people loved to hate, and many critics didn't want to see us find glory. Chief among them was former Liverpool and England player Emlyn Hughes: 'If Howard Wilkinson sent out eleven vestal virgins and whistled up the Angel Gabriel to captain them, folk would still loathe Leeds United. Me included,' he wrote in the *Daily Mirror*, going on to explain how he longed for us to be torn apart, and lose the title. We responded by thumping Sheffield Wednesday 6–1 at Hillsborough, Lee Chapman scoring a hat-trick.

We then suffered a couple of bad reverses in the spring, getting thumped 4–1 at Queens Park Rangers on 11 March, my fortieth birthday, and then 4–0 away at Manchester City at the start of April. It was hardly the form of champions. Come 12 April, with four games to play, we were top of the table with 72 points. Manchester United were second on 71 but with two games in hand. It was their title to lose, and they buckled under the pressure, losing crucial games in hand against Nottingham Forest and West Ham.

Suddenly, our destiny was in our hands. The mere talk of such a possibility was enough to discharge electricity through the veins of every Leeds fan.

When we beat Sheffield United 3–2 at Bramall Lane in an early kick-off, leaving us four points clear, everyone waited on the result of Liverpool versus Manchester United at Anfield. I watched the match live on ITV at Peter Gilman's farmhouse in Derbyshire, and how we screamed out the Peak District when Ian Rush and Mark Walters put the title out of Alex Ferguson's reach.

The feeling was immense. We phoned Bill. We then phoned Howard. He'd not watched the match. He'd chosen to eat Sunday roast with his family instead. His five-year-old son Ben had told him the news after watching the match on a television upstairs. We both congratulated the manager.

'Thank you very much, it is a dream come true and I look forward to celebrating with you all. But we've got another game to play at home to Norwich, remember,' he said, ever the grounded professional.

When that final game came and Sgt Wilko blew the whistle, and his players could fall out and throw their caps in the air on 2 May 1992, the scenes were memorable as the team paraded the trophy around the pitch. It was an incredible feeling to return to the glory days, courtesy of Lukic, Sterland, Fairclough, Whyte, Dorigo, Strachan, Batty, McAllister, Speed, Wallace, Chapman, Cantona, McClelland, Hodge, Newsome, Shutt, Varadi and Kamara.

I'll never forget Cantona standing on the steps of Leeds Town Hall, before a crowd that thronged the city centre with a mass of brilliant white, to mark the civic reception, and, as each player held the trophy aloft, Cantona's English was restricted to four simple words: 'I . . . love you . . . Leeds!!' and the place went berserk. They idolized him. He referred to them as part of the 'Cantona family'.

I'd joined the open-top bus on its route to the civic reception after driving to the stadium with sons Matthew and Joe, and wife Jackie, with the windows down on a warm, sunny day. 'Marching On Together' blared from the car stereo.

As we boarded the bus and it crawled out of Elland Road, it turned right outside the main gates and pulled alongside Jackson Boilers, and I pointed out to the boys and Jackie where I'd spent the night queuing for that first FA Cup final ticket twenty-seven years previously. In that moment, I had everyone around me who mattered: the family, the Leeds team, the fans. But I so wanted Dad to be there to share in the occasion, even though he never really liked football. I wanted him to see there had been a purpose to my blind passion, and this was the reward. I missed him not being there to witness it all, not being able to share what it meant to be a director of a championship-winning club.

I suppose a lot of people got nostalgic that day, and many older fans would have flashed back to the Don Revie days. For the Leeds United team of 1991–92 had one remarkable thing in common with the great Revie side of 1963–64: both won promotion and became champions in the First Division. These days, promoted clubs would find it impossible to accomplish such a feat; that it's happened twice in our history speaks volumes for the skills of both managers.

Some commentators have argued that both men earned the titles on the back of dull football, and that far too often the ball was passed back to the likes of Gary Sprake or John Lukic, allowing players to push up and play 'Route One' football. But the game is about creating goalscoring opportunities and putting the opposing team under pressure, and the champion Leeds teams executed that strategy with effective, winning football. We might not have had the flair of, let's say, a pass-and-run 'invincible' Arsenal team under Arsène Wenger but we were, nevertheless, deserving champions.

As the *Daily Mirror*'s John Edwards and Harry Harris said in an article under the headline 'WE ARE THE CHAMPIONS' on 27 April 1992: 'While Leeds may not be the classiest champions of all time, Wilkinson deserves the honour of becoming the first manager since Don Revie to bring back the glory days to Elland Road – and that is no mean feat.'

No one can ever forget Don Revie. He'll forever remain a God-like figure at Elland Road. But, equally, no one should forget what Howard Wilkinson masterminded. His form might not have been as sustained as Revie's run but the scale of his achievement remained Herculean, and he built the foundations for an even more exciting future.

•

In the dressing room, I pulled on the Leeds United yellow away strip, sucked in my paunch, and prepared to make my debut as Howard finally made my dream come true, and gave me the call-up.

Turning out for the First Division champions certainly beat playing for Adel Memorial Hall.

It was Tokyo, and the summer of 1992, and the champions of England were in Japan to play an exhibition match against the champions of South America. Sadly, the reality was that my debut was limited to the training pitch in Japan. I'd been drafted into the reserve XI as a stop-gap measure for a match against the first XI. I'd asked Howard if it would be okay to attend training.

'You can put a pair of boots on if you like, we need someone to make up the numbers,' he'd said.

And that was how I found myself in the right-back position, man-marking the gazelle-like Rod Wallace. For the first five minutes, I'd fooled myself into thinking I was doing okay. Then Rod ran at me with the ball, stopped just in front of me, the ball trapped under his left foot. He winked, smiled and then darted inside and ran past me so fast that I didn't even see him move.

'I thought you wanted to play, Peter!' yelled Howard from the touchline. 'If you're not up to it, get off the pitch!!' I was ribbed mercilessly. What a pathetic sight I must have been – an unfit, unathletic, breathless director, deluding himself a million miles from home.

I lasted twenty minutes and then collapsed. 'Enjoyed it?' asked Howard, laughing. It's fair to say the boss wasn't that impressed with my trial.

As we prepared to defend our title, no one seemed in more scintillating form than Eric Cantona. He scored a memorable hat-trick in a 4–3 victory over Liverpool in the Charity Shield at Wembley, and two weeks later he scored the first ever hat-trick in the new Premiership in our 5–0 home drubbing of Spurs. The man was on fire, and it was the perfect way to tee up our return to the European Cup in a first round, two-leg tie against the German champions VfB Stuttgart. Only it seemed no one knew the extent of an injury he'd been carrying going into the first leg at the Neckar Stadion. We'd held out 0–0 in the first-half but then Cantona uncharacteristically slipped up, playing a loose ball across the field, and gifted Stuttgart a goal.

We went on to lose 3–0 that night; it seemed like we'd never pull back such a deficit, and it was the beginning of the end for Cantona in a white shirt. Behind the scenes, he and Howard started to have disagreements, sparked by Howard having a go at him over gifting Stuttgart that goal.

You'd think all would have been forgiven after the return leg. No British side had ever come back from a three-goal deficit in Europe. But 'Super' Leeds evoked the majestic European nights from the Revie era, and defied the odds with a titanic effort and an all-out attack. Cantona set up one and scored another as we romped to a 4–1 victory. We should have been out on away goals but the drama wasn't over because Stuttgart admitted breaking UEFA's foreign player rule with a substitution, and a replay was ordered for Barcelona's Nou Camp. Leeds completed a magnificent comeback with a 2–1 win, to set up 'The Battle of Britain' tie against Glasgow Rangers in the second round. The Scots beat us 2–1 in both legs and our European adventure was brought to an end.

And then *everything* seemed to go downhill.

There were clearly ructions in the dressing room, and Eric Cantona and Howard Wilkinson's feud had come to a head three days after the first leg against Rangers when we travelled to London to play Queens Park Rangers. Howard had decided to make changes, and drop the Frenchman. The ensuing explosion was always going to happen when a direct Yorkshireman's no-nonsense manner was primed to upset the delicacies of a Frenchman's football ego.

I was sat reading a newspaper in the Royal Lancaster Hotel, London, where the team was staying. Howard was on the other side of a set of double doors, dropping his bombshell in a team meeting. The next thing I heard was a clatter – perhaps a chair going over? – and a single door flew open, banging against the wall. Cantona stormed out in a whirlwind of red mist, shot down the stairs and hailed a taxi. He went to Paris instead of Loftus Road, and from then his days were numbered at Leeds United.

Howard had walked out after him, and stood seething in the hotel corridor.

'I told him he was dropped, and that was it,' he said. 'Don't breathe a word about what you've just seen. But I won't be treated like that by anyone – and he won't be playing for Leeds much longer!'

Disciplinarians like Howard don't tolerate tantrums from their troops, and whatever was done or said in that meeting room was enough to sever player–manager relations for ever. And that was when Wilkinson made it clear to the board that Cantona must go. Meanwhile, Cantona, unable to tolerate being dropped, faxed in a transfer request.

Two league games later, and to the disgust of Leeds fans, he was transferred to Manchester United in November 1992.

Bill Fotherby had rung Martin Edwards at Old Trafford to inquire about full-back Paul Parker but he wasn't for sale. Martin asked if we'd release Lee Chapman. Bill said no, but out of the blue offered Eric Cantona instead. That's when Martin fell off his chair. Bill's only conditions were that negotiations must be kept secret, and a deal worth £1.2 million had to be completed that night.

Manchester United must have done cartwheels – Cantona, scorer of two hat-tricks already that season, was offered on a plate for little more than one million. No wonder Edwards went on to describe it as 'the greatest deal in the history of English football'. But it also illustrated how much Howard wanted rid of him.

Leeds fans felt betrayed by club and player. In the distant past, Joe Jordan and Gordon McQueen had caused upset with a double transfer across the Pennines but Cantona was different – he'd joined our title rivals, and it was tantamount to swapping religions.

Howard tried justifying the sale in his programme notes: 'Eric Cantona left here because he wanted to go or, to put it another way, he wasn't prepared to stay and abide by the rules and conditions which operate for everybody. He wasn't prepared to stay unless he was playing in the team. He can't have his cake and eat it . . .' He added: 'Mark my words, this club will continue to win and grow.'

Sadly, the reverse happened. Our decline became unstoppable, exacerbated by the loss of Cantona. That season, we didn't win a single away league game, and finished seventeenth. Between 1993 and 1996 the team broke up; we lost the likes of Strachan, Batty and Chapman and in came players like Tony Yeboah and Tomas Brolin – and a certain David O'Leary.

I felt for Howard as he struggled to rediscover the touch and strategies that had brought such success. It was as if he'd run out of ideas, and the biggest sadness was to hear the fans chant, 'Wilko out! Wilko out! Wilko out!' at the end of our 3–0 League Cup final defeat to Aston Villa in 1996. The following autumn, Howard was sacked after seven games of the new season, and George Graham was said to be waiting in the wings.

•

In the Ridsdale household, life had been just as hectic.

That mogul of the US media, Barry Diller, had purchased a $25m stake in the QVC teleshopping network and, together with his Australian counterpart Rupert Murdoch, he hired me to launch QVC in Europe, the first retail shopping channel of its kind on this continent. Barry Diller was an inspiring but fierce character to come up against. If a phone rang four times and wasn't answered, you'd be sacked. At least, that was the rumour that kept everyone on their toes.

The channel was to be launched in October 1993 and, after an initial interview at Sky TV in London, I was flown to the QVC HQ in Westchester, Pennsylvania, that August. When I faced this formidable bald eagle across his desk, I was genuinely quivering in my boots. Unlike Sir Ralph, who was able to relax and crack a joke, Barry Diller had the stare of a boxer, totally business, totally focused, and he wasn't in the mood for quips from an Englishman. He grilled me, discharging questions at the rate of a machine-gun spilling cartridges. The interview lasted no more than twenty minutes.

'What are you still doing here then?' he smiled. 'You've got a black tie dinner in London to celebrate the launch of Sky Multichannels – and to celebrate your appointment. Congratulations.'

On 1 October 1993, QVC Europe went live on air with its first product – a plastic VW beetle alarm clock. Within seconds of going live, the phone lines lit up like Regent Street at Christmas, and we knew we were in business.

By then, I'd retained a new PA called Sophie Hobhouse. She would become my third wife in 1995 after Jackie and I, who had been unable to repair our marriage, divorced the previous year.

I'd known Sophie for a number of years because she'd been PA to one of my best friends, Matthew Luthos, then chief executive of an advertising agency. Sophie was outgoing, self-confident and very attractive; her personality, looks and intelligence knocked me out. She convinced me she knew lots about football. That was, until one of her friends told me she thought I was a director at Leicester . . .

We married on 22 April 1995 in Somerset. As I was getting ready, best man Mike Spencer handed me a waistcoat as a gift from the bride-to-be. It was embroidered with 'No.3' on the back, not because I was a left-back but to signify that this was third time lucky! Our first daughter, Charlotte, was born on 13 May 1996, and Olivia followed on Boxing Day 1997.

It was all change at the club, too. At an extraordinary general meeting Leslie Silver, Bill Fotherby and Peter Gilman had pushed through the creation of a new holding company that sat above the board; we directors were officially frozen out of the key decision-making process. Voting shares and ultimate power had switched from being in the hands of hundreds of small shareholders into the hands of just three chiefs. It felt to me that, as a director, I became nothing more than a glorified season-ticket holder.

For me, it was a particularly remote and disillusioning period. I went to matches but felt no involvement or inclusion. I wasn't even hearing anything on the grapevine any more. The *Yorkshire Evening Post* seemed to hear rumours before we did. The restructuring of the board left a bitter taste in a lot of mouths, and I'd been dead against it from the outset, never thinking for a minute that an EGM would grant approval.

I'd made my opposition clear and maybe that's why I received a phone call from someone suggesting that I 'give some consideration to joining the board of a London-based club to save all that travelling time from London to Leeds every other week'. It was pointed out that 'the path could be smoothed' to a seat on the board at Charlton Athletic. I reminded the caller that my passion was Leeds United and under no circumstances would I be going anywhere.

It was clear that my questioning of the holding company wasn't welcomed. I'd been asking some awkward questions. There was nothing improper in this restructuring, but I could not help wondering why it was being done. Why was it necessary to disenfranchise hundreds of people for whom it meant so much to have that Leeds United share certificate framed on the wall? Maxwell Holmes quit his seat in protest. I wasn't so principled, and wasn't going to give anyone the satisfaction of seeing me walk away.

It seemed clear to me the restructuring of the board in 1993 was always going to be a precursor to a future attempt to sell the club and sure enough, three years later in 1996, Leeds United was sold for £6.5m. Leslie Silver, Bill Fotherby and Peter Gilman each walked away with around £2m for shareholdings that had initially been worth around £35,000.

London-based Caspian Media Group plc were the new owners, having beaten a rival bid from Conrad. Bill, forever thinking ahead, had been clever in his negotiations with the buyers, ensuring they publicly stated that the football club's chairman would be local. And with Leslie Silver stepping down, and Bill and me as the only Leeds lads on the board, that left him walking into the role of club chairman, answerable to Caspian plc.

One of the first things he did was treat himself to a green Bentley, which purred into the car park with the private registration 'WJF 271'. I've always said that when it's Bill's turn to die, he'll arrive at the Pearly Gates and somehow persuade God to give him a second chance at life.

As many had suspected, George Graham was a Caspian appointee, installed as Howard Wilkinson's successor. He arrived pledging to build 'a George Graham Leeds' but didn't want anyone getting carried away with huge expectations. 'We are not in a position like some clubs who can go out and spend £20 million so ours will be a slower progress,' he wrote in his programme notes one day.

The chairman was a frustrated manager, and would soon clash with the new boss. Ever since the days of Billy Bremner, Bill had tried having an input on team selection, sharing his wisdom on team selection. Some would view it as interference; some, like Howard Wilkinson, regarded it as an enthusiasm to work with. And no one was more eager than Bill to be chief scout, chief buyer, chief power broker.

In 1994, after the World Cup, Bill was despatched to Italy by Howard to sign one of the tournament's hot-shots, Faustino Asprilla, from Parma. On his return, Bill was absolutely buoyant over the success of his mission. Then it was announced he'd signed Tomas Brolin instead, for £4.5m. Sadly, that acquisition put on more pounds than points for Leeds United, never really impressed Howard and earned the unfortunate tag of 'the worst signing in Leeds' history'.

But the best story about Bill's forays into the transfer market concerned one of Howard's last signings, Lee Sharpe from

Manchester United. Bill was a man on a mission as he headed across the Pennines, and I learned all about his hard bargaining tactics many years later from Martin Edwards, his counterpart at Old Trafford.

Unbeknown to Bill, Martin had discussed the imminent transfer with Alex Ferguson, knowing that the emergence of Ryan Giggs meant there was no realistic place for Sharpe. Manager and chairman both agreed that, if they could get £1m for the player, that would represent good business.

So in walks a poker-faced Bill to negotiate with Martin Edwards. 'I really want that young man but I'm not going to pay over the odds,' he asserted. Martin fully understood, he said.

'I'll pay no more than four million,' said Bill.

Martin thought about it for a moment. 'Make it four and a half and you've got a deal,' he said.

'Done,' said Bill, knowing he had authorisation from the board. And that's how Lee Sharpe was brought to Elland Road. Another new recruit to Leeds was a young man called Lee Bowyer, a whippet of a midfielder signed from Charlton for £2.75m – then making him the most expensive teenager in the game.

George Graham didn't take too kindly to Bill's attempts to influence team selection, as Bill himself explained. He'd suggested to the manager that Tony Yeboah be selected against Chelsea. He felt the striker wasn't being given a fair chance. George, one of the most professional, impressive and self-confident managers I've known, was having none of it. He felt Yeboah was unfit and overweight, and refused to pick the Nigerian striker. He made it clear he didn't appreciate being told how to do his job.

Bill then pointed out that he was the chairman. George, with his inimitable Scottish directness, made the position even clearer. 'And in my contract with the club, it states *I* pick the team,' he said.

Bill took umbrage and rang Caspian plc, seeking its backing. That was his mistake. Chairman Chris Akers, managing director

Jeremy Fenn and non-exec director Richard Thompson were all fierce allies of George. When his call backfired, Bill sensed his days as chairman were numbered.

To be honest, I didn't see a future for me at the club, either. Privately, I was thinking of walking away. The mystique surrounding Leeds United had been stripped away by the reality of the politics, the takeover, and I still loitered on the periphery of involvement, wondering what the point was. I was as disillusioned as the Leeds supporters.

'I'm seriously thinking of giving it all up,' I told Sophie one night.

Sophie was right behind me, and felt it would be fantastic to spend whole weekends together instead of having life interrupted by the constant travelling, home and away.

'About bloody time too,' she said. 'I'm fed up of being a football widow, and wouldn't mind the children seeing their father as they grow up.'

As we returned home from the victorious second leg of the FA Youth Cup final in May 1997, in which we beat Crystal Palace to lift the trophy, I was contemplating my last season as a director. On the coach, our teenagers sang and cheered; among them were Paul Robinson, Harry Kewell, Jonathan Woodgate and Alan Maybury. Also on the coach was a young Irish lad who was the substitute keeper. Nicky Byrne, they called him. He never made the big time in football because he was too small. But he made the big time with his voice, going on to be part of the boy band Westlife.

The trophy, with its yellow ribbons still tied round the handles, was on the table between the seats as we headed up the M1, and I was sat with Bill, Paul Hart and corporate sponsor Adriano, owner of the Flying Pizza restaurant, a regular haunt for players and management.

'I'm on my way out of here,' said Bill, alluding to his run-in with George. Then he turned to me and asked: 'How would *you* fancy being the next chairman of Leeds United?'

I looked at him, wondering if it was another Bill ruse. 'I'm not sure it's in your gift to offer it to me, is it?' I replied.

That was an affront to his ego. 'I will determine who'll be the next chairman of Leeds United!' he reminded me.

What he didn't know was that the matter had already been tentatively raised – while paddling in the Indian Ocean. I'd been on holiday that February with Sophie in Mauritius, and we started talking to a couple called Andrew and Nicki Reagan, who happened to be best of friends with Chris Akers. Thousands of miles from home, we'd discovered the small world around Leeds United. In the conversation that followed, it became apparent that Caspian would be looking for a new chairman that summer. Andrew was curious to know if I'd be interested.

'I haven't really thought about it but, if it were to come up, I'd be very interested,' I said.

Suddenly, all thoughts evaporated about walking away from Leeds United. Sophie sensed she'd forever be the football widow but understood it was something I wanted to do. 'It's the stuff of boyhood dreams,' she said. 'If you want to go for it, I'm behind you 100 per cent.'

Three months later, and just a couple of weeks after the Youth Cup final, I found myself having drinks with Chris Akers and Andrew in a bar in Fifth Avenue, New York, after we'd discovered we'd be in Manhattan on business at the same time. I didn't waste time selling my credentials, my passion for the club and my history as a supporter.

'I would love the opportunity to become chairman of Leeds United,' I said, brazenly. I'd since left QVC and joined Tulchan, a 3i company, as chief executive, and it was a job that saw me move back to Yorkshire. Being back in Leeds could only have fortified my credentials to be chairman.

Over the next couple of weeks, the wheels turned and quiet discussions took place. Then I received an excited call from Bill, inviting Sophie and me to dinner at the house he'd bought from Geoffrey Richmond. Yet again, I found myself in the same house where we'd first contemplated my role as director a decade earlier.

'Peter, they've said to me that I can recommend my successor and I've told them that I'm going to suggest you,' announced Bill.

I played the diplomat. 'Bill, thank you. If offered the position, I'd be delighted to accept but let's wait to hear formally from Caspian,' I said.

Bill cracked open the champagne anyway. It was *his* recommendation, and that was that. We went to dinner at the Flying Pizza. Then, when the waiter came over to our table, Bill announced far too loudly for my liking: 'Can I introduce you to the next chairman of Leeds United?'

It was typical Bill – loud, brash and over the top.

Heads turned, the waiter overdid the congratulations and Sophie winced. I've never been so embarrassed. Even if it was true – and nothing concrete had been conveyed to me – Bill was forgetting that Caspian plc first needed to make an official announcement to the Stock Exchange. He couldn't just shout off his mouth willy-nilly in a restaurant! Besides, a highly respected lawyer in Leeds, Peter McCormick, was also rumoured to be in the running. It was not the foregone conclusion he'd painted it out to be. But Bill *had* to be seen as the power-broker, the key influence.

It wasn't until 24 June 1997 that my appointment was confirmed to a banqueting suite full of 300 corporate sponsors at Elland Road, just one hour after I'd been given the news myself. The next day, I was publicly unveiled as the new chairman at a press conference. I remember standing in front of a bank of photographers as their flashes went off, and it was both blinding and bewildering.

Was I just a puppet chairman to deflect attention from the real power-brokers in London? Just how does a fan become a chairman? As a chairman with no experience, have I taken on more than I can chew? The questions came thick and fast for this particular 'no-mark'.

In response, I wore my heart on my sleeve, deflected most of the barbed questions and said, 'It is a great honour and responsibility to be chairman of Leeds United, and a task I shall relish as the club embarks on a new and exciting era.'

That same morning, one of the first calls I made was to Ray Fell, chairman of the Leeds United Supporters' Club. I wanted to tell him I was a supporter first and foremost, and that he had a direct line to my office at all times. 'Remember, Ray, I'm one of you,' I told him.

I genuinely felt more supporter than chairman, and it was odd because the chairmanship had never been a dream – it had seemed so unattainable. Directorship was as good as it would get, I'd always told myself. Club chairmen were typically multimillionaires with big chequebooks, not working-class businessmen from Hyde Park. I was no Leslie Silver, let alone a Jack Walker at Blackburn. But football was becoming more business-like, and so its revolution presented me with an opportunity.

I flew to Hong Kong on Tulchan business that same day, a buying trip coinciding with the official handover of the colony to China. As I arrived at my hotel room, a faxed press cutting had been stuck to my door, and the headline read, 'PETER WHO?' The buyers from Tulchan had written a little note beneath it saying, 'Welcome to Hong Kong Mr Chairman.'

When the new season kicked off in August 1997 with an opener against George's former club, Arsenal, I wrote my first message as chairman for the programme, and used words that would, in time, come back at me: 'It doesn't matter what people think about where the funding is coming from; as chairman of the football club, I am ultimately accountable.'

IN THE HOT SEAT

I almost didn't want to sit there, in that blue-cushioned seat in the directors' box; the seat earmarked for the chairman. I felt like an impostor, someone with the wrong ticket for a reserved seat, hoping like mad that the rightful owner wouldn't show up.

It was Saturday 9 August 1997, Arsenal at home. The atmosphere seemed more charged than normal. Or was that just my senses on the day, heightened by the occasion? Or my nerves intensifying everything?

'You must feel bloody fantastic!' whispered lawyer Peter McCormick into my ear, leaning forward from the row behind me as almost 38,000 fans erupted into cheers to greet the teams on to the pitch.

I took my seat, Sophie to my left, and a suited George Graham to my right. He turned to me, shook my hand, and I wished him all the best. 'Thank you, Mr Chairman,' he replied.

That was the moment when the fan within me couldn't quite pinch enough skin to believe it. I looked down to the pitch, and a gaggle of yellow-bibbed press photographers stood with their long lenses trained on me.

I swivelled round to look up into the stand to find Reg and Audrey Glover, a couple who, for many years, had stood with me and Mr and Mrs Beesting in the West Stand Paddock. Their obvious excitement for me mirrored the emotions simmering beneath a chairman's decorum. I looked back towards the pitch and there, about twenty yards in front of me, was my old seat, occupied by a young father, screaming so loudly that the veins on his neck looked like they were going to burst. Sophie said he looked mental. I described it as the passion of being a Leeds fan.

Earlier, in the boardroom, I'd welcomed the Arsenal directors, the likes of David Dein and Peter Hill-Wood. I passed through the formalities on auto-pilot that afternoon.

There is no training to become a chairman, nothing that prepared me for the switch from peripheral director to being at the helm of a PLC club with the public profile to match, and the pressure of expectant supporters' dreams. I felt that pressure squeeze me from that very first kick-off. Even before a ball had been kicked, I'd heard the murmurings from fans asking, 'Where are the big-name signings?' They'd known that Caspian had made £12 million available after the takeover, and some had already started questioning our forays into the transfer market. George's new additions that summer didn't seem to instil high confidence.

I knew that each fan would be reading my notes in the programme, trying to suss out what the new man was all about, and what he had to say. 'Chairman's Pledge – it's time to reward fans' patience' – so said the headline across my two-page introduction, written by editor John Wray. I scanned the main stand around me, looking for people who had found that page, and how long they stayed on it. This was what I had written: 'I cannot always guarantee that what the fans want will be delivered but I will guarantee that their voice will be heard . . . I don't have my head in the clouds and I am not saying that I have a magic wand that will conjure up a fairytale, but I do believe we have to be challenging for Europe . . .'

Yet fans will always demand that chairmen are gods that come armed with a magic wand. And if you can't find the magic wand, you'd better at least have the golden – and ever open – chequebook.

So I'd stated my intentions from the word go. Europe had to be the goal, and the club's strategy needed to be built around that very ambition. Slowly but surely.

I felt George was frustrated within the transfer market, though. I sensed he wanted to run before we could find our stride. Nevertheless, he brought in David Robertson, Bruno Ribeiro, Rob Molenaar, Alfie Haaland and a Dutch striker few had heard of from Portuguese side Boavista – Jimmy Floyd Hasselbaink. He was a revelation, scoring twenty-two goals that season. George also appointed our former player David O'Leary as his assistant. That would prove to be his most astute move.

George was impossible to get close to. That's not a criticism; it's an observation of a private man. Nor did I get the sense that his heart was in Leeds United, more the job. I always felt he was passing through. But he deserves credit – he brought structure, discipline and stability to the club, and established a platform for a broader vision.

I didn't really know how to deal with an inherited manager with such a massive reputation and record of success, however stained it might have been by allegations of corruption that had led to a one-year ban from the game for accepting illegal payments as part of transfer deals when manager at Arsenal.

I was still 'green' as a chairman, still finding my feet, and it felt daunting working alongside him. It's different when, as chairman, you employ a new manager because there is a defined chairman–employee relationship. With George I couldn't escape this feeling of being the pretender alongside the master.

But he understood I was learning with each day, and my first real lesson came after we'd lost an FA Cup sixth round tie 1–0 at home to Division One Wolves on 7 March 1998. It was a game we expected to win, and everyone was gutted. That Saturday night, I rang George at home in an attempt to be helpful and said, 'If there's anything I can do to help you strengthen the squad . . .'

He interrupted with a fierce snap: 'And why should I need your help!' and he slammed down the phone. To his credit, he came to my office on the Monday morning to apologize. He was out of order, he said. But he then issued this piece of advice:

'Peter, you must learn in football to always give it at least twenty-four hours before you discuss things like that. Let it settle.' I've never forgotten that, and never made the same mistake again.

Aston Villa chairman Doug Ellis also dealt me a salutary lesson. We both wanted to sign Bolton's left-winger Alan Thompson. At a summer meeting of Premier League chairmen, I sat up late with the wily Doug, discussing our mutual interest.

'Look, Doug,' I said, breaking the ice, 'we both know Alan has a clause in his contract that with any offer of £3.5 million, Bolton would have to accept . . .' Doug listened, appreciating that neither of us wanted to get sucked into a Dutch auction. 'So I suggest we both offer £3.5 million and let the player decide where he wants to go,' I continued.

Doug smiled, said he was relieved I'd shown such common sense and shook my hand. 'Agreed,' he said, and we stayed up late to enjoy another drink.

The next day, Leeds United made our £3.5m offer. Aston Villa also showed its hand – and won the player with a £4.25m bid. When I learned we'd been outbid, I phoned Doug immediately. 'I thought we had a deal!' I fumed.

Booming laughter greeted my protests.

'Peter,' he chuckled, 'the first lesson you have to understand as a chairman is this: don't trust anyone in football.'

I had to take it all on the chin. Gentlemen's agreements that might have existed in the menswear world were not going to be honoured in the cut and thrust world of the Premiership. It was an unsettling, uncertain first year as chairman, feeling around, trying to find my way and understand the politics.

I had no grand office at Elland Road, no name above the door. On my first day, I had to find a table and a seat to work from, and ended up sharing an office with managing director Jeremy Fenn. Or, when George wasn't in, I'd commandeer his office. I didn't care about the trappings of office. I'd have been happy working out of a cardboard box. As non-executive chairman,

I was paid £16,000 a year. But I wasn't in it for the money. I wasn't in it to make a fast buck. I wasn't in it for the profile. I was in it for Leeds United, and all that was important was carrying out the job to the best of my ability, doing justice to the club and fans. I spent those early days counting my blessings. It was to be the start of the most exciting and turbulent five years I'd ever know.

•

I fastened my seatbelt, gazed out of the window across the plane's wing, and looked into the pitch darkness, calculating how many more points we'd need to claim a top five UEFA Cup spot. Behind my emergency exit seat, the remainder of the fifty-seater British Aerospace 748 twin-propeller aircraft filled with the rest of the glum-looking squad, staff and corporate fans. We'd just been thumped 3–0 away at West Ham, live on Sky's *Monday Night Football*, leaving us fifth with seven games to go, and the Hammers and Blackburn were breathing down our necks. George Graham was livid afterwards and didn't join the flight home from Stansted to Leeds-Bradford airport, preferring to stay in London. It was 30 March 1998, the end of a forgettable day, and the time was nearing midnight.

At the back of the plane, my son Matthew, then thirteen, was probably the only excited one among us, still star-struck at being on 'the players' plane', preferring to sit with the team rather than Dad. Travelling by a chartered, private jet was a rare luxury for all of us back then. It was unusual not to travel by coach but, because of congested fixtures over Easter and to ease the fatigue on players, we'd opted for air travel, even though managing director Jeremy Fenn took some persuading. When I first saw the Emerald Airways plane earlier that day, with its two green stripes running beneath its ten, tiny porthole windows, I laughed and realized Jeremy had hardly splashed out. It looked like something straight from the Second World War.

Commercial director Adam Pearson sat to my left in the aisle seat. Across from us, sat in the other two emergency exit seats, David O'Leary and coach Eddie Gray were in animated conversation. As the small, cramped plane trundled on its taxi towards the runway, two female stewardesses, wearing jackets as green as any goalkeeper jersey, demonstrated what to do in the case of an emergency. When the players realized that for one of the girls this was her maiden flight, a few of them started making faces, and she blushed and giggled, and the point of the exercise was lost in her embarrassment.

None of us on that plane would ever again ignore an emergency demonstration.

The stewardesses took their seats, the lights dimmed for take-off, and the drone of the propellers drowned out the subdued murmur of idle chatter. I was chatting away with Adam as we powered down the runway, and felt the ground detach from beneath us.

Then, within seconds of being airborne, it happened.

A clattering boom of an explosion rocked the entire plane. Jolting shock. Then sparks to my right. Screams coming from behind me. I looked out of the window. Flames were licking around the right engine, leaving an orange tail as the plane continued to climb. A piercing alarm sounded.

'*Stop! Stop!*' someone screamed. And then everyone started yelling. But how do you suddenly stop in mid-air, mid-ascent?

It was then that pilot John Hackett made the best decision of his life, and ignored all the rules of civil aviation, which state he should have circled the airfield and made an emergency landing. A subsequent Civil Aviation Authority report said that, had he done so, we'd have exploded into smithereens. We were minutes away from certain death, and he knew it.

He suddenly ditched the plane, despite being laden with fuel, and we dropped like a stone. We all tucked into the crash position. 'This is it . . . *This is it!!*' someone screamed. Then I heard someone else's terrified wailing. All I could think about, as I closed my eyes and prepared for impact, was Matthew at the back.

As we made that stomach-lurching drop, none of us knew how far we'd travelled, how high we'd climbed, and where we'd come down; whether we'd be nose-first or belly-flopping. Were we landing or crashing? For all we knew, we were just dropping out of the darkness and there could have been a housing estate below. That wait was the stuff of nightmares. Luckily – and our luck was in that night – Stansted has one of the longest runways in the country. We hit the ground, bounced violently, bounced again and then bobbled. The plane lurched forward, falling onto its nose, scraping along the tarmac.

I braced myself for impact with God knows what, as we slewed out of control. No one was screaming any more. Everyone must have been in silent prayer. We kept sliding for what seemed like an age. Then a crunch. And everything stopped; the nose of the plane ditched into the field at the end of the runway.

I looked up. Heart racing. Still breathing. I felt a burning sensation in my right shoulder. My jacket was smouldering – the window beside me had started to melt because of the intense heat from the fire now engulfing the wing. The emergency floor lights came on. David O'Leary shoulder-barged the emergency exit hatch to our left. '*Get out – everyone get out!!*' I heard someone shout, panic in their voice.

The plane's darkness was bathed in an orange glow from the flames that threatened an explosion.

But I didn't want to get off. I wanted to find Matthew. I shouted his name as loud as I could. I tried rushing up the aisle, running back up the plane, against the tide of panic but hands pushed me back. '*Get the fuck out . . . Get out Peter!!*'

I jumped into the turf from the middle emergency hatch over the left wing. People were jumping and running from the other two exits at the front and rear. I saw Harry Kewell and Ian Harte running for their lives. I found Matthew nearby. He'd escaped via the rear door. He was shaking uncontrollably. In the distance, sets of blue lights were racing towards us. We all ran, and kept running. Then we stood in a huddle, in shock, and looked back at the plane, its chin on the soil, its tail in the air, flames raging from the other side. It was like we were in a disaster movie or something not real and not really happening.

Rod Wallace stood there, looked up at the plane and calmly said: 'Best result of the night.'

Pilot John Hackett was stood there, in as much shock as the next man. All the players went up to him to shake his hand. The newspapers, in the following days, quite rightly labelled him a hero.

I rang Sophie on my mobile while watching the fire brigade douse the flames. I could hear Olivia, then three months old, screaming in the background. Before I could get a word out, she said, 'What are you doing ringing me at this time of night? Can't you hear I've got a screaming baby? Phone me in the morning,' and put down the phone. My next call was to Matthew's mother, then to the manager to tell him his squad was safe and sound before the accident broke on the news.

A coach turned up to return us to the airport terminal. Cups of tea and snacks were handed round. One of the players noticed that barbecue flavoured crisps were on offer. 'Barbecued – shit, that could have been us!' and we all laughed for the first time that night.

David O'Leary and I went to the check-in area to talk to the press that had started to gather. When I look back at those TV interviews, I was white, shaking and not making much sense. We returned to Leeds via coach, not plane.

As we arrived in Yorkshire, my mobile rang. It was Sophie. She'd been woken by a friend, asking, 'Has Peter survived the plane crash?'

'Why didn't you tell me the plane had crashed?' she asked. Priceless.

One of the comments I did make in the aftermath, and I still feel strongly about this today, was that we were so close to suffering the same fate as the 1958 Manchester United team, and yet a small minority of Leeds fans still sing that appalling

'Runway Song', poking fun at that tragedy. No Leeds fan, had they been at Stansted that night, would ever chant that song again if they knew the fear we had faced, and how we close we came to an entire squad being wiped out.

•

Soon after Wolves had turfed us out of the FA Cup, the sports editor-in-chief of the *Yorkshire Evening Post* wrote an open letter to the board, airing frustrations 'that Leeds supporters have become used to have [sic] to bear'. It went on:

> Every failure brings its own crop of excuses but the simple reality is that Leeds do not have enough high quality players . . . without substantial investment, Leeds are never going to hit the big time. The statistics speak for themselves. The average price for top players in the Premier League is £5m to £7m. Leeds United have bought 10 players for £11.5m – average price £1.15m. What is the priority of Leeds Sporting plc? Is it profit or success on the pitch?
>
> You began by giving us one of the best managers in the game. Now let's get the players. As George himself says: 'It would be lovely to be in a position where I could go out and buy players at £8m . . .
>
> No one could disagree with that.

> – *Stephen White, Sports Editor-in-Chief.*

I felt my blood boil, as well as the pressure crank up. That's all I needed – the evening newspaper whipping up the fans with spend, spend, spend demands. We were fifth in the table, going well and had invested £16m in new players since the Caspian takeover, and negotiated to buy back the stadium from Leeds City Council for around £10m. By that time, Allan Leighton, then chief executive of Asda, and Richard North, then finance director of Bass, had been appointed to the board after the parent company had changed its name to Leeds Sporting plc, and Richard Thompson and Chris Akers had stood down.

Allan Leighton became the non-executive deputy chairman, and I was reassured with having someone of his stature and reputation by my side; he was seen as the big turnaround-man at Asda and had multiple non-exec directorships at Bhs, Selfridges, Dyson, BSkyB, lastminute.com and later became chairman of Royal Mail. With someone like him as an ally, we couldn't go wrong, I thought. He would become my confidant and sounding board in every move, and I valued his judgement. To some degree, I felt others on the board were in awe of his presence. People would respond to his input and leadership as much as anything I contributed but far from undermining my position, he bolstered it. We had, I felt, the best and most experienced board of directors in football, and each one of us was equally responsible for the successes and mistakes that occurred.

In the meantime, I became full-time chairman, both of the club and of the plc, and left Tulchan, retaining a consultative role. Leeds United had become my day and night job on a basic salary of £110,000. I was determined the club would be run with proper corporate governance and needed the two City-respected heavyweights to act as non executive directors to check and counterbalance the business decisions being taken. They would prove invaluable allies in the long run.

What hit a nerve with that open letter from the *Evening Post* was that we clearly didn't have the spending power to buy the type of players George Graham wanted. Yet, in my view, there's a big difference between a lack of ambition and a lack of money. That our ambition as a club was being questioned irritated the hell out of me. I'd stated my objectives in the first programme notes as chairman: 'We have to be challenging for Europe . . .'

That season, led by the shrewd eye of George Graham, we qualified for Europe and a UEFA Cup place, finishing fifth behind champions Arsenal, Manchester United, Liverpool and Chelsea. I felt like writing back to the sports editor-in-chief and saying, 'The statistics speak for themselves.'

In my first season as chairman, I'd delivered on my promise. Leeds United were back in Europe.

Some might say that such a statement sounds egotistical; that it self-importantly inflates my role and input. How could I possibly claim that it was I who had delivered Leeds into Europe? In fact, that point has been made in the past, that getting into Europe had nothing to do with me and everything to do with George Graham. And I wouldn't disagree. But on the other side of the coin, what has it got to do with me when everything goes awry, when performances slip, when we don't qualify for Europe, with all the acute consequences for the club's finances? It can't be the manager that takes 100 per cent of the credit when things go right, and then the chairman who takes 100 per cent of the blame when things go wrong.

George Graham deserved the credit, and felt good about his achievement. Which is why I ended up sitting in the conservatory of his ground-floor flat in north London with the 1998–99 season still in its infancy. It would precipitate one of my first testing periods as chairman.

The first thing I noticed about his place was a room which was a virtual shrine to his days at Arsenal. I was stunned given his career as player and manager elsewhere. Here was a constant reminder of what he'd achieved, lost – and wanted to get back. It made me feel that, whatever he was doing at Leeds, it was to demonstrate to his old club that they'd been wrong to sack him in 1995 for receiving an unsolicited backhander from agent Rune Hauge – over £400,000 stuffed into a bag, proceeds of the transfers of Pål Lydersen (from IK Start) and John Jensen (Brøndby) to Arsenal in the early 1990s.

I felt George was more committed to success and proving his point than to proving his worth to Leeds United fans. But that hunger for success was something we could harness to our benefit.

We sat down over coffee, and George, quite rightly, said he'd delivered the goods, returned Leeds to Europe, and if we wanted him to commit himself to the club, he'd like us to commit to *his* future with a renewed and improved contract. He wanted a salary of £1m a year plus a £1m signing-on bonus.

I almost spat coffee all over his lush carpet when he came out with his proposed package. He stared at me with the intent of a poker player who knew he had a royal flush. He knew, and I knew, that we couldn't afford to lose a manager who had just taken us into Europe. He also knew he was testing our ambition as a club. I was professionally paralysed in that instant, and said I'd take it to the board for consideration, knowing this would mean doubling his salary.

George held a view then that many managers still hold today – that they are the most important part of the management process, that they build winning teams and, therefore, should have parity with some of the highest-paid footballers at a club. It's a sentiment I don't agree with. Being blessed with an individual talent, like a David Beckham or a Wayne Rooney, is wholly different than *finding* that talent. Players, and combined talent, maketh the manager. That doesn't stop me recognizing that a manager is essential, and that boards should seek the best manager they can afford in the league in which they're performing. That's why I felt we needed to retain George.

The Leeds board agreed to his improved package but we wrote into the contract a compensation clause that, in the event of him leaving of his own volition, any new employer would have to reimburse the £1m bonus plus compensation for any unexpired portion of the contract. It would prove to be a wise move.

•

We drew 0–0 at home to Aston Villa in the September of the new season when George approached me and asked a bizarre question: if another club came in for me, you would tell me, wouldn't you? Of course we would, I said. 'But no one has so it's not an issue,' I added. It was just six months since we'd improved his contract, and newspaper speculation over his future had already overshadowed our European opener at home to Portuguese side CS Maritimo in the first round, first leg of the UEFA Cup, which we won 1–0, four days earlier.

After the Villa match that Saturday, I'd attended a Supporters' Club dinner at Elland Road, and Clyde Wijnhard, one of our new players, was driving me back to my hotel on the outskirts of the city when the mobile rang. It was Alan Sugar, chairman at Tottenham Hotspur, asking for permission to talk to our manager. Clyde dropped me off at the bottom of the hotel's sweeping driveway so I could walk and talk on the phone in private. I'll never forget what Alan said: 'Despite what I've said about George Graham, I think we need him.'

I politely refused permission, saying: 'The last thing we want is for George to leave.'

On the Monday morning, having confirmed with my colleagues that we should refuse permission, George phoned and said, 'I thought you gave me your commitment that if anyone asked to talk to me, you would let me know?'

'Well, what makes you think anyone has – unless you already know?' I replied. He didn't answer, but it was clear to me that someone had had wind of Spurs' approach and tipped off George. He just reiterated his request to be kept informed *should* such an approach be made. That's when I told him we'd received a call from Alan Sugar and, as a board, had declined his request. George expressed his frustration, and made it clear that he would like the chance to speak to Tottenham 'just to hear what they would have to say'.

He then spoke openly of his ambitions, and said Tottenham might stand a better chance of breaking through than Leeds. By this, he meant Spurs were more capable – and had the financial clout – to sustain a more realistic championship bid. It didn't seem to matter that they'd finished behind us the previous season. And, I thought, what better way of proving his point to Arsenal than to achieve ultimate success at their north London arch-rivals? His entire attitude seemed to belittle Leeds United and its potential. But my stubborn instinct was to fight to keep him.

Over the next week or two, we batted away further calls from Alan, and yet he had seemingly worked out what I'd not reconciled in my own mind – that George wanted to leave; his vision lay elsewhere. Alan was a true gent and a professional throughout the entire cat-and-mouse game and I had the utmost respect for the way he handled such a delicate matter. In contrast, I lost some respect for George. Having backed him with his hugely improved package, and shown the commitment he'd wanted, I felt let down as both a supporter and chairman.

As so often happens in football, as speculation came to the boil, the fixture list threw up a timely irony with our next game – Tottenham away. It was played out as a tug-of-war fixture, with George Graham torn in the middle. The press argued he wanted to be nearer his home in London. That always bemused me because he spent half his week in the capital, anyway. It was no wonder his assistant David O'Leary seemed to have a better relationship with the players.

Before the game, I appeared on BBC *Grandstand* and, in another naive moment, declared on national television that I expected to succeed in keeping George. The reality, as it turned out, was that I never stood a bloody chance. But I was relieved to arrive at White Hart Lane to find Alan Sugar was in Los Angeles on business till that evening. Not that it diminished the media's focus on George and me, sat together in the directors' box. All the photographers' lenses were trained on the manager with his Leeds United AFC emblem on his blazer, and desire to join Tottenham Hotspur worn on his sleeve. In the ground, the vociferous Leeds United support didn't know what was happening. Spurs fans, loathing George for his Arsenal pedigree, didn't even want to comprehend what was happening.

'*Stand up . . . if you want the truth . . . Stand up . . .*' sang the Leeds contingent.

'*Stand up . . . if you hate Arsenal . . . Stand up . . .*' sang the Spurs fans, louder. Both sets of fans then stood and applauded one another.

I looked at the man who'd united an entire ground in vitriol, and registered nothing on his face. I looked across to the Leeds fans and saw the banner: 'Who are you supporting today, Judas?' and felt their dismay, but what could I do with a man who didn't understand what it was to feel Leeds in his bones? Elland Road had been his rehabilitation centre, and he was desperate to check out and move on.

Three minutes into the match, Gunnar Halle put us a goal up. If ever you needed a photo to tell its own story, it appeared in the following day's papers: there's me leaping up, both arms in the air with unrestrained joy. And there, rooted to the seat next to me, is a glum-looking George Graham, motionless, expressionless. He wasn't the most animated man but he normally showed some glee when a goal went in. But at White Hart Lane that day, he sat like a manager who suspected he would be swapping dug-outs. '*Fuck off Graham! . . . Fuck off Graham!!*' shouted our fans. My heart echoed their sentiment; my head needed him to stay.

Further goals from Hasselbaink and Wijnhard had put us 3–1 up. But Spurs went on to score two late goals. The match ended 3–3: the perfect result for George. I approached him after the game and offered him the position of director of football, with David O'Leary as first-team coach, freeing George to spend more time in London. It was my last throw of the dice. He rejected it within seconds. He stayed in London; we boarded the team bus back to Yorkshire.

I'll never understand, bearing in mind the intense pre-match hype, why the Metropolitan Police didn't give Leeds an escort away from the ground but we were hopelessly exposed as the coach turned out of the ground and into Tottenham High Road. I was sat at the first table, facing the front, with David O'Leary, and we didn't think much about the moron walking in front of the bus, deliberately idling and hurling abuse; just another mindless idiot. We didn't realize he was part of a planned ambush until he stopped dead, forcing the driver to brake, just as we pulled up alongside a pub. That was the cue. A gang of Spurs fans burst out of the pub and into the street. Stones and coins rained on the windows. A brick smashed into the front window, shattering a corner section.

Then the automatic doors swung open. Someone had pressed an emergency switch from outside, and a handful of hooligans stormed up the steps, shouting abuse at George Graham, yelling that Spurs didn't want him. But the man they came hunting wasn't even there. Our players had to manhandle those yobs back into the road before the driver spotted an escape route and got us out of there. It had been a scary moment that illustrated how highly charged the whole George Graham episode had become.

On the Sunday morning, as the newspapers heralded the 'Graham Deal Is Dead' and reported that 'Leeds United slammed the door on Tottenham's attempts to recruit George Graham', I capitulated. Alan Sugar agreed to reimburse the £1m bonus plus £2m in compensation. My only condition was that George couldn't speak with Spurs until after he'd taken charge of the UEFA Cup first round, second leg at Maritimo. It galled me to see him in the dug-out that night, going through the motions, both of us knowing it was his last game, even if no one else did. Maritimo won 1–0 on the night but we went through to the second round 4–1 on penalties, and Lee Sharpe wheeled away in celebration after scoring the decisive spot-kick.

We flew back to Leeds-Bradford airport, where George made his quick exit to meet Alan Sugar, and I announced to the media that we'd given him permission to start talks. That evening, the deal was done. He'd left at lunchtime, driven to London, met with Alan, agreed terms and I'd faxed the forms to release him from his contract by seven o'clock. But there was no point in debating how he had handled himself. George didn't want to stay. Full stop. You learn to be pragmatic as a chairman. George would, in time, learn to rue his short-sightedness over Leeds' potential.

At our training ground at Thorp Arch, near Wetherby, the next morning, I met the players in the changing room, and explained we'd be making a Stock Exchange announcement, that I was going to talk to both David O'Leary and Eddie Gray about the future but, first, wanted to sound out the team on its thoughts. I stood there, all these eyes looking at me from beneath sweaty brows, and asked, 'What do you want? What should I do?'

I saw a collective, embarrassed smile grow around the changing room. 'Well, that's your job, Mr Chairman,' said one player. 'We're footballers, and we're paid just to get on with it.'

I was attempting to consult them, to involve them. But it was, with hindsight, a mistake which made me appear indecisive and anxious. Another lesson learned. As I walked away, and the door closed behind me, I heard cackles of laughter.

Bollocks, I thought, cursing myself.

I went straight into a meeting with David O'Leary, George's right-hand man, half-expecting him to be zipping up his bags to leave with his mentor. We had a frank chat. He told me that on the day of the Aston Villa game, George had suggested it might be their last match in charge. David had told him his family were happy living in North Yorkshire, and he had no desire to return to the capital, where he'd played with Arsenal. So I asked if he'd like to be considered for the manager's job. He said he didn't think he had enough experience but agreed to take temporary charge until we found a new manager.

I didn't know who that could be. But then, in our very next fixture, Leicester City visited Elland Road and, out of the 1–0 defeat we suffered, I found the ideal solution sitting in the visitors' dug-out – Martin O'Neill. He'd done a great job at Filbert Street with not a lot of money, and he was seen as a rising star. The press had already linked him with the vacancy, while Gordon Strachan, then manager of Coventry City, was also mooted as a leading contender. Clearly, Coventry chairman Bryan Richardson was rattled by such talk and sent a faxed letter, 'pre-empting any thoughts you or your board may have', making it '100 per cent clear that under no circumstances whatsoever, including any figure that may be offered in compensation, would we allow any approach directly or indirectly to be made to Gordon Strachan'.

But it was Martin O'Neill we wanted. We approached Leicester for permission to talk. They refused. But our target had let it be known via the newspapers that he was interested in talking, believing he had a verbal agreement that allowed that freedom. But his club chairman John Elsom and plc chairman Sir Rodney Walker said otherwise, and refused to open the door. I was convinced, however, that we'd get somewhere in the ensuing two-week gap in the fixture list because of the noises that were emanating from Leicester. 'Martin wants the Leeds job,' someone who knew him told me.

In the meantime, acting manager David O'Leary was letting it be known through friends on the coaching staff that he was relishing the challenge, and did, after all, want to be considered. 'He feels he is ready. He believes he's the man for the job,' a well-placed source told me.

But we still wanted Martin O'Neill. In fact, my mind was fixed on him being our next manager.

Then everything changed in Rome, venue for our UEFA Cup second round, first leg tie with AS Roma. On the Monday night, the day before the match, we all sat in the team hotel watching the live Sky TV game – Leicester City v Tottenham; O'Neill v Graham. Ironically, I later came to learn that Martin had sounded out George about the Leeds vacancy. 'The most magnificent job at a brilliant club with an unbelievable chairman and fantastic money,' was, apparently, George's summary.

It was no wonder then that all the media talk was of the Spurs game being Martin's last as manager at Filbert Street. The

Leicester fans sensed as much, and demonstrated a terrific show of strength with banners and placards that pulled on his heart-strings with pleas like 'Don't Go Martin!' I could tell, after seeing his face on TV as he saluted the crowd, that there was no way he was leaving.

'There's been plenty of emotion tonight and I haven't had much sleep for the last two weeks, to be honest. But I have a decision to make . . . and I'll make it in twenty-four hours,' he said.

He stayed, as I knew he would.

The next night, in the Olympic Stadium, our fans chanted the name of David O'Leary. We lost 1–0 but the lads played out of their skins. At half-time, I turned to Jeremy Fenn, and told him 'This man is going to be our next manager.'

But not everyone was so readily convinced. When I told Allan Leighton, who knew we'd been after Martin, he queried whether I'd properly thought through the matter. As the most senior independent non-executive director, Allan held some con-siderable sway on the board, and seemed unsure. He took some persuading, to the point where I had to lay it on the line.

'You have to back me on his one, or that says something about our relationship,' I insisted.

'If that's how strongly you feel about it, then that's good enough for me. I'll support you,' he said.

After returning to England, Jeremy Fenn and I travelled to Harrogate to formally offer David the job, and undertake the simple task of appointing the new boss! If only it had been *that* simple . . .

David suddenly played hardball. He was grateful for the offer but wanted time to reflect and would give us his decision before the next home match, he said. I couldn't believe it. There we were, offering a coach with zero managerial experience the post at Leeds United, a job many would kill for, a break we *knew* he wanted and yet, instead of snatching our hands off, he played at procrastination. If I'd had the balls, and more experience under my belt, I'd have given him twenty-four hours and no more. But maybe the chants of the fans in Rome were still in my head; maybe they'd even gone to David's.

Over the years, I would come to understand that such bravado and self-confidence was all part of the O'Leary style. 'Surprised I may have been but I wasn't at all fazed when Peter Ridsdale told me I had the job,' David recalled in his book, *Leeds United on Trial*. Over the years, our differing recollections of events would be a hallmark of our differences. But give David his credit – the man had a vision for the club, and it matched mine.

When he stopped playing games and accepted our two-year-contract, he excited me. We built high incentives into his contract, with very lucrative bonuses aligned to performance. With Eddie Gray as his assistant, he convinced me that the Englishman, Irishman and Scotsman could go far together. He wanted to entertain, to win and challenge Arsenal and Manchester United, and not settle for playing in the UEFA Cup but the Champions League. He wanted to achieve what Don Revie and Howard Wilkinson had done before him. You could almost hear his hunger rumbling in the empty belly of Elland Road.

DREAMS, GREED & GAMBLES

Every football club wishes it could touch the dream but, for many, the chances of competing among the top clubs in Britain, and then the elite of Europe, remain as fanciful as finding pots of gold at the end of the rainbow. But David O'Leary's appointment brought with him a cast-iron belief in, and a shared vision of, a new future where that dream was within touching distance. But our clear sight of that bright new future also brought cold financial realities if we were to put money where those dreams were.

As a club, we felt galvanized, wanting to push further forward and make gains on our considerable progress; push higher than fifth in the league table; push for the Champions League; establish Leeds United as one of the most entertaining and talked-about clubs in the country. David was talking up exciting, attacking, winning football with flair.

I'd learned from Howard Wilkinson's successes that it wasn't necessarily a reckless strategy to speculate to accumulate; pursuing honours in the top flight involved an element of gambling. Under George Graham, and as a plc, we'd spent only what we could afford. But David persuaded the board that we'd challenge the very best if we invested more in top-quality players. A collective attitude of 'it's now or never' dawned on us all.

Maybe, with hindsight, we shouldn't have been so swayed; should have stuck to the prudence maintained with George. Maybe I was scared of the backlash from the fans, and the

Yorkshire Evening Post, who'd been clamouring for us to invest in the future. Maybe the fan within me overruled the chairman.

Either way, we sat down, devised a winning strategy and knew what was required: we had to spend. Our choices were simple yet complicated: we either aimed for the moon because that's where we'd find the television income and future European revenue. Or we settled for a mid-table survival strategy with all the restrictive prudence attached. Aim for mid-table and it goes wrong, and you're in danger of being relegated. Aim for top three and it goes wrong, and you're mid-table, ready to fight another day. It was that more aggressive, albeit riskier, strategy that was approved by all shareholders, and it was the right decision to take for that time. If you're Leeds United, having tasted the championship in 1991–92, you're never going to countenance a strategy to settle for safe mediocrity. If you stand still, you go backwards. We needed to push on – and that meant chasing the money; the teams with the biggest income streams, and therefore maximum spending power, would be the teams that finished highest in the league and qualified for Europe.

Having secured the rights to broadcast Premier League football, in what was a £670m four-year package in 1997, Sky TV's deal meant that each club would receive £500,000 for each position its team finished in the league from twentieth to first. Finish twentieth and it was £500,000, finish nineteenth £1m, eighteenth £1.5m, and so on. So to finish fourth, and qualify for Europe, meant earning around £8m, leaving aside the basic £625,000 received for each live Sunday game. Also, a UEFA Cup position would mean an extra £7m per season. A Champions League spot would earn £20m.

TV rights had made the rewards for winning massive, and the cost of failure almost unthinkable. In today's game, if you're promoted into the top flight and go straight back down, you can withstand failure. But if you're promoted, climb and become one of the top five teams, and *then* get relegated, the consequences can be catastrophic. Football's fate is ruthless with its destruction of successful clubs who then fail on the pitch. And therein lies the inherent nightmare of pursuing a thriving and successful business from the boardroom – because the control of events lies with the team on the pitch.

What we needed to do is the challenge that faces every club – build a team capable of delivering the trophies. That meant investing. We needed to drive every aspect of the business to generate income, and look to the banks to raise money to afford the £4m and £5m players. As the Sky deals transformed football, the financial gulf between success and failure was vast; the difference between life on a council estate and life in a stately pile; the rich getting richer, the poor getting poorer. The structure of the Premier League, and the financial rewards, were – and remain – geared to benefit the top five clubs. Some would argue it's a league sponsored by 'Greed', and I couldn't argue too vociferously against such a view. Few have the interests of football at heart these days, just the interests of the top echelons of the Premiership. And unless there is a redistribution of wealth trickling down from the Premiership and into the Football League, I can't see ninety-two clubs surviving in England and Wales. But in a plc environment, you've got to look after No.1; the shareholders demand that income is maximized, and fans demand that the profits are reinvested in the club and players.

So it was obvious why Leeds had to follow the gravy train and aim for a top spot, and why team performances were vital. 'Living the dream' was never about overspending. It was about football and success on the pitch, funded properly, by building the brand that was Leeds United. There was no reason in my mind why, from performances on the pitch to season ticket sales to merchandise, we couldn't match Manchester United. We engaged in a strategy we believed in. Each year we would outline our strategy presentations to our four main shareholders – Jupiter Asset Management, Schroders, USB Warburg and, later, BSkyB – and each year they would be approved. My job as chairman, from beginning to end, was to echo a collective strategy to aim high in the Premiership.

Previously, the club had little or no management structure capable of developing the Leeds United business. Furthermore, the club wasn't in a position to invest in a playing squad capable of challenging for top honours and, therefore, lost the confidence of the supporter base.

All that had changed, and it's the same in any business – you need to invest to become successful. Football is a volatile market but we had the prospects, and the manager, that allowed us to be bold. No business can be led by the fear of failure, only by a positive drive towards success.

As faceless analysts examined our strategies, one told *Business Age* magazine that I was engaged 'in a dash for glory. If he pulls it off, he will be a hero . . . If he gets it wrong, the knives will be out.'

•

'I'm coming over to your house tonight – Sky is interested in having a stake at Leeds,' said the urgent-sounding voice on the other end of the phone. Trevor East, managing director at BSkyB, said Rupert Murdoch's company wanted a 9.9 per cent share. (BSkyB's overall takeover of Old Trafford had just been blocked by the government on the recommendation of the Monopolies and Mergers Commission.)

Trevor, with in-house lawyer Jonathan Sykes in his wake, pitched up at my house late at night, and we stayed up until the small hours working on the finer details to present to the board. It would be some weeks before the deal reached a conclusion but ultimately it meant £8m was made available for new players; it gave BSkyB influence on TV rights for the clubs in which it held a stake, and it was good business as a club to forge an alliance with a media company that was driving football as an industry.

Bleary-eyed after that meeting at my house, I travelled down to St Andrews the next morning for a pre-season friendly against Birmingham. The travelling Leeds fans barracked Jimmy Floyd Hasselbaink as he warmed up on the pitch. The goalscoring hero of last season was now reduced to villain of the piece. Word was out that he wanted away from Elland Road, and had made exorbitant wage demands, thrown in with a like-it-or-lump-it attitude. As George Graham had discovered, there is nothing the fanatical Leeds fan detests more than what they see as disloyalty, aggravated by ambivalence, towards their beloved club.

Jimmy had been an unstoppable goal machine since George unearthed this bargain find languishing in the Portuguese league; any Premiership club would have wanted such a powerful and prolific striker on their books. And that reality wasn't lost on the player or his Holland-based agent, Humphrey Nijman, as we entered into talks about renewing his contract. Nijman felt in such a powerful negotiating position that he called the shots from the off, which is why I ended up flying from Leeds to Amsterdam when, if I'd had more about me, I should have insisted *he* travel to see me; dancing to his tune was not such a good starting point, and I was annoyed at myself for demonstrating such weakness.

At numerous meetings at a hotel near Schiphol airport, Nijman said Jimmy 'had earned the right to be the highest-paid player at Leeds', and yet the sheer size of his demands made it clear he had zero interest in signing a new deal; naming figures he knew were out of our reach. Jimmy wanted his £15,000 a week more than doubled to £40,000 – silly money back in 1999 – with goal and performance bonuses stacked on the back. What many fans don't realise is that these bonuses can be anything around £5,000 appearance fee per game and, say, a £2,000 win bonus per game; all this on top of a player's weekly salary. And by today's standards, those bonuses are small. More significantly, what Jimmy was asking for was almost double the contract of our then highest-paid star, Lucas Radebe.

'Even if we made Jimmy our highest-paid player, it wouldn't

be enough!' I pointed out. 'This is not about him being the highest-paid player at all.'

He nonchalantly shrugged his shoulders. 'If you can't afford that sort of money, we'll just have to go elsewhere.'

The moment we first sat down, I sensed he was negotiating to extricate Jimmy from his contract. But all I could think about was the backlash from the fans, and the forty-two goals he'd scored in two seasons. I'd be guilty of allowing Roy to leave the Rovers. As Humphrey played hardball, I sweated and worried, just as anyone would when a gun is pointed at your head and you are being held to ransom. Not just that, he wanted a clause that said he'd *always* be the highest-paid player.

His requests were, to me, outlandish, ridiculous and unrealistic. But what choice did I have? I turned the issue inside out and back to front on the return flight home: if we don't keep him, how do we replace someone of his calibre? . . . He'll leave us in the lurch, then blame the board for not backing him . . .

I got out the calculator and scribbled desperate mathematics on scraps of paper. But there was no escaping the brutal conclusion: it would have been madness to cave in to such demands; the wage hike was unjustifiable. We'd been out-priced by our own player.

It was my first unsavory taste of player-power; the loyalty of the likes of Bremner, Hunter and Lorimer belonged to a different age, and such loyalty remained only in the hearts of the diehard fans who deluded themselves into thinking players like Jimmy Floyd Hasselbaink were as loyal to the club as they were. Naively, I felt *all* the squad would have given everything to play for Leeds. But how could I expect a player with roots in Holland having the same allegiance to Leeds as I did.

Jimmy's single-mindedness on the pitch was also his single-mindedness off it; it was an attribute as much as it was an annoyance. If he wasn't so strong-willed in his self-belief, he would not have been the player he was. It was part of his brilliant package, and I became resigned to losing him. We couldn't afford to put him streets ahead of other players, both in terms of finances and status, but Jimmy felt he was entitled to the rewards he had earned.

The only way to resolve the impasse was to insist on him submitting a written transfer request. Such requests were relatively rare and Jimmy grew suspicious about our motives. He feared we would use it as a lever to stop paying outstanding signing-on fees; he rang me late one night, arguing that we were trying to pull a fast one. He was agitated to say the least.

Signing-on fees are usually spread over the term of a contract. If a player has a £500,000 fee on a five-year deal, for example, he'd be paid £100,000 a year for that term. But written transfer requests nullify that right to remaining payments, and maybe that's what Jimmy, with two years left on his contract, was worrying about. I promised we would honour his outstanding fees. I wanted that request for another reason – to prove to the fans that we weren't cashing in on our top scorer, just in case he or his agent tried to be cute with the PR.

In an earlier conversation, Jimmy had asked: 'Why won't you give me what I want? Chelsea would. Why won't Leeds?' It seemed the football grapevine had been working overtime.

'How do you *know* Chelsea would?' I asked.

'I just know they would pay,' he replied.

The Roman Abramovich era hadn't begun but Jimmy was convinced that his demands would be accommodated. He must have got wind that Colin Hutchinson, then managing director at Stamford Bridge, had already been on the phone, asking if we were interested in selling him.

Over my dead body, I thought. There was no way we'd ever have given permission for Jimmy to join one of our biggest rivals in the Premiership. Anywhere but Chelsea. And that's the position I made clear to both agent and player, suspecting they had a preference for life in south-west London.

By the last week of July 1999, Spanish side Atlético Madrid entered the ring with a bid for £10m that gave Jimmy exactly what he wanted. On the 29th, a fax rolled off my machine at home: 'TRANSFER REQUEST – The undersigned, Mr Jerrel Floyd Hasselbaink, hereafter called "player", herewith requests Leeds United for a transfer of player to another club,' it read. I ensured it was leaked to the *Daily Mail* and the *Yorkshire Evening Post*. The fans deserved to know the truth, not the spin of others.

Two days later, as that transfer request hit the papers, we played Birmingham in that pre-season friendly.

'*Yer just a greedy bastard!*' sang the fans. How Jimmy hated the truth being known.

His agent later protested that the player had wanted to stay at Elland Road, but it was our insistence upon a written transfer request, and stories that appeared in the newspapers, that changed his mind.

After one season in Spain, he returned to the Premiership – and joined Chelsea for a reputed £15m. When they came to Elland Road, the players strolled out on the pitch for the pre-match walkabout. I saw Jimmy in the tunnel and walked up to shake his hand. He recoiled, and pulled away.

'Fuck off!' he said.

I'm not someone who holds a grudge, and I remain disappointed Jimmy wasn't big enough to accept the realities of a business transaction that fulfilled his wish to leave Leeds, and Leeds with a handsome profit on a player bought for £2m. In that respect, we were both winners and, ultimately, his departure didn't adversely affect team performances.

It seems perfectly okay for players to hand in their ticket, expect clubs to recognize the realities of the commercial world, and then get their agents to issue the positive PR messages. But when clubs play equally tough and PR-savvy, players start moaning and take it personally. Jimmy must have been aware that, because of his popularity with fans, we had to defend the position *he* had put us in. It was imperative that the fans understood it was the player who had initiated the move. And why shouldn't players be held to account? Or does the hero-worship, even when it's blind, really matter that much to them?

I asked myself the same question about David O'Leary. Clearly, the opinion of the fans mattered to him just as much. In discussing the Jimmy situation, he'd made it absolutely clear to me, and others, that if the club couldn't afford his demands, then he had to be released. So you can imagine my surprise when I read in one newspaper that he was being quoted as saying that if Leeds sold Jimmy Floyd Hasselbaink, he would have to consider his position.

This was in stark contrast to his earlier reported comment in the *Yorkshire Evening Post* when he said it was 'unsurprising that some people have formed the opinion that he [Jimmy] is a greedy son-of-a-bitch'. But David had never intended that opinion to be made public. He had been caught off guard during an introductory meeting – which he thought was off the record – with the paper's new chief sports writer, Phil Rostron. I was in the office with them both when the comment was made. David was furious. 'I'll never trust that man ever again,' he vowed.

Phil Rostron didn't do himself any long-term favours with the manager but had succeeded in doing what few had achieved before: illustrate the unguarded, spontaneous and raw comments of a man who prided himself on his public image and his measured diplomacy with the media.

I would quickly learn that David was capable of saying one thing privately within the club, and saying something else, or acting differently, in public. It would become a feature of our ongoing business relationship, and a source of future frustration and conflict.

•

One of the first things the new manager did was to unleash the exciting youth of Leeds United on the Premiership. Having spotted obvious talent on the training pitch, in came teenagers like Jonathan Woodgate, Ian Harte, Harry Kewell, Stephen

McPhail, Alan Smith and, when keeper Nigel Martyn was injured, Paul Robinson. David's attitude echoed the thinking of Eddie Gray – if the lads were good enough, they were old enough. These young guns were the end product of the legacy Howard Wilkinson started and left behind – the youth academy.

It's worth mentioning here that a peculiarity of football business is that you can't list homegrown talent as assets, even if they grow into huge Premiership stars. Buy a player for £10m, and he's a depreciating asset on paper of £10m. But with the likes of Harry Kewell or Jonathan Woodgate, who would rapidly develop into Premiership stars with a transfer market value, they had a zero value on the balance sheets because we didn't buy them in the first place. Therefore, the true value of the company, and the assets it could realize, was never accurately reflected.

Aside from our young guns, we were also aware we needed to strengthen the squad from the outside, using the money from BSkyB's injection, and the sale of Jimmy Floyd Hasselbaink. Not forgetting the £7m we'd bank for the UEFA Cup qualification. David remarked how he now had money to spend on 'diamonds'. This was a time when I personally oversaw all transfer and contract negotiations but, as with every player, each transfer needed, and received, board approval.

David's initial player wish-list took us to the North Yorkshire home of Sunderland chairman Bob Murray to negotiate the transfer of Michael Bridges. David and I sat in the lounge as Bob held out for £4.5m, with me determined not to pay a penny more than £4m. I sat on the sofa facing the extremely business-like Bob in his armchair, both poker-faced, both digging our heels in. His wife Sue, the perfect host, popped in periodically with drinks and refreshments, and kept saying, 'I can't believe we're selling him – I love Michael.' David sat on another chair sipping his tea and observing the brinkmanship with increasing impatience.

'Four point five million,' said Bob.

'Four,' I said.

'We shouldn't be selling Michael at all,' Mrs Murray chipped in.

David couldn't stand much more. After half an hour of stalemate, he stepped in. 'Look,' he said, 'let's come to an agreement and split the difference. Let's agree £4.25m.' He stood up and shook Bob's hand. I had no chance to react. The manager had shaken on a deal, and undermined my position. I said nothing to David then or afterwards. I just shook Bob's hand. He chuckled. Sue Murray got even more depressed, and the transfer was concluded. I'd learned there and then never to take a manager with me again into transfer negotiations; their desire to get the player can override the subtle art of negotiating to get the man but at the best price.

David had got the man he wanted to join Harry Kewell in attack, even though we still searched for a replacement for Jimmy. On the upside, we had stolen Bridges from under the noses of Tottenham and George Graham. He soon looked like a steal too, banging away a hat-trick in a 3–0 win in only our second game of the season, at Southampton.

Meanwhile, David Batty had also rejoined Leeds from Newcastle for £4.4m, having been inexplicably sold to Blackburn Rovers in 1993 by Howard Wilkinson and Leslie Silver. It was a sweet signing for me because it was like bringing the hero back home; the fans had never wanted to see him go in the first place. It was also symbolic: David making a statement of intent that we were serious about our assault on the top echelons of the Premiership. With 'Bats' in the engine room of midfield, we meant business. There is no one tougher or hungrier than him, and here was a player whose heart was tied to Elland Road.

Other exciting additions for the new season were Darren Huckerby (£5m from Coventry City), Danny Mills (£4m from Charlton Athletic) and Eirik Bakke (£1m from Norwegian side Sogndal). David Weatherall, Gunnar Halle and Lee Sharpe were all released to Yorkshire neighbours Bradford City.

Our more ambitious forays into the transfer market were

funded by a scheme set up by former Manchester City and Birmingham City player Ray Ranson. Having hung up his boots, he'd gone to work for Chelsea vice-chairman Matthew Harding's insurance company, and devised a product which allowed clubs to fund a transfer over the length of a contract, as clubs did in Europe. This was in stark contrast to Premier League rules, which stated the whole transfer fee had to be paid within twelve months. Ray offered us an insurance-backed facility which allowed us to compete within the British transfer market. The funding mechanism meant we borrowed the money from Ray's institutions, paid the fees up front, and then paid back the money, plus interest, over the length of the contract. It was ingenious and helped us attract a better calibre of player.

In that summer of 1999, David wanted two more players: the exciting striker Kieron Dyer from Ipswich and the resolute defender Michael Duberry from Chelsea. But I had to stand up to the manager and be firm. 'You can't have both; there's not enough money. So it's a choice – Kieron or Michael?' I said. We ended up buying Duberry – one of the nicest guys in the game – with the last £4m in the kitty.

Looking back, I've often wondered whether I should have stood up to the manager more often over the years, and said, 'David, we can't afford it.' But, as we all know, I didn't and that was a weakness I'd come to regret.

But, in those initial years, David's persuasive argument that, if we invested in players, we'd reap rewards, started to bear fruit – and we'd soon have Manchester United looking over their shoulder in the race for the 1999–2000 Premiership title.

●

After away games, which consistently ended in victory, everyone on the coach would be singing; everyone was buoyant, and an incredibly tight team spirit often carried us back home up the M1, across the M62 or down the A1. Times were good, Leeds were flying high. By early October 1999, we sat atop the

Premiership with a 2–1 win at Watford. And there we stayed, apart from a two-week hiatus, until the following January. Midfielder Lee Bowyer was a prime mover in getting us to the top, putting away eight goals in the league and tournaments before the holiday period in support of Bridges and Kewell.

No wonder the atmosphere on the coach trips home was of a team buzzing with belief. 'You're Still The One' by Shania Twain would belt out from the coach stereo, and players at the back would bellow along, disrupting the concentration of those playing cards. Then, more often than not, a few of them would burst into 'Flying Without Wings' by Westlife. Somehow, 'Marching On Together' found itself relegated behind these two numbers! I'd sing my heart out as usual, standing in the aisle between the seats, soaking up every bit of an unforgettable camaraderie.

David O'Leary would sit there, shaking his head and smiling as he observed his chairman acting like an excitable teenager on a supporters' coach.

'You'll always be one of the lads, Peter!' he'd say. Let's face it, we had a lot to smile about in those days. Cars passed us in the outside lanes, horns beeping, white scarves trailing out of the windows and flapping in the wind. Radio phone-ins on BBC Five Live and Radio Leeds raved about a new era for Leeds United, and how the team had taken the Premiership by storm. Fans and neutral observers alike asked serious questions about us being championship contenders. The dark horses from Yorkshire had crept up on the inside rail.

After an epic 4–4 draw at Everton, David Maddock wrote in the *Mirror*: 'Leeds, as leaders of the Premiership, were simply magnificent, stunning in their imagination and refusal to give up, despite ending their consecutive win record at 10 games.' As the manager had intended, everyone was talking about the team and their style of football.

After home games, I'd not want to be in the boardroom for all that post-match chatter. You'd find me, first, visiting the dressing room, where you'd decipher laughter and banter among the steam from the showers, and then, second, in the manager's office together with the rest of his management staff: Eddie Gray, Roy Aitken and Brian Kidd. We'd dissect the game like *Match of the Day* pundits, check the rest of the results, calculate the points and work out where that left us; what games were coming next; who were Manchester United's next opponents; what points we'd need for Europe, what points we'd need for the Champions League. I was with a management depressurizing and relaxing over a glass of cold white wine and some scampi. Eddie Gray would always wind me up about being a frustrated coach, asking if my place was in the boardroom not the manager's office.

David would often smile when I offered opinions about the match and certain players; he was open to me chipping in, and saw it as a passionate fan speaking, not a chairman interfering. I think ... And if I ever sniffed around for inside information about the team, David would say nothing.

'Mr Chairman, it's a need-to-know basis. David will tell you when he's ready!' said Eddie, and the place fell about laughing. The management team was second to none in my book.

Not all ex-players make successful managers, especially in the Premiership, and David was as green, unproven and inexperienced as any aspiring coach when he landed the job. But he took to top-flight management like a natural, and seemed to thrive on the pressure. For someone so new to the role, he had an air of authority and confidence that belied his inexperience. He was professional, diligent, ambitious and an absolute perfectionist, scrutinizing every minute detail from the opposing team's tactics and danger men, to the length of the blades of grass that either facilitated or hampered his brand of pass-and-move, free-flowing football. What I also admired was a passion and belief in Leeds United that translated into winning results.

David O'Leary was highly popular with the fans, while the respect he won in the dressing room was, for a long time, immense. Like his predecessor, he wasn't the easiest of men to get close to but we built an effective working relationship and a great rapport. Away from the ground, I'm not sure we had that much in common but, in my eyes, we made a brilliant chairman–manager partnership. I also think we bonded because we walked the same learning curve together, even if mine was that little bit steeper. But there was an excitement to the journey we shared; even more so because we were sitting at the top of the Premiership. We also, perhaps, shared a similar naivety in thinking, and then believing, that whatever we touched turned to gold. We'd hit a rich vein of form, everything was going right, and we had no fear as a team or a club.

But, for the apprentice manager and apprentice chairman, were we really learning anything? We'd had a dream start, and it was almost too easy, but you don't learn lessons in the good times, you learn lessons when things are going wrong. The problem we didn't appreciate was that we didn't think the good times would stop. Failure was a taboo thought at a club drilled with a winning attitude. Don't get me wrong, everyone provided their sweat and toil. But no one stopped long enough to think what it was that was working so well; no one gave due care and attention to the road ahead. We just kept thundering on.

•

The mix of youth and experience had worked wonders. Michael Bridges – with nineteen goals in thirty-four league matches – and Harry Kewell scored for fun, and we went on to finish third that season, qualifying for the Champions League with title-winners Manchester United and runners-up Arsenal.

Our gamble on investing in a team capable of pushing for third spot had paid off, and earned us a £20m reward from qualification. The press started talking about David O'Leary being a natural successor to Alex Ferguson at Old Trafford. It would become even harder to say 'No' to a manager everyone was raving about, and with results that spoke for themselves on and off the pitch.

Interim financial results for the six months ending 31 December 1999 showed our operating profit was up 89 per cent to £6.4m; attendances climbed from 35,773 to over 39,000; season ticket sales were up 30 per cent; revenue from TV had reached £7m.

I'll never forget the away game at Chelsea, just before that Christmas. In the dressing room, David simply told the lads: 'You're not afraid of going top of the league. Now go out and prove it.' They did just that, and with a swagger. Stephen McPhail scored his first league goal, then added another from a free-kick. Chelsea boss Gianluca Vialli tore the woolly hat from his head and threw it on the ground. David O'Leary leaned against the dug-out, as calm as you like. Then the Leeds supporters sang my name: 'One Peter Ridsdale . . . there's only one one Peter Ridsdale . . .'

The hairs on the back of my neck stood on end.

Going into the new millennium, it was as if we could do no wrong. Our success at the end of the season was even more remarkable when you consider what we'd had to contend with as a club for the final four months of the campaign.

For in that January of 2000, in the days after the lads had just blown Manchester City out of the FA Cup with a breathtaking 5–2 victory at Maine Road shown live on television, the first bolts started to come loose on the wheels of our juggernaut.

Commercial director Adam Pearson and I were stopping off in Hong Kong after flying down under to meet with the Australian Soccer Federation to forge commercial links and discuss a nursery club feeder system that would nurture the cream of Aussie talent, so impressed had we been by the likes of Harry Kewell.

We were sat in the Horizon Club at the top of the Shangri-La Hotel, enjoying the views and a well-earned glass of white wine, when my mobile rang. It was Liz Dimitrevic, our club PR officer. The *Yorkshire Evening Post*, she explained, were running an exclusive story that Jonathan Woodgate and Lee Bowyer were to be arrested by West Yorkshire Police in connection with an assault on a nineteen-year-old student in Leeds city centre, three days after the Manchester City game.

'I wanted to make you were aware but there's no need to return early because I've spoken to the two players,' said Liz. 'They say it's got nothing to do with them and there's nothing to worry about.'

DARKEST HOURS

Student Sarfraz Najeib was mauled by a pack of animals, and left lying in his own blood. His left leg was fractured, his cheekbone smashed, his nose broken in three places. He'd need twelve stitches to a gash in the back of his head. Teeth marks were embedded in his face, and a foot had left its imprint on his cheek. Witnesses thought he was dead when his attackers ran from the dimly lit side street where they'd beaten him to within an inch of his life.

The victim – who was in hospital for a week – had been with his brother and three friends in the same nightclub, The Majestyk, as a handful of Leeds players. The students were in the main club with 800 people, and the players upstairs in the VIP lounge. Both groups coincidentally left the venue at the same time, spilling outside into City Square.

Jonathan Woodgate and Lee Bowyer, our two £7m-rated stars, were out with some of Woody's mates from Middlesbrough, Neale Caveney, Paul Clifford and James Hewison. Our players, by their own admission, were smashed out of their heads, having downed pints of vodka and rum-based cocktails, wine and beer during a marathon drinking binge. James Hewison was particularly drunk and 'acting like he was ten men'.

In the blur of the incident that followed, there was an altercation between the two groups, then a chase. Woodgate was seen flashing past witnesses; Bowyer spotted coming late out of the club, then jogging after his team-mate. Club doormen watched them disappear down the main thoroughfare, Boar Lane.

The next thing witnesses were clear about was that Sarfraz Najeib tripped and fell on the pavement in street called Mill Hill. Before he could get to his feet, he was punched, kicked and beaten unconscious. Even as he lay motionless, the 'barbaric' attack continued; Paul Clifford was seen bending down to bite him on his cheek, shaking him like a dog with meat in its jaws.

All these details would emerge much later. At first, there was nothing but a fog of confusion and conflicting accounts. But one thing clear from the start was that attacks don't come more despicable than the one carried out on that young man in the early hours of Wednesday 12 January 2000.

That our players were within a mile of such an incident was a grave concern. What *were* they thinking, rolling around drunk in Leeds city centre? How stupid can you be in a city where every passing pedestrian is bound to recognize you?

Michael Bridges and Harry Kewell had been sensible enough to remain inside the club's VIP room, keeping out of harm's way on a night which also saw reserve players Tony Hackworth and Brian McCrystal out and about.

The full enormity of what happened that night began to emerge upon my return from Hong Kong, and Woodgate and Bowyer's assurances that 'there was nothing to worry about' proved flimsy.

The *Evening Post* was spot on with its information, and the police had arrested both players six days after the assault. As the news made national newspaper and TV headlines, it was the wider ramifications of the incident that also disturbed me as the ripple of this episode spread nationwide.

First impressions, based on the way it played out in the media, were that it was 'Whites v Asians'. From that moment on, the question of racism hung over Elland Road like a sinister cloud. In a place like West Yorkshire, where racial tension is often palpable, the connotations of the incident, regardless of the facts or the evidence, were that this was a racist attack. That suggestion would be inflamed much later on when it emerged that the victim had heard someone shout, 'Do you want some, Paki?' As one barrister would later state in court, the racial elements surrounding the case had 'seeped into the public consciousness'.

As an individual, I abhor racism. As a club we couldn't have been more anti-racist. We'd recruited South African-born Albert Johanneson in the 1960s, one of the first black players to star in the Football League, and the first to play in an FA Cup final at Wembley in 1965. I was there, witnessing 'The Black Flash' and his legendary speed. In the year 2000, Harpal Singh was an exciting winger in our reserves. A section of supporters had long before set up 'Leeds United Against Racism'. We had one of the best community programmes in the country, and had spent years ridding ourselves of a fascist, hooligan element that had tarnished our reputation in the 1980s. One drunken night out had, in the public perception, transported us back to Victorian times.

It was catastrophic PR in such a diverse community. Everyone talked about the 'Leeds United street attack', and the case would escalate into one of the most politically sensitive and abhorrent crimes since the 1993 murder of Stephen Lawrence in south-east London, applying pressure on the club, the police and the British judicial system.

All our positive hard work since David O'Leary's appointment seemed to unravel overnight. We were at the mercy of events outside our control. All we could do was attempt to understand what had happened that night – and only two people knew the truth.

•

Jonathan Woodgate and Lee Bowyer, dressed casually in trainers and jeans, sat like delinquent schoolboys summoned to the headmaster's office. By the looks on their faces, I got the impression that's also how they viewed their predicament. Once you've survived the questions of West Yorkshire Police, and been released without charge on bail, maybe the prospect of coming up against the Leeds United chairman didn't seem that intimidating. I was treated with the same scorn as a probing detective; there was a stiffening in their body language with each question, an irritable twitching in their responses, and a clear suspicion about our motives. As a result, there was a lot of tension, and no desire to tell the full story in that first difficult meeting at the Thorp Arch training ground.

Club secretary Ian Sylvester was a fascinated but crucial witness, and David O'Leary was there for a substantial portion of the discussions, held around a table in the secretary's office. David looked like a man who couldn't quite believe what was unfolding. He was also understandably frustrated and angry that the player's behaviour had led to such a distraction from the job in hand. He'd already had a private chat with them but, like me, hadn't got the lads to open up.

I'm not sure any of the management knew whether we were facing barefaced bravado that day, or the naivety of children who somehow didn't quite comprehend how much trouble they were in.

'Just so you're both aware, I will continue to dig to determine the facts because I need to know what happened to understand the full impact on this club, as both a plc and as your employer,' I said, my own assertiveness masking deep anxieties within me.

I then made clear that they both needed independent legal representation, and that the club solicitor, Peter McCormick, would not – *could not* – act for them. I offered the club's support throughout the legal process but it was not a Leeds United matter; in the same way a driving offence wouldn't be.

And, as futile as it would turn out to be, I wanted to put clear daylight between Leeds United and its arrested players; we were employers, not legal guardians.

'I don't see what all the fuss is about – nothing happened, we weren't there,' Bowyer snapped.

I looked at Jonathan, slouched back in his seat, pretending to be as cocksure as his team-mate, but that's the difference between those two: Bowyer has a convincing poker-face, Woodgate does not. Bowyer's entire attitude suggested we were making a mountain out of a molehill. I truly think he felt that if they kept their heads down long enough, the whole thing would blow over. I treated their intransigence with increasing frustration.

I turned to the weaker of the two. 'Jonathan, I'm seeing your father in a few minutes and I suggest you meet with him privately and tell him all there is to know.'

Alan Woodgate had requested to see me. When he arrived, I met him in the corridor and he was furious, saying we were treating his son unfairly, and overreacting to a media circus. I understood his reaction because he, too, had been reassured with a sketchy outline of events from a player who didn't want to confront the truth, and let down the two people he respected the most: his father and his manager.

'Look, Mr Woodgate,' I said, calming him, 'I know sufficient information to know Jonathan is potentially in a lot of trouble. Go and spend a few minutes with him, and if he continues to tell you there's no problem whatsoever, then he's not the lad I thought he was – because he'd be lying to his own father.'

Father and son disappeared into a side office, and there they remained for around twenty minutes.

Alan Woodgate emerged first and, to his credit, apologized. Jonathan's defiance had cracked, and he'd said things that he'd clearly been holding back. 'I've told him to trust you, and co-operate,' said Alan, forlornly. I was told there were tears in that room as Woody broke down. When he emerged, and had dried his eyes, he did so as a changed character, contrite and co-operative, if not completely open.

There were no tears from Lee. I'm not even sure he has tear ducts. He is a tough character.

Of course, Bowyer already had 'form'. In 1996, within weeks of joining Leeds from Charlton and in the days before I was chairman, he was convicted of affray and fined £4,500 after hurling chairs around a McDonald's after a dispute with an Asian server over his food order. That criminal record meant, that, if he was proved to have any involvement with the Leeds attack, his liberty would be at stake. But he must have been convinced of his innocence – it's the only thing that can explain his defiance and cockiness in such circumstances. Not that his stone-walling mattered. We had other ways of getting to the truth.

•

In Hong Kong, as news of the arrests broke, I'd received a phone call from Dave Richards, chairman of the Premier League. He had the name of a private investigator he highly recommended. Within days of returning to Leeds, the club hired Mark Castle. He'd never be cast in a drama as a PI because this baby-faced, chubby, balding individual was anything but your smouldering, shadowy type. But he was thorough and clearly knew how to obtain the information we so desperately needed to know. Forearmed meant we could be forewarned.

It meant that we were hiring someone to investigate our own players, to determine where the lies were, and what the truth was, alongside the inquiries of the West Yorkshire Police. We checked everything: from CCTV cameras to phone bills, witness statements to taxi drivers and their whereabouts at given times, and what they'd been up to.

Within weeks, Mark knew everything and his information ultimately proved spot on. Once I'd read the confidential file, with witness statements, evidence of phone records, and details of what had been captured on CCTV, a disturbing picture began to emerge. I was even more determined that this must not become a Leeds United issue. On the back of what we'd discovered, I worried for Woodgate and Bowyer.

•

'We expect you to suspend these two players *immediately*, and send out the correct message to the rest of the community, and the rest of the country,' said one of the men gathered in my office, all thunderous and frowning.

There was Imran Khan, a solicitor well known for his involvement in such sensitive high-profile cases, Suresh Grover, representing the National Civil Rights Movement – 'there to provide support to victims of racial injustice' – plus Piara Powar, from the anti-racist group Kick It Out. And then there was Neville Lawrence, the father of murdered teenager Stephen. They were impatient for me to take swift action. It mattered not to them that an arrest implied nothing more than suspicion and, even if charges followed, that the British justice system is built on sturdy foundations that insist a person is innocent until proven guilty before a jury, judge or magistrate. As uncomfortable as that meeting was, as much as I felt the enormous pressure of politics and the media circus squeezing my conscience, I was not going to buckle, however much others were keen to prejudge matters, however much I felt on the back foot, however much I felt the hostile mood in that room.

'The normal thing for a blue-chip company such as yours would be to suspend your employees on full pay. Mr Ridsdale, these are very serious matters – you *must* suspend them,' I was told. At times, I felt harangued, and I privately resented being told what to do. The fierce stares and irritability focused on me suggested they weren't happy with my refusal to back down.

Towards the end of the meeting, Neville Lawrence – the diplomat in the room – calmed matters and asked for a private word. We were left to talk in that room alone. This man has my utmost respect and so that conversation will remain private. But I can say that he never raised his voice, or made a demand. He just asked me to listen, and think carefully. Speaking calmly and softly he gave a poignant account of what his family had endured, and the injustice they'd suffered in knowing their son's killers had slipped through the net. He made me understand better why Sarfraz Najeib's father, and his representatives in that meeting, were so intent on ensuring justice; history and experience had taught them painful lessons about slack responses and procedures after such incidents.

But that realization was not enough to break my resolve that we were right to stand by the players, and stand by this country's presumption of innocence until proved otherwise. I had no right to deprive two employees of their ability to perform their duties. I was acutely aware that such a decision – outlined in a public statement – would cause outrage in certain parts of the community but I had to stick to my guns.

Meanwhile, the Football Association caved in. Kevin Keegan was told he couldn't select either player for England. As a club, we weren't consulted, and both the manager and I were stunned by the decision. Indeed, Keegan told me he'd have been more than happy to have selected our players. For me, the FA made a kneejerk decision that followed a political mood, simply to make themselves look good. In my book, it just made them look weak and reactionary. But I had too much on my plate concerning the impact on Leeds United to get too vexed about it.

Those initial weeks seemed to be a conveyor belt of meetings with players, parents, manager, Sarfraz Najeib's lawyers, the private investigator, the players' lawyers. Then West Yorkshire Police's senior investigating officer, Supt Eddie Hemsley, arrived at Elland Road, but he was in no mood to concede too much ground, either. I made it clear that the club would be protective but not obstructive, and we would co-operate fully with his inquiry. But I felt he eyed me with suspicion, and didn't want to share too much about the investigation's progress; in his eyes, we were on the players' side. He did nothing to dissuade my growing fear that, as much as we tried to plead the contrary, Leeds United were also going to be in the dock.

The whole episode became all-consuming. It seemed to dominate every part of football life except for the ninety minutes on match days.

The hate mail started almost immediately. The postbag went from five or six letters a day to hundreds. Most letters or scrawled slogans followed the same tack: we were 'irresponsible not to suspend such scum'; we were 'shielding suspects'; I was 'a racist'; David O'Leary was 'a racist'; everyone at Elland Road was 'a racist'.

We would get our comeuppance, we should keep looking over our shoulders, we had blood on our hands. 'How do you sleep at night, Ridsdale?' asked one. 'You're not fit to run a public company,' said another. 'Hang your head in shame!' wrote someone else, in black marker pen.

We were 'white trash' and, for not suspending the players, we'd all face the retribution of a *jihad*, a holy war, declared on Woodgate, Bowyer and Leeds United. Racial elements were not just confined to the incident in Leeds city centre. Chairman and manager were being treated like the accused.

Then, the hate mail turned more sinister. David started receiving letters that suggested he was being watched, that threatened physical harm, and then targeted his wife, Joy, with language that was sick and extremely disturbing. We treated the threats so seriously that we ended up calling in West Yorkshire Police, and the manager had to take extra security measures around his home. As for the letters that targeted me, they reduced my PA, Lindsey Culley, to tears on several occasions. It was a mentally exhausting time. But, in the end, I went from shock to hurt to tired to immune – the relentless wave of misguided hate, bile and insults began to roll off me like water off a duck's back.

When you become used to opening an envelope and reading insults and threats, the shock wanes after a while, and I began to scan and read on auto-pilot. I viewed most of the people who wrote to me as either ignorant or cowards; middle England cast its verdict in advance, believing that what it read in the newspapers was enough to be armed with the full facts. All this coincided with my becoming chairman of Leeds education authority, and that allowed me to go out into the community schools, two or three times a week, to spread a positive, anti-racist message from Leeds United. But that was like dropping a pebble in the ocean and expecting a ripple. It was as if the world hated us, and Elland Road retreated into a siege mentality.

Strangely, the intense spotlight and pressure seemed to gal-vanize the team; there was a reinforced steel of determination not to allow the 'leisure-time' antics of two players derail the achievements on the pitch. As for the individual players, they couldn't have coped more differently.

Woodgate began to psychologically fall apart; the more I saw him, the thinner he became, as the shadows under his eyes grew darker. But Bowyer met fire with fire, thrived on the pressure and played out of his skin, undeterred by the chants at every single away match that screamed, *'He's going down, He's going down . . . Bowyer's going down!'* Like the current-day Cristiano Ronaldo, Bowyer took a crowd's hostility as fuel to rev him up, and even if he couldn't silence them, he knew how to answer them in the most effective way he knew how: with his speed and his feet.

I didn't think matters could get much worse as the season reached its climax, and we pushed for that third spot, racing Liverpool to the wire. But then, at the start of March, defender Michael Duberry was arrested, on suspicion of perverting the course of justice, and reserve striker Tony Hackworth in connec-tion with the actual incident. I didn't know what to think; just when we felt we had a grasp of events, we were thrown into more confusion. It seemed to be never-ending.

I knew 'Dubes' was innocent. He'd been the sober one who had picked up Woody and his mates after the incident, and taken them back to his home seven miles out of Leeds city centre – and yet Woody had rooms booked at a hotel just yards from the attack scene. At the house, Paul Clifford changed into a tracksuit. Several phone calls were made. Out of misguided loyalty to friends, 'Dubes' had been dragged into a set of circumstances which made it appear, wrongly, that he'd helped cover the tracks of those involved in a crime. What made it worse was that he then 'lied and lied and lied' out of misisguided loyalty to Woodgate.

As for Tony Hackworth, I was puzzled why his name was in the frame. As far as our information was concerned, he was nowhere near the incident. But West Yorkshire Police and the CPS had collated all they needed to know. On 14 March 2000, Woodgate and Bowyer were charged with causing grievous bodily harm to Sarfraz Najeib, and causing an affray in Leeds city centre. Sixteen days later, the same charges were made against Tony Hackworth, while Michael Duberry was charged with attempting to pervert the course of justice. The case was going before a jury. In reality, it would become infamously known as 'The Leeds United trial'.

Meanwhile, our UEFA Cup run had mirrored our domestic form as we saw off the challenges of Partizan Belgrade, Spartak Moscow and AS Roma. It was almost a relief to escape Leeds and arrive in Geneva for the semi-final draw – a welcome chance to concentrate on football matters. We waited for our name to be called for the two-leg fixture: 'Galatasaray . . . will play . . . Leeds United.'

Not the draw we'd wanted. We'd have to run the gauntlet of hate in Istanbul, and visit Galatasaray's notorious stadium, where the Turks don't put out the welcome mat, they just unfurl the banners – at the airport and inside the ground – that warn, in blood red letters, 'WELCOME TO HELL'.

•

Aboard a floating restaurant in the middle of the Bosphorus, the atmosphere couldn't have been more cordial. Leeds and Galatasaray directors, and their wives, and one UEFA delegate, extended the hand of friendship at the traditional eve-of-match dinner, where we couldn't have been made more welcome. There were a lot of smiles and raised glasses, and lots of well-meaning diplomatic talk about forging new alliances.

I'd just got to my feet to thank the Galatasary president for his warm words and hospitality, and had started looking ahead to the following day's first leg, when I spotted our operations director David Spencer fish around in his pocket for his vibrating mobile phone. I was irritated that he was taking a call in the middle of my speech. His eyes looked up and caught mine. From the look on his face, I knew instantly that something was wrong.

When I sat down, and the formalities relaxed, he pulled me to one side, and whispered in my ear. He'd just been notified by his British police liaison officer that there had been an incident in Taksim Square, and some Leeds supporters had been injured and taken to hospital.

'One of them is described as being in a bad way, and the rumour is that it might be fatal,' he said.

. . . and the rumour is that it might be fatal . . .

I looked around the room, still engaged in lively conversation, still smiling through the language barriers, everybody being social, coffees being served.

. . . and the rumour is that it might be fatal.

'Peter,' said David, refocusing my attention, 'we've been advised to return to the safety of our hotel as soon as possible. We must get everyone together and leave.'

Cordialities were abruptly broken. The UEFA delegate's phone rang. My wife, Sophie, asked if I was okay, mistaking my ashen face for illness. Quietly, as the host directors looked bewildered over our sudden farewells, the group boarded the launches back across the water to return to the team hotel. But there was no way I was heading back to twiddle my thumbs and make calls.

It was inconceivable, to me, to head in the opposite direction to our fans. Instinct drove me to the hospital, accompanied by David Spencer and our driver. I didn't know what had happened, what we'd be encountering or how grave the situation was. I just felt a need to get there.

As we neared the hospital, it was chaos. Blue lights flashed, sirens screamed by. People draped in red and yellow flags blew whistles in the street. Crowds were everywhere. TV crews, with cameras perched on their shoulders, ran through the gridlocked traffic. We had no choice but to park up, get out and weave through the same maze; two suited directors wearing the official Leeds United ties.

As we neared the bedlam around the hospital entrance, someone with a Yorkshire accent ran up to us and said: 'Thank God you're here! You've got to get in there . . .' In the bombardment of shouting voices clamouring to be heard, I grasped at two phrases that came out of the noise: 'it just kicked off' and 'ambushed'.

I was breathless as we walked into the hospital. It was eerily empty, no hint of an emergency unfolding. There was no reception, and seemingly no one in charge. It was like walking into a deserted outpatient ward. Our driver walked off to find a doctor. I looked down a long corridor that stretched in front of us, and spotted about eight of our fans standing in a huddle; one was slouched against the wall, another was pacing. They looked up, and started running towards me, crowding me with their panic and their desperate need for information.

David and I had to shout to make ourselves heard, calming them down, needing clarity. That's when we first heard about the friends they were searching for: a man called Christopher, and a man called Kevin. 'No one's telling us anything!' screamed the friends.

'Is anybody else missing?' I asked.

'Christopher's brother is in the ward,' said one.

An agitated doctor arrived, speaking loudly in Turkish, as our driver acted as interpreter.

'I'm the chairman of Leeds United,' I said.

He grabbed me by the arm, led me in a hurry down the

corridor and down one flight of stairs. Only David and the driver were allowed to follow. The concrete staircase grew darker as we reached a basement area, turned left and opened a thick steel door, as if we were entering a vault. Inside, we were confronted with floor-to-ceiling rows of what looked like giant filing cabinets. Our voices echoed around that room. We were stood in the hospital morgue.

The doctor suddenly pulled out one giant cabinet, and there was the body of a bare-chested man. For the sake of his family, it's not necessary to go into morbid details but it was clear he had been attacked repeatedly with a knife. The doctor impatiently asked for me to identify the body.

'I can't . . . I don't know who it is!' I said.

We rushed upstairs to find the friends, and they led us to the brother on the ward. We found Darren behind a drawn curtain, sat on the edge of a bed, having received attention to stab wounds. 'Where's Christopher?' he asked, getting to his feet.

I told him he'd need to be brave and follow us. We wheelchaired him to the top of the stairs, and then he limped down each step. I started to shake in anticipation of the reaction I dreaded. In my mind, I prayed – I desperately prayed – that the man on the slab wasn't his Christopher; that, somehow, the white body wasn't English; that there had been a mistake – that rumours of a fatality were misleading.

That heavy steel door heaved open. David and I stood back as the brother walked forward and the doctor pulled out the giant cabinet again. The screaming that echoed around that room will live with me for ever; a man screaming for his brother to wake.

'Wake up, our kid! Wake up, our kid!'

Those screams identified the body as one of our own: Christopher Loftus, aged thirty-seven.

We went back upstairs, first to break the news to the rest of the lads, and then to locate the man we knew to be Kevin Speight, aged forty, a pub landlord, from Pudsey. He was in the operating theatre and desperately needed blood, but the hospital had no blood stocks for transfusions.

'They can get blood from another hospital but you pay,' said our driver-turned-interpreter. David Spencer gave his credit card for a purchasing order, and rushed the driver on his emergency errand.

My phone kept ringing – '23 missed calls', said the screen. The British media had got wind of an incident. By now, the British ambassador had also arrived.

Turkish TV crews had been allowed in, and stalked us through the hospital corridors, lights beaming on our every move. 'Where the fuck is he?' someone shouted, desperate for the blood to arrive. Our driver seemed to take an age but did his best in the chaos outside. He burst through the doors and we ran to the operating theatre. But it was too late. Kevin Speight had died from his stab wounds minutes earlier. I was numbed. I was then told he had two children. All I wanted to do was get home and hold my two girls. The fans around me leaned into each other, crying.

I sat down and put my head in my hands, unable to comprehend reality. Then the phone rang again. It was the police liaison officer, saying UEFA had called a meeting at the police HQ to decide whether the semi-final would go ahead. My head was spinning. We had supporters' planes already in the air, Istanbul-bound. More were due the following morning. I didn't want to contemplate the consequences of Leeds fans arriving by the hundreds, knowing two of their number had been murdered. I had to snap out of all my swirling emotions, and think practically.

I travelled to the police station with David, as the ambassador liaised with the British Embassy over the bodies. I made sure our travel manager, Stuart Priestley, co-ordinated with the team leaders on each incoming flight of supporters to ensure they were shepherded to their hotels, and stayed indoors. I phoned my wife, Sophie. I needed her to get a message to the manager.

'Find David and tell him not to go to bed until we get there. Two of our supporters are dead. Tell him I need to speak with him as soon as I get back.'

At the hastily arranged UEFA–police meeting, we decided to allow any planes in mid-air to land but to cancel all other flights. Having managed the supporter situation, the police chief, backed by his two lower-ranking officers, told the UEFA delegate that they were in control of the streets, and policing the match wouldn't be a problem.

'I don't think we should play the game. We should call it off, manage the situation, and rearrange,' I said. A Galatasaray director disagreed. The UEFA delegate went out of the room to make a call and returned, saying his instructions were that, if we didn't fulfil the fixture, we would forfeit the semi-final. All eyes looked at me.

I had to think on my feet. I couldn't shift the sight of Christopher Loftus's body from my mind. I couldn't stop hearing his brother's screams. And football had lost all its importance. But, in that split second, I also pictured his murderers, and the Galatasaray fans draped in red flags, dancing in celebration that we'd forfeited the match; dancing on the graves of our two fans.

'We'll honour the fixture,' I said in a snap decision.

Of course, when it came to explaining this difficult decision to the British media, I never did mention – for reasons of diplomacy – how UEFA had demanded a decision in the most impossible situation. All I said was: 'It is UEFA's view that the match should go ahead . . . and we accept that.'

I got back to the hotel about 5 a.m., eager to speak to the manager. David had gone to bed. He could not have realized the seriousness of the situation. At 7 a.m., the hotel was besieged by the media. At 8 a.m., I held a press conference in the business centre. It had become clear that Turkish hooligans, armed with knives, had ambushed Leeds fans in Taksim Square. Christopher Loftus and Kevin Speight were not hooligans; they were ordinary, passionate fans who'd saved money to travel to Europe, and had been guilty only of wearing the wrong colours in the wrong place at the wrong time. We were told categorically by the police that they were innocent bystanders.

David wandered down for breakfast at around 9.30, still seeming oblivious to the gravity of the events the previous night.

'Look, David, there has been a major incident, and the first thing you need to know is that I've taken a decision to go ahead with the game,' I said.

He looked nonplussed. 'Well of course it will go ahead – why wouldn't it?'

I pointed out that, had he stayed up like I'd asked, he'd have had an explanation earlier. 'All hell has broken loose out there, two of our fans have died, I've had long conversations with UEFA and they took the view that the game must go ahead. I had to agree.'

'Peter,' he said, still ignorantly nonchalant, the seriousness of the situation having not yet sunk in, 'we couldn't cancel the game, why would we?'

I was overtired, a little fraught and not in the best of moods, and his reaction angered me. There was a man, who went to bed knowing nothing, questioning me, the man who'd stayed up and helped identify the bodies.

'You just do not understand the gravity of all this, do you? Two of our supporters have been murdered!' I repeated, losing my temper. Without giving him the chance to answer, I then made it absolutely clear that, as a mark of respect to them, the team will be wearing black armbands for the match.

David was not impressed. 'I'm not sure about that,' he argued. 'We don't even know what happened. You know what our fans are like – how do you know they weren't to blame?'

I was staggered, and for probably the first and only time during my tenure as chairman, I gave him an order. 'David, I've been up all fucking night, I know exactly what happened and what those lads didn't do. I rarely tell you what to do but now I'm instructing you – you and the team *will* wear black armbands tonight.'

In fairness to David, and because of his focus on the match, he'd not fully understood the situation; in the bubble of the team hotel with its police cordon he had been separated from reality. But it hit him hard when we returned to Leeds, and he witnessed the mourning that took place at the gates of Elland Road. Shirts, scarves, flowers and photos, in blues, yellows and whites, turned those gates into a shrine.

One bouquet summed up the futility of it all with an attached card that read, 'Football?' It was a fair question. At that time, the beautiful game could not have appeared any uglier.

I know from comments David made to me days later that he respected the decision to wear armbands, and recognized it would have been 'calamitous' had they not done so – particularly if it had emerged that it was the manager's decision not to wear them.

Match day in Istanbul was the scariest experience of my life, even more so than the Stansted plane crash. There was a premeditated mood to intimidate and frighten us, and everything about that night was sinister, not accidental. Those banners at the airport warning us of Hell were no idle threats. There was not a hint of respect towards our dead; just goading threats that further death was possible.

It lashed with rain as the team coach neared the ground. We saw armoured tanks, and water cannons; riot police and dogs straining on the leash. Not that they did anything to hold the crowds back because baying mobs banged on the sides of the coach, jumping up at the windows, sneering men pretending to cut their throats with their fingers. It was as if they treated the two murders as a prelude to something even bigger, even more tragic. And you don't feel safe when you have, what was in my experience, an indifferent police, appalling organization, and the worst security for protection from the Turkish authorities. I looked at the players, their faces as bewildered and scared as the directors and their wives.

UEFA had shoehorned us into that cauldron, and refused our requests for a one-minute silence because they felt it could 'provoke' the home crowd. When you looked at the caged animals foaming at the mouth behind the fencing, you wondered how it was possible to provoke them any more.

We never stood a chance in such intimidating conditions, and were beaten 2–0. I'm not sure the players had the appetite for football anyway. In the dressing room beforehand, there was not a single spark of enthusiasm from anyone, just a resigned sense of going through the motions. I saw them wrap the armbands round their biceps, and saw soldiers going into battle not footballers entering a semi-final.

As they walked from the dressing room in a basement area beneath the stadium, they emerged from the tunnel, protected by a wall of police riot shields held high to deflect the missiles that rained down. A woman's voice came over the Tannoy, in English, expressing regret about the tragedy but her words were lost in a deafening cacophony of whistles, chanting and howling. All around us, apart from one pocket of white, the Galatasary fans bounced on their feet, crazed and high on the intimidation they had stirred. I focused on one man flailing his arms around, jumping up and down, eyes wide and bulging. In any other situation, you'd have said he was on drugs. But this fan's crazed behaviour was somehow deemed to be acceptable within the Ali Sami Yen stadium. I looked down towards the pitch and saw the Leeds players applauding their fans, spending longer than usual in acknowledging their support; players and fans with their arms aloft, being brave for one another.

In the absence of a minute's silence in respect of Christopher and Kevin, those same fans greeted kick-off by turning their backs to the pitch, and raising both hands in the air; defiance over the two empty seats among them. You can't tell me there are better fans anywhere else in the world. Because I will never believe you. Christopher Loftus and Kevin Speight included.

I've often wondered whether it was right to play the game that night, and the *Daily Mail* foamed at the mouth with its criticism of us for doing so. 'GROTESQUE' said its headline. It even claimed we'd done it to make money; that greed had been our motive. Such claims were grotesque in themselves. But maybe the *Mail* was right? Maybe, in thinking on my feet, I called it wrong. We weren't afforded the time to make a well-considered decision, and perhaps my decision was emotive instead of sensible. I know that, for the first time in my life, football didn't matter. Maybe it just wouldn't have mattered if the tie had been awarded to Galatasary because the result was irrelevant anyway.

But I felt I must have done something right when, at half-time in our next league game at Villa Park, all the Leeds fans started singing my name. I listened for a few seconds, acknowledging them. Then, following my instincts again, I raced down to the tunnel, turned left and walked to the corner flag, stood there and applauded *them*. I didn't want to be in the directors' box with the rest of the board. I wanted to be among the seats. I didn't want to be remote from the fans.

'*Leeds, Leeds, Leeds!*' they chanted, their one-fisted salutes punching the air, and I swelled inside with a pride that had nothing to do with being chairman.

One supporter came right down to the advertising hoardings to shake my hand. 'What you did for those lads . . . you'll always be one of us, Peter!' he said, gripping my hand. After the most traumatic three days of my life, I had to wipe tears from my eyes.

People, in the stands and in the media, have said it was my 'finest hour as chairman of Leeds United'. The local BBC awarded me a crystal vase for 'Sports Achievement of the Year 2000'. But the plaudits were embarrassing. I cannot agree that it was my finest hour. How can it possibly be my finest hour in the wake of two murders? It truly was the most horrific hour of my time as chairman.

I didn't do anything extraordinary. I instinctively did what was right: to be there for a set of fans who needed help. And if it was my 'finest hour' then why did I feel so pathetically helpless, as helpless as I've ever felt in my whole life? I always said I was the fans' representative on the board, and I meant that. It's why I attended supporters' club meetings all around the country, from Cheltenham to the Isle of Man, from Scarborough to Pontefract, from London to Leeds. It's why I had to be there that night in Istanbul, and why I attended both funerals, together with David O'Leary.

An article in the *South China Morning Post* best summed it up:

> It would be understandable if Ridsdale was left reflecting on the extraordinary nature of the job. When he was voted into the chairmanship, he no doubt suspected . . . he might have to endure supporters' jibes. But nobody could ever have warned him that he would be attending their funerals.

When Billy Bremner died in December 1997, one of my first acts as chairman was to commission the bronze, life-size statue in commemoration of my childhood hero, now immortalized on the corner of Elland Road and Lowfields Road. After the deaths of Christopher Loftus and Kevin Speight, tributes were laid at Bremner's feet, and scarves draped around his arms and neck, as well as the gates to the ground. But those lads deserved their own tribute, we decided. So a stone, engraved with their names, was placed in the wall of Elland Road, just behind the Billy Bremner statue; the memories of one legendary player and two dedicated fans symbolizing all that is magnificent about Leeds United.

The following season, long after we'd drawn the meaningless UEFA Cup semi-final return leg versus Galatasaray 2–2 and gone out of the tournament, and finished third in the league, there was a special moment at Elland Road just before kick-off. I stood at the front of the directors' box, watching more intently than usual for the arrival of the teams on the green turf. The roar that greeted them brought a lump to my throat as my eyes caught the one person I'd been looking out for, a boy mascot trotting out in his all-white strip.

Little George Speight, the son of Kevin, ran out that day in his father's name, and you couldn't wipe the beaming smile off his face. He wasn't just the team mascot that day. In my eyes, and in his bravery, he represented all that was indomitable about the spirit of not just Leeds United, but the ordinary football supporter.

And I cheered for him louder than I've ever cheered before.

QUESTIONS OF JUSTICE

Ex-England manager Graham Taylor once said that all football agents should be lined up against a wall and shot. I'm not sure such a summary execution is something I'd agree with. But if Graham ever found his luck was in, and ended up shepherding players' representatives to the execution wall, I can almost imagine what the final requests would sound like:

'If you shoot and miss – 10 per cent of the price on my head, plus £250,000 for compensation.'

'If you shoot and only cause injury – 7 per cent plus £200,000 for medical expenses.'

'If you shoot and kill me – 5 per cent to my family and £150,000 for funeral expenses.'

And if the agent leading such negotiations was a man called Dennis Roach, then Graham would, inexplicably, find himself sucked into a typically persuasive and forceful argument about why the agents *deserve* such commissions.

Dennis, who has represented Glenn Hoddle, Mark Hughes and Duncan Ferguson, is one of the game's real characters and, in his day, was both a skilled manipulator of circumstances, a polished negotiator of contracts, and the ubiquitous 'Mr Fix–it' of football who got into the business after apparently meeting Johan Cruyff on holiday.

Such was his network of contacts among players, managers and clubs that he seemed to have this uncanny knack of cropping up in deals where there'd be no obvious link between club or player. Any club can retain any agent to help acquire any player

– it's commonplace and not illegal. Dennis was, on the face of it, a freelance operator, floating around the transfer market. His skills around the negotiating table were so highly respected that he was much in demand.

Often, so I've been told, his arrival on the scene would be greeted with an incredulous 'Why is this player being represented by Roach?' or 'What the hell has Roach got to do with this?'

And so it was that I first encountered Dennis during the transfer of Olivier Dacourt to Leeds from French side Lens, one of three signings in the summer of 2000 to reinforce our team for its bow in the Champions League. David O'Leary had identified Dacourt to provide impetus in midfield, having been impressed with what he'd seen in France and his previous club, Everton. It was my first 'big-money' transfer, and it proved to be an eye-opener.

'Sorry David, but on what basis are we using Dennis Roach?' I asked.

'Well, he's assisting us because he's bilingual,' he said.

'Have we made any commitment to him?'

'None whatsoever, Mr Chairman. I'll leave that to you and him to sort out.'

He had organized through Dacourt's agent, Bruno Satin, for us to fly to France from Leeds-Bradford airport, and meet the Lens president, using a private jet we'd hired for speed of business. The only drawback was having to land in Bourne-mouth to collect Dennis Roach. Call me naive, but I genuinely believed Dennis was merely there as a favour to David, acting as an interpreter with no strings mentioned let alone attached.

You can imagine my surprise, therefore, when we get to Lens, and are met by Dacourt's agent – and he speaks near-perfect English!

I managed to grab a quiet word with the manager. 'I thought you said Dennis was here to translate? You didn't tell me the agent speaks English!' I said, through the corner of my mouth.

David didn't see my point. 'But he's Dacourt's agent so how

do we know what we're saying is being translated accurately in French to the president? *That's* why Dennis is here.'

I placed my unease at the back of my mind.

At the club, negotiations with the president and agent got underway. As they raced through their conversation in French, and Bruno relayed the English translation, I sat there looking at Dennis, on the edge of his seat, listening intently. He kept nodding – his confirmation that, yes, we'd been given an accurate translation.

Don't give up the day job, I thought, your future as a UN interpreter wouldn't last three minutes. It was nothing short of hilarious, and I, for one, couldn't see the point of him being there. I'm not doubting Dennis's French but his purpose that day was, in my eyes, effectively redundant.

After several hours, and some adjournments, the £7.2m deal was agreed, leaving only the formalities of paperwork.

On the return flight home, after the stop-off in Bournemouth, I queried with David if his friend was expecting anything other than a day out and a nice lunch. That's not a matter for him, he reminded me again.

Days later, Dennis rang me. He'd be invoicing the club for £200,000 plus VAT for his 'role in the Olivier Dacourt transfer' through his company PRO International.

I confronted David O'Leary, asking if he knew anything about it. He did not, he said. 'You know I can't get involved,' he said, 'all the transfer fees are down to you, Mr Chairman.' But he knew full well that he was *already* involved because *he* was the one who brought Dennis to the table, even if he hadn't made any commitment to him.

Interestingly, in his book *Leeds United on Trial*, David acknowledged that hiring agents was not within his remit. He wrote: 'We have a clear working practice at Leeds. With help from my backroom staff and scouting staff, I nominate the players ... and my chairman acts as chief negotiator on Leeds United's behalf.'

But, in reality, I felt he had left me in an impossible position with the Dacourt commission to Roach. I didn't have a legal leg to stand on, especially as I'd allowed Dennis to remain present during discussions.

Look, I'm a businessman and, in the business world, if you came across an acquaintance who said, 'I know the president of Lens, I'll do you a favour, put in a good word, or facilitate this or that,' then you don't expect a whopping invoice afterwards; it's not how business works. But it *is* how football works and in the circumstances Roach was perfectly entitled to feel he could invoice.

You'd be hanging around a long time if you had to listen to the gripes of managers and chairmen who felt a third party had needlessly become involved – or interfered – in the transfer and then submitted an invoice for 'assistance, promotional activities, consultation services, communications' as a crucial go-between.

If an agent – and especially those with an influential network – knows well a manager or chairman and then drops in a good word about a player, or engages in an enthusiastic discussion about the theories of a transfer, and then that player consequently makes the switch, you'll hear the 'Ker-ching' sound from the agent's wallet. Because what measure is there on 'assistance provided'? Is it the odd phone call here and there? Is it one active discussion over dinner? Or is it some advice imparted and some gentle arm-twisting over cigars and whisky in a hotel bar? In the majority of cases, most 'assistance and consultation services' are genuine and in good faith, and these agents work their socks off to make deals happen, and overcome complications and political stumbling blocks.

In my case, I felt that Dennis Roach was superfluous to requirements and I should have been tougher with him and David and made it crystal clear that it was the board's responsibility to decide which agents, if any, to use. It's a lesson I'm putting into practice nowadays but, back then, I behaved like a mug.

The episode left a bitter taste in my mouth, and was a foretaste of how David O'Leary would behave in the future, undermining the trust and respect I'd long held in him. Dennis and I spent months haggling over the fee but, in the end, I had to settle the invoice, with two staggered payments, because I was in an impossible position. By July 2001, Leeds United had paid £200,000 plus VAT to Dennis Roach for his 'translation services and assistance'. I felt sick writing the cheque.

Dennis wrote to me soon afterwards to thank me and said, 'They say that everything comes to those who wait! I was beginning to have some doubts.' The man's certainly got a nerve.

Sometimes, there is no escaping a Dennis Roach invoice. As ex-FA chief executive Graham Kelly explained in an article in the *Independent*, Dennis – now president of his self-founded International Football Agents Association – is a figure whose deals have never been besmirched by anything other than unsubstantiated allegations.

Mr Kelly wrote in 2004: 'Shortly after I joined the FA in 1988, I challenged Manchester United over their employment of Roach following Mark Hughes's £1.5m transfer from Barcelona, but unfortunately I could not get behind his company's £25,000 invoice for "promotional activities".'

One year after the Dacourt transfer, another one of Dennis's deals was seemingly lost in translation, and led to him being charged by the Football Association following Costa Rican striker Paulo Wanchope's £3.5m switch from West Ham to Manchester City. Dennis received £250,000 from City for making the deal happen but Maine Road's management then heard he was also due £250,000 commission from the player – a clear breach of FA rule No.22, which states a licensed agent can only receive one payment in relation to each transfer; 'double-dipping' – taking from club and player – is forbidden. Roach explained that Wanchope was clearly mistaken, and that he had never asked for that second payment. He challenged the charges, and forced the FA to back down when he argued that he was FIFA-registered and therefore not governed by the English association. Besides, he said, Wanchope was wrong about the second payment. 'It was a misunderstanding because of his poor English,' he said.

Clearly, Dennis' Costa Rican tongue was nowhere near as accomplished as his French.

Meanwhile, Leeds had another player within its sights – West Ham defender Rio Ferdinand. While David couldn't quite persuade me of the need for someone to translate east London into proper Yorkshire, he hadn't finished delivering his surprises.

Unbeknown to me, thirteen days after we'd finalized negotiations over Dacourt, David had *already* put pen to paper and signed the paperwork to 'exclusively authorize' another FIFA-licensed agent to get involved 'on behalf of Leeds United Football Club'. But it would be a further six months before I'd discover the full truth of the situation.

●

Centre-forward Mark Viduka represented the bargain-buy of my whole time at Leeds United. In that summer of 2000, we saw off competition from clubs in Spain, Portugal and Italy to land him for £6m. The impact he would have on our Champions League campaign would prove enormous, and he must be one of the most underrated footballers with his selfless team qualities, his quick feet and great awareness. He was the true replacement for Jimmy Floyd Hasselbaink, and I'll never forget his four goals in the epic 4–3 victory over Liverpool in the November, plus his brace in the 4–3 win against Spurs a few weeks earlier.

Our third key purchase was the versatile Dominic Matteo from Liverpool. This £3.75m deal almost ran aground when he failed his medical with a knee problem that would mean five weeks on the sidelines. An injury curse that would blight our start to the new season had started to infect our transfer targets before they'd even arrived at the club! I saw a disconsolate

Dominic trudging into the Malmaison Hotel in Leeds, distraught that his big move was over.

'Don't worry,' I said, 'we've done a deal with Liverpool. We'll pay a nominal sum for the transfer, and pay the balance as soon as you're passed fit. We're buying you for the long term, not for next weekend.'

He nearly shook off my hand. 'I can't believe you're taking that view. Thank you! I promise not to let you down,' he said, and he never did. Whether he played as a left-sided defender or as a centre-back, he was a superb addition to the squad.

We'd spent almost £17m on three players but that only told half the story. We still had to reward our 'young guns'. Or 'the babies', as the manager so often called them. Those 'babies' would make up a mean team in their maturity today: Paul Robinson, Scott Carson, Ian Harte, Gary Kelly, Jonathan Woodgate, Stephen McPhail, Aaron Lennon, James Milner and Harry Kewell; all at varying stages of their development, and all bursting on to the scene.

One of the issues in relation to the success of youth academies is that if a significant number of youngsters push through to the first team, your wage bill is artificially depressed at first, and then suddenly explodes as they become successful and seek parity. Take Jonathan Woodgate, a player who started on around £3,000 a week, broke into the first team on around £8,000 a week and then became an ever-present England contender about to star in the Champions League; he'd expect to be earning around £15,000 a week seven years ago. All these young players become prize assets we can't afford to lose to our rivals, so we pay the competitive wages they deserve. Harry Kewell, as another example, went from academy novice to one of Leeds' best-paid players, with a basic salary in excess of £2m. As our team grew in stature and skill, the total wage bill in 2000–01 was around £30m. But what was the alternative? Especially when our strategy was working – investment was a road that led to the Champions League.

Injuries blighted our start to the season, leading to jitters around the ground. High expectations brought a shorter tolerance within Elland Road. Our league form was patchy but we did overcome 1860 Munich to make the group stages of the Champions League.

That meant going to Monaco for the draw, and this was the apogee of my time at Leeds. A frisson of excitement, pride and disbelief shot through me as club secretary Ian Sylvester and I took our seats among the greats of Europe. Nothing prepared me for the buzz of that supercharged draw. I don't care whether you're a fan, player, manager or chairman – there is something that feels brilliant about rolling around the inside of a drum with the likes of Real Madrid, Juventus, Barcelona, Lazio and AC Milan. If you think the FA Cup third round draw is special, the Champions League draw takes the sense of anticipation into another stratosphere. I looked around me, and saw Peter Kenyon from Manchester United, Rick Parry from Liverpool and David Dein and Danny Fizman from Arsenal. I'd be lying if I didn't admit to thinking, What am I doing here?

I was in awe of the magnificent Monaco conference centre, the people, the clubs and the occasion.

But I was beaming. *We are back*, I thought.

And how. For in the first group stage we were drawn alongside heavyweights Barcelona and AC Milan, with Besiktas the fourth club. Danny Fizman turned to me and said, 'Never mind, Peter, there'll always be next season!'

As much I laughed it off, I felt he had a point. Not even I – the eternal optimist – believed it would be the start of a memorable European odyssey, or that we would become the flag-bearers for English football; the last men standing. As the draw concluded, I was still talking excitedly about visiting the Nou Camp and the San Siro. I'd not thought about Besiktas, who they were, or where they came from.

Then it all went manic as the press pushed forward their notepads and microphones, seeking my reaction about returning to Istanbul. At that moment the realization dawned about a return to Turkey just months after the murders in Taksim Square.

As things turned out, and as hard as the memories were, we had nothing to worry about; the contrast could not have been starker. From start to finish, Besiktas provided hospitality that could not have been warmer, and the atmosphere within the ground was subdued and incident-free. We beat them 6–0 at Elland Road and drew 0–0 away, the only depressing feature about our return to Istanbul being the leg injury to Michael Bridges which would see him missing for the next two years, and almost end his carer. He'd certainly never be the same player at Leeds again.

I'm not sure many within the club would have put money on us finishing in the top two in that strong group, what with our injuries and suspensions. We walked into the Nou Camp and its 85,000 crowd with the likes of Jacob Burns, Danny Hay and Tony Hackworth in our team, and, with all due respect to those young lads, it was understandable why Barcelona tanned us 4–0. They were in a different class. I thought it was going to be the shortest, most miserable stint in Europe.

None of us foresaw the tremendous performances that would take Leeds United and its fans on the most incredible journey, starting in the next match with a 1–0 victory over AC Milan and Shevchenko at a rain-lashed Elland Road, thanks to a long-range dipping shot from Lee Bowyer two minutes from time. 'David O'Leary's youngsters answered his call for courage last night and grew into Champions League men,' said the *Daily Mirror*.

There was an abundance of memories and newspaper cuttings to treasure. But the clearest recollection for me is the deafening sounds of the Leeds faithful, cheering us throughout Europe. Their support was incredible, and to see the Union Jacks, St George's flags and white and yellow banners hanging over the fencing and mid-tier advertising hoardings in such impressive stadiums was a sight I'll never forget. The letters

'LUFC' were everywhere and every group of fans, with every flag, told us which part of the country they supported us from: 'Barnsley Whites', 'Worksop Whites', 'Batley Whites', 'Salisbury Whites', 'Kendal Whites', 'Hampshire Whites' and 'Old Goole Whites'. It was as if we had a supporting representative from each town and region in the UK!

Paul Robinson's performance against Barcelona at home was a warning to the rest of Europe, not just England, about what a keeper he was destined to be. As deputy for the injured Nigel Martyn, he almost single-handedly kept them at bay with some incredible shot-stopping until Rivaldo scored an agonizing injury-time equalizer in a 1–1 draw. Robbo was simply outstanding, and already growing into England's heir apparent for the No.1 jersey.

That draw meant we had to do the unthinkable if we were to qualify for the second group stage: go to AC Milan and avoid defeat. Win or draw, anything but defeat.

On the eve of the match, I couldn't wait to get into the San Siro to watch the team train, and marvel at the stadium while it was empty. But there was a mix-up over the transport at the team hotel, and I ended up getting left behind! That, in turn, led to a new superstition among the team – that the chairman should never watch training sessions ever again on the eve of a big game. Being superstitious myself, I could hardly argue.

That night in Milan will probably go down as one of my proudest moments as both fan and chairman. Shevchenko missed a penalty. We took a 44th-minute lead through Matteo. Milan equalized. Milan pressed forward. Robbo was in outstanding form between the sticks yet again, and pulled off two spectacular saves. We were hanging on. Really hanging on. The desperate whistling of the Leeds fan sounded like a collective screech. Then the referee blew. It was a euphoric moment.

The nerves we'd shredded in the stands made an England World Cup penalty shoot-out feel tame by comparison. Afterwards, as Milan fans drifted away, our fans stayed put and savoured the moment, singing and dancing around, letting off flares. Even as the players showered, our supporters kept the jubilant delirium boiling, and their songs echoed around the stadium as it emptied. I went down on the pitch, walked across to their stand and stood in front of that 7,000-strong army and saluted them; the hairs bristled on the back of my neck. We were living the dream, every single one of us. Then the team came out in their suits: Leeds players saluting Leeds fans in the most memorable celebration and show of unity. As BBC Five Live's Alan Green described it on the radio for those back home: 'This is the most powerful bonding between fans and players I have ever witnessed.'

The squad and management kept the celebrations going back at the team hotel, Villa d'Este, overlooking Lake Como, and Gary Kelly ended up serenading my wife, Sophie, during one of many sing-songs with his version of 'Lady in Red' (even though she was wearing pink!).

The second-stage draw would pit us against equally formidable opposition: Real Madrid, Lazio and Anderlecht in Group D.

Once we'd returned to the sobriety of Elland Road, the injury curse and suspensions continued to stretch the depth in our squad. We were having a glorious run in Europe but we were thirteenth in the table come New Year's Day. But things would turn around, and one of the key factors behind our recovery was the arrival of central defender Rio Ferdinand, our record signing at £18 million.

●

Rio's name had been 'top priority' on the manager's wish-list since the end of the previous season, and the Leeds board took the unanimous view that we should pursue him. The stark truth was that we also needed a replacement for Jonathan Woodgate, a colossus who had been reduced to a shadow of his former self by his pending trial, and, let's face it, was someone who had an even chance of going to jail. Had Woodgate not fallen apart and not been charged with an offence that carried a maximum sentence of life imprisonment, there was no way the Leeds board would have sanctioned the Rio deal. In our mindset at the time, we were not looking for 'cover' for Woody, but a replacement, a new first-choice centre-back: Matteo in for the injured Lucas Radebe, Rio in for Woodgate. David O'Leary and Eddie Gray have since denied this, and suggested we'd have still bought Rio. We wouldn't, I can assure you.

The wheels were put in motion on the last day of the 1999–2000 season after we'd qualified for the Champions League at West Ham. After the match, I spoke with Hammers chairman Terry Brown to ask if he'd be willing to release his twenty-two-year-old centre-back. 'Not a chance,' he said, but we maintained dialogue throughout the summer and into the autumn. Rio was a Rolls-Royce of a central defender, the entire package, and we weren't going to let him slip away.

By the time West Ham visited Elland Road in November 2000, we'd already had a £12m offer rejected. After the game, which they won 1–0, I approached Terry Brown in the board-room and floated in a renewed offer of £15m. 'We're not interested at that price,' he said.

'Terry,' I said, exasperated, 'there's *got* to be a price you'd sell him for.'

He looked at me, his resolve diluting, and said, 'If you offer £18m, we'd have a deal.'

It wasn't my decision. I wasn't bidding up from £12m to £18m. I needed board approval. I pulled Allan Leighton to one side, and he approved, as did the other directors on the Monday. West Ham's board accepted our offer that same day, 20 November 2000.

People immediately questioned the wisdom of us spending 'crazy money' but we'd properly calculated that the Champions League run, with its profits of between £15m and £20m, would pay for the deal, and it did. It would turn out to be both a wise football move, and a sound business investment.

That same afternoon, the phone rang. It was Norwegian agent Rune Hauge asking for £1.75m for 'assistance and advice provided . . . in connection with the transfer for Rio Ferdinand'.

I didn't know whether to fall off my chair or hit the roof.

I stormed into the office of Stephen Harrison, our chief operating officer, and told him about the outrageous fee Rune was asking for. 'Leeds United is being raped by this agent!' I spluttered.

This transfer, and the matter of that £1.75m payment, has been the source of much speculation and sly innuendo that ultimately brought the FA investigators rushing in, and led to a searching internal audit at Elland Road, with suspicions that questioned my honesty and integrity. Now, it's the time for the detailed truth about a transaction that unsettled many supporters and commentators.

Certain people started pointing fingers at me after journalist and author Tom Bower published his 'definitive exposé of British football corruption' in a book called *Broken Dreams* in 2003. In an updated edition, he wrote:

> The revelation that Peter Ridsdale had employed Rune Hauge to buy Rio Ferdinand, costing £900,000 in commission to Hauge, surprised Allan Leighton. The subsequent revelation that Hauge had in fact received £1.75 million astonished the non-executive director. On Leighton's orders, an internal audit . . . unravelled the background to the transfer.

There were two problems with these 'revelations': first, I don't know where Mr Bower ever found the figure of £900,000 in commission – such a figure never came into the equation; and second, I was not the person who had employed 'Rune Hauge'. The truth is that David O'Leary hired him without my knowledge, and without board approval. He acted unilaterally, and invited the Guernsey-based agent into the commission-rich deal.

The whole focus within *Broken Dreams* lent astonishment to Allan Leighton and sympathy to David O'Leary, and heavily suggested it was I who had the crucial relationship with Rune.

It led to a headline in the *Daily Mail* which screamed: '£1.75m Transfer Scandal Leads To Ridsdale'. The meaning of those words built into a dubious picture that questioned all I stood for. Indeed, two people within the football industry told me how 'word on the street' was that I had retained Rune, and taken a kick-back from his £1.75m – in the same way George Graham had – to pay for the conservatory in which I'm now writing this book.

The truth is that I did everything possible to block Rune's commission, only to find my hands were tied by an agreement O'Leary had put in place. He authorized the agent to act exclusively on behalf of Leeds United. It was his signature that allowed Rune 'to contact the player, player's agent and club representatives on our behalf'. David signed the form on 15 May 2000, three months *before* Pini Zahavi informed me of Rio's interest in joining us, and six months before the actual transfer. The form, faxed to Rune's company Libero Limited by club secretary Ian Sylvester, stated: 'We hereby confirm that we have exclusively authorised FIFA-licensed agent Rune Hauge to act on our behalf in connection with the acquisition of the player's registration for the professional footballer Rio Ferdinand.'

Ian Sylvester's office was opposite the manager's at the Thorp Arch training ground, and it was from there – not Elland Road where my office was based – that the forms were faxed to Libero Limited. I was completely in the dark over what they had done.

As the award-winning sports columnist Martin Samuel wrote in the *News of the World* on 2 March 2003, when he was condemning me: 'Giving Hauge the job was not bent – it just wasn't particularly bright.' I couldn't agree more. Had the decision been mine, it would never have happened. As far as I was concerned, discussions were at an advanced stage with West Ham; we didn't need an agent to act as a fixer.

I explained the background to Rune's involvement in a sworn statement provided for both the FA inquiry, and its compliance officer, Graham Bean, and the subsequent internal audit carried out by Deloitte & Touche. I submitted the following:

> Rune had first called me following initial conversations with David O'Leary about the Rio Ferdinand transfer. The agent then said he was having dinner with West Ham boss Harry Redknapp, and he would be happy to assist because he knew Harry well. I said I was already in discussions with the chairman of West Ham but if his discussions may assist with a transfer then I would be grateful. But I made it clear to him that it was neither normal practice nor that of the club to engage agents on a fee basis. If the club ultimately signed Rio, and Rune demonstrated he had brought the player to the club, then I would discuss with him, at that stage, whether the club would be prepared to pay him a fee. During those discussions with Rune, he did not mention the authorisations which were signed by David O'Leary. I did not authorise David O'Leary or anyone else to sign such authorisations.

In their subsequent review of transfer payments, Deloitte & Touche stated in its final report: 'There is no evidence that the authorisations for exclusivity given by David O'Leary or Ian Sylvester were covered by written company policies applicable at that time.'

How Rune must have been smiling, though. None of the politics mattered to him. He could wave his signed form and start calculating a near 10 per cent commission for advice he believed he'd given in conversations with the manager, myself, Rio's agent, Pini Zahavi, and Harry Redknapp. The minute his 'exclusivity arrangement' was in place, we were stuffed. If we were raped by Rune, our arms were pinned down by the manager's mandate.

Stephen Harrison and I toyed with the idea of not paying. Ten per cent was a lot more than the usual 5 per cent we'd pay someone for representing our interests. But, in a call we received from a third party, it was made clear to us that if we didn't agree to the £1.75m commission, the £18m deal would collapse. Within twenty-four hours of our offer being accepted by West Ham, the whole deal was in jeopardy because of a dispute over an agent's role and fee. Can you imagine the bad press we'd have received at a time when there was such a buzz over Rio's impending arrival? That the world-record deal for a defender had fallen through because we refused to pay an agent his fee?

In the end, we felt compelled to pay. It was either that or losing Rio. I sent a letter to Rune Hauge, confirming we would honour the agreement, and pay him in two separate instalments, one for £1m, the other for £750,000.

In a funny way, I can't blame him, and I understood the stance he took. In his eyes, he'd been retained by senior management. Full stop. What I can't understand is David O'Leary's decision to act unilaterally. Since all this came to light, I've been asked on many occasions why he would give exclusivity to Rune, without informing the chairman. It is a question to which I cannot provide a satisfactory answer.

What's more, his actions caused me a lot of subsequent grief and opened me up to false accusations. I faced an internal audit and the FA's compliance officer, Graham Bean, alias the 'sleaze buster', investigated me over the commission but concluded, and has repeated this statement since, that everyone 'was pointing the finger at the wrong man'.

I co-operated with every inquiry into these transactions, and made available for scrutiny and inspection every one of my private bank accounts and statements. I cannot have been more honest or transparent, and the constant innuendo has been a scandal in itself.

I was also grateful to Rio's agent, Pini Zahavi, who contributed this statement: 'I believe Peter's reputation for honest dealing is unparalleled within the industry and that he has never, to my knowledge, ever benefited directly from the proceeds of any transfer.'

With the 'small matter' of the £1.75m fee cleared up, we were able to meet Rio and his mum, Janice, at Pini's London flat. I like Janice enormously. She's proud, she's sharp, she's funny, and she insisted on being there for the discussions about personal terms. We forget that however big and wealthy these young footballers are, they're still sons with worried mothers, and the move north from east London was an upheaval for all involved. Janice and I got talking and discovered that we had both worked for the Burton Group at the same time, she for Top Shop, me for Top Man, and we were enjoying a nostalgic chat when Rio made his first intervention.

'It's all very interesting and that,' he said, 'but is there any chance we can now turn our attention to the contract!' He signed up for £35,000 a week plus bonuses, and a £300,000 signing-on fee, paid over a five-year contract.

Rio and Janice flew north on a private jet we'd laid on for reasons of expediency; we wanted to get the formalities of the medical and paperwork out of the way in time to unveil our new signing before the televised home game with Arsenal the next day. When he cleared the medical, and the ink dried on the contract, I looked at Rio and thought, How can someone who has just signed an £18m deal look so down in the mouth?

'Cheer up!' I said, slapping him on the back.

'He is happy,' his mum reassured me, 'that's Rio that is! He's not one to dance all over the place.'

Rio Ferdinand: cool under pressure, and even cooler under the weight of an £18m price-tag.

David had been away in Ireland all week because his father had undergone heart surgery but he'd returned in time for the Sunday afternoon so I fully expected him to join me, as he had done for every other new signing, at the one o'clock press conference before a four o'clock kick off. While it might not be his job to hire agents, it is his job, in my view, to showboat new players, especially when he'd listed Rio as a 'top priority' and after we'd gone out on a limb to land his target.

In his own mind, David expected us to do a deal at £12m or, at a stretch £15m, not £18m. I got the impression that such numbers made him nervous, and he made it clear that his wife Joy thought such numbers were 'obscene'. More than that, though, he was suddenly in charge of the world's most expensive defender, and our record signing; the manager who always made a thing in the press about being 'naive' and 'still learning' was faced with the pressure of no failure, no excuses.

Maybe that is why, when we unveiled our new star, the man who had been so intimately involved with the Rune Hauge set-up was suddenly nowhere to be seen. I'd asked him to attend the heaving press conference to unveil Rio, but he declined, as if he was somehow distancing himself from the sharp media focus, and inevitable questions about the fee; another example of 'Nothing to do with me, guv.'

That impression has been subsequently strengthened after reading his book, which states he 'didn't know how the Rio talks were going until the Friday' before the Arsenal game. This baffles me. David was abreast of everything six days earlier. Even the price. I'd spoken to him in person after Terry Brown accepted, in principle, our £18m offer. He told me he would leave the matter in my hands, and trusted we'd reach a suitable agreement.

He was also keen to leave the press conference in my hands, saying he couldn't afford the distraction before such an important match. 'We've got a match, you did the deal. I'll leave it to you, Mr Chairman,' he said.

So it was I who faced the bright lights, and I who walked out on the pitch with Rio to introduce him to 38,000 people inside Elland Road. The fans who had chanted for Rio just eight days earlier in our previous game against West Ham, imploring him to sign, gave him a huge reception as he held aloft his No.29 shirt. As Rio saluted them, I thanked the heavens that we'd agreed to honour the £1.75m to Rune.

It was a strange feeling being out on that pitch with the world's most expensive defender because I had worried about the size of the fee, and thinking about it had kept me awake at night. I had the support of the board but it didn't ease the burden. I knew we needed Rio but I couldn't get my head around paying £18m for a footballer. My working-class background agreed with Joy O'Leary, although my football head would have countered, 'Obscene but necessary.' As a sign of my insecurity, I'd even phoned three of our largest shareholders to talk it through, not for approval but to hear their confidence. I *needed* to tuck their confidence under my belt. It's always irritated me in subsequent years to hear people talk about 'Peter Ridsdale spending £18m on one player' when the truth was that, along with me, it was Allan Leighton, Richard North, Stephen Harrison and David Spencer who, on all occasions, approved the expenditure of Leeds United plc.

It also jarred with me when, on the Tuesday before the Arsenal game, I was in London with the FA International Committee to be measured for our new suits and, as I walked into the room, Doug Ellis turned to me and said: 'Peter, tell me it's not true that you've bid £18m for Rio Ferdinand. You must be mad . . . you will never get your money back!'

We beat Arsenal 1–0 on the day Rio joined. As a club and as a team, we were at our peak. Ian Edwards wrote in the *Daily Mirror* about 'the first signs of a Premiership power-shift at Elland Road' and added:

It began with confirmation of their naked ambition to put a stop to Manchester United's domination . . . with the

parading of £18m record signing Rio Ferdinand. His hunch
that the £64m investment made by manager David O'Leary
over the last two years is about to start generating rewards
in silver appears to be a shrewd assessment. Ridsdale's
smile at the end was almost as broad as Ferdinand's . . .

I think that what Ian Edwards really saw that night was utter
relief.

•

The new year brought the case we'd dreaded: 'The Queen v
Woodgate & Others'. The biggest drama in the club's history
took place sixty miles away from Elland Road, in Court No.4
inside Hull Crown Court. What we didn't expect was that I
would be the first person to face accusations in the witness stand
before the jury was even sworn in. I'd said all along in media
statements that it wasn't Leeds United in the dock and yet there
I stood, facing the prosecution.

Nicholas Campbell QC, leading with the suspicions of West
Yorkshire Police, launched a legal argument that claimed we, as
a club, had launched some kind of Machiavellian conspiracy and
leaked news of Woodgate and Bowyer's arrests to the *Yorkshire
Evening Post* 'in order to taint the envisaged identity picture',
thereby encouraging such a welter of pre-trial publicity that the
players' barristers could argue that a fair trial was impossible.

'The publication of the names . . . [was] nothing to do with
the police. It was down to Peter Ridsdale,' he said.

I stood in the witness stand, nervous and angry over being
accused of something I hadn't done. I was in Hong Kong at the
time, and hadn't received the news until around 3 p.m. UK time.
Yet there was the prosecution suggesting I'd tipped off the
media at 1.30 p.m. It was impossible. Besides, with my plc hat
on, why on earth would we encourage bad publicity when there
was no certainty of the players being charged? There was nothing
to 'taint' at that juncture.

If this is the accuracy of the prosecution case, God help the players, I thought.

With the nation's press crammed into seats behind me in Court No.4, Nicholas Campbell, with the looks of a studious, bespectacled headmaster, attempted to skewer me, suggesting there was a motive to our leaking the story. We had only ever released a media statement *in response* to the *Evening Post* 'exclusive'.

'Your young players were being accused of being racist thugs?' he suggested.

'Certainly, at one point, it was speeding towards a suggestion that that was the case. It was an enormous concern and, clearly, it was disturbing,' I said, 'but I was out in Hong Kong.'

Thankfully, the testimony of *Evening Post* editor Neil Hodgkinson persuaded the judge of the madness of this prosecution claim. 'Did your story come as a result of the press release from Leeds United?' asked the prosecutor. 'No, it did not,' said the editor, but refused to reveal his true source.

Within our camp, and from what we heard from friends in the media, we had always believed the leak emerged from someone within West Yorkshire Police. As its own press officer, Michelle Laister, would later testify, the first media inquiry came on 13 January from a *Sun* reporter asking about 'an incident involving a Leeds player' – five days before our statement. The CPS and West Yorkshire Police clearly had no idea how the media worked, and were trying to heap the blame on us. It illustrated what we were up against from the word go.

I'd driven to Hull that morning with our new communications director, ex-*Daily Mail* man David Walker, a man we'd recruited as our PR shield and filter because of his experience working in Fleet Street. Bowyer, Hackworth and Duberry were staying with their legal teams in a hotel overlooking Hull Marina. Woodgate was some miles away, staying in a more remote hotel. It seemed to me that his legal team and management, Sfx, took a deliberate decision to put distance between him and his fellow defendants. Even in the lobby outside court, where all the reporters hovered, Woody didn't stand with his team-mates but his co-accused Middlesbrough friends, Neale Caveney and Paul Clifford.

I was tense as we walked into court that cold January morning. I dreaded to think what the following weeks had in store.

As the press photographers and TV crews stalked our entry through the police cordon, everything was surreal; I felt detached from and yet entwined within the same experience. I'd already met Bowyer and Duberry in the hotel lobby, looking uncomfortable in their smart suits. Lee seemed not to have a care in the world. 'Dubes' looked pensive and agitated. Outside the court, I saw Woody, and was shocked by how pale and gaunt he was; completely haggard – the stress of the trial really getting to him. He and Bowyer exchanged nods but didn't talk.

Then it was time to walk into court, through two sets of double doors, for day one of the trial. It was ticket-only for the public gallery and media seats. To see four of our players sat behind a Perspex shield in the dock at the back of the court was a shock; they seemed suddenly stripped of all the stardom and glamour that the Premiership had coated them in. Woodgate resembled a terrified schoolboy; Hackworth just looked bewildered; Duberry was on the edge of his seat, hanging on every word of counsel; and Bowyer the cocky rebel on his best behaviour, in his Sunday best. However much they were regarded as overpaid footballers with enviable lifestyles, no one in the world would have swapped places with them there and then.

In the hushed court, Nicholas Campbell QC got to his feet and began the prosecution's opening statement: 'This case concerns events that took place in the city of Leeds on a night in January last year . . .'

At the end of that first day in court, Allan Leighton phoned me after watching the wall-to-wall TV coverage. He issued some sound advice: that this wasn't the club's trial; that I should not be publicly linked to the players, and we should put distance between them and us. I didn't attend the trial again.

•

In the Premiership, Leeds had turned their 2000–01 season around from January; only Newcastle and Arsenal would take all three points from us before the end of the season. From thirteenth, we shot back up the Premiership.

Another supporting factor for this turn in fortune was the appointment of Brian Kidd from youth-team development manager to first-team coach at the beginning of March, seen by many as a promotion over Eddie Gray's head. His input for the crucial run-in to the end of the season, and the Champions League, was invaluable, however hard it might be to accept for those Leeds fans who never took to him because he used to be the No.2 at Old Trafford.

During a goalless draw at Everton the following season, I had to remonstrate with a section of our supporters because of the vitriolic abuse they were dishing out to Brian. I couldn't bear to hear it from the directors' box and so went down to talk to them at the final whistle. It landed me in a spot of bother with the FA and Merseyside Police – because I should have known my place, apparently. But supporters get behind teams, and that also must also mean the first-team coach. I was glad when results vindicated both Brian and David.

•

Don Warters, a journalist who reported on Leeds for more than thirty years, reminded me of a quote Don Revie came out with at a dinner in the 1970s.

'Mark my words,' he said during the glory years, 'a team as good as this, and the successful times it brings, come along only once in a lifetime. So make the most of it while it is here.'

That night in Madrid on 6 March 2001, his wisdom taught

me to savour the moment, as we took on Real Madrid in the Champions League – and took the lead.

'We are beating Real Madrid!' I screamed inside my head as everyone around me celebrated Alan Smith's sixth-minute goal.

We're actually beating Real Madrid. Beating Real Madrid in the Bernabéu.

The ghost of Don Revie must have been smiling down on us; the man who had changed our strip to all-white so we would at least 'look like Real Madrid' was no doubt witnessing, like the rest of us, the modern-day Leeds team emulating the Spanish giants on the pitch, and matching them in every department. I saw the fans dancing around, my legs bouncing in tune with their chants in the directors' box: 'We are the champions . . . champions of Europe!'

We'd already qualified for the Champions League quarter-finals. Real Madrid had also qualified so the match was viewed as the Group D decider. They had handed us an object lesson in football the previous November with a 2–0 defeat at home, but we'd gone on to beat Lazio 1–0 in Rome, and had swept aside Anderlecht home and away.

In the rain inside the Estadio Santiago Bernabéu, the 10,000 Leeds fans outsang 70,000 Real Madrid fans, even though we lost a pulsating fixture 3–2.

This elite tournament of Europe, when staged in one of football's finest theatres, is like one of those dramatic operas that leaves you spellbound, from the ceremonial moment both teams walk out to that famous theme tune – Handel's 'Zadok the Priest' – to the those ballboys lifting the huge circle of the black and silver Champions League logo, stretching it, and rippling it like a giant trampoline above the centre-circle. You don't need alcohol on such occasions. You can just get drunk on the atmosphere, and we celebrated our entry into the quarter-finals.

Our European dream was astounding everybody, and high praise had been rolling in from all quarters, including Man-

I remember when you
were this big! Walking
under Dad's wing

Dad pushes me in
a pram along the seafront
in Bridlington, with Mum and Judy

Father and son in the
back garden at home in Hyde Park, Leeds

Dreaming of becoming Gary Sprake . . . as keeper with Adel Memorial Hall FC

Tasting championship glory
under 'Sgt Wilko' in 1992

Our young fans: wife Sophie
with new-born daughter Olivia and
sister Charlotte in 1997

Crunch match:
Spurs v Leeds United,
and George Graham's mind
is made up

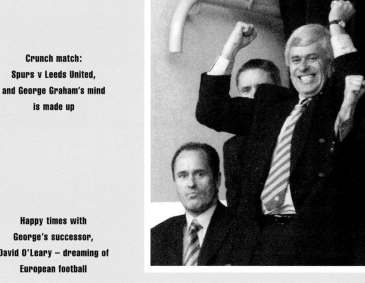

Happy times with
George's successor,
David O'Leary – dreaming of
European football

The Mighty Whites who helped revive the memories at Elland Road . . .

. . . and their lucky escape: the first team cheated death in 1998 in the Stansted plane crash. David O'Leary injured a shoulder forcing open one of the emergency exits

When football meant nothing: the tragedy in Galatasaray united players and fans. I applauded our brilliant supporters before the game in Istanbul in a stadium filled with hate, while the players had to come onto the pitch shielded by riot police. In Leeds, the Billy Bremner statue became the focal point for tributes

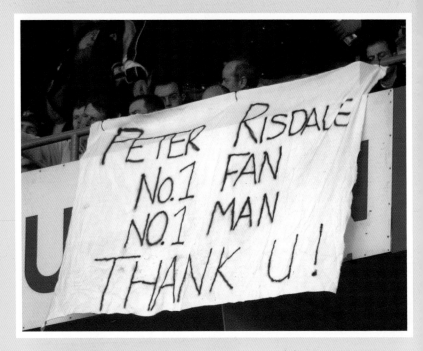

Glory days: when my popularity
and Leeds' success in Europe
was at its height

This is me jumping into the
arms of David O'Leary, celebrating
another triumph in the Champions
League, in the San Siro in
December 2000

The infamous 'Leeds United trial' brought me to Hull Crown Court to give evidence.
Here I am walking into court with fellow director David Walker

A grim moment: announcing the sale of Woodgate, and the rift with Venables begins

From hero to zero: with Woodgate gone and, as Leeds slide down the table, the fans turn on me, unfurl their banners and make their feelings clear

chester United boss Alex Ferguson. 'What Leeds have achieved in the Champions League, and what David O'Leary has done at Elland Road is terrific. Leeds have found a way of playing in the Champions League . . . and they might be the surprise package,' he said.

What made our run even more remarkable was that it was being played out against the backdrop of a high-profile court case; the scales of justice above Hull Crown Court balancing the Champions League trophy in one hand and the liberty of our footballers in the other. It meant that stresses and strains of running a football club, and getting a winning team mentally prepared, were ratcheted up more notches than we would have liked. As the manager said in his programme notes once: 'The disruption off the field here this season has been immense. There's been a shadow over this club for 12 months now . . . but I've been so delighted with the way the players have stuck together and battled on.'

As a football fan, you want to see your players show guts, dig deep and scrap for every ball and the team spirit and camaraderie at this time were exceptional. Woodgate was reduced to watching our Champions League adventure unfold on television; officially he had an ankle injury but, in reality, the stress of the trial meant he had fallen apart. He became such an isolated figure, and I felt for him.

Bowyer, by contrast, was a man transformed. Despite sitting in the dock all day, he would turn out for the team and play the best football of his career. He scored six goals in the 2000–01 European campaign when the pressure must have been intolerable. Bearing in mind he wasn't training properly, because his weekdays were spent from 10 a.m. to 4 p.m. inside a court room, it makes his contribution even more outstanding. Say what you like about Lee Bowyer but, if you went to war – as the players say – you'd want someone with his guts, focus and passion in your team. His spirit and determination not to let the trial stand in the way of his football was typified by the visit of

Anderlecht to Elland Road, on the thirteenth day of the prosecution evidence. Bowyer raced back from Hull, made it just in
time for kick-off and scored the winning goal three minutes from
time. No wonder the Leeds fans screamed, '*Bowyer for England!
Bowyer for England!*'

It required a Herculean effort to get Bowyer to our games.
Saturdays were easy. It was the midweek fixtures that became a
nightmare, and the trial ruled him out of away European games.
Getting Lee Bowyer, an indispensable player in the form of his
life, to matches was as important as the tactics. The one match
that proved problematic with timing was actually a midweek
Premiership game at Everton. We had to resort to flying him by
helicopter to Liverpool from Hull. It cost around £2,000 but,
bearing in mind that each place in the league was worth
£500,000, it was worth the investment.

At the other end, I saw Lee scrambling for the dressing room.
'How was the helicopter?' I asked.

'Never want to do that again, Mr Chairman – it was horrible.
Scariest ride ever!' he said. We never did hire another helicopter
for him.

At Hull Crown Court on 3 April, the jury began its deliberations after hearing all the evidence from the defence and prosecution. That evening, reigning Spanish champions Deportivo La
Coruña arrived at Elland Road for our eagerly awaited quarter-
final. Nerves were frayed for different reasons. But there was
much to celebrate. In the match programme that night, I wrote:
'Coming this far is a dream few of us could have anticipated last
August. Last Friday, we reported our half-year financial results
to our shareholders. The operating profit . . . increased from
£2.3m to £6.2m on turnover of £41m. There is no doubt that
results are starting to pay back our investment.'

The match itself was sensational. Deportivo's pre-match
psychology was to suggest Leeds would be a walkover but their
mind games didn't work – we won 3–0, and Ferdinand scored

his first goal. In the away leg, it was a different story. The Spaniards laid siege to our goal and cruised into a 2–0 lead. It required the most magnificent defensive performance to hang on and take us through to the semi-finals versus Valencia, conquerors of Arsenal. We were the only team left flying the flag for England; two legs and 180 minutes from the final. I looked at David O'Leary, quietly celebrating in his own way, leaving the fans to go wild. Then I thought of George Graham, and his decision to leave because he felt Spurs had more potential. As journalist Richard Sutcliffe says so perfectly in his book on Leeds' European dream, *Marching On Together*, it was 'a decision that now looks as astute as that of the record company boss who turned down the Beatles'.

We drew the first leg of the semi-final 0–0 at home but had denied Valencia a crucial away goal. All we needed was one at the Mestalla stadium, and they would need two. Three days before our trip to Spain, we'd lost 2–1 at Arsenal, knocking us from third to fourth in the league. Liverpool were now odds-on favourites to clinch that last Champions League place. It meant we had to win the second leg, then win the final.

On the eve of the Valencia match, the entire Leeds team turned up without a hair between them. Every single player had shaved his head. Some commentators in the media criticized it as an act of folly but, for me, it illustrated the togetherness and spirit that bound that squad so tightly; all for one, and one for all going into the club's biggest match in a quarter of a century. Not since the Jimmy Armfield side had reached the final in Paris in 1975 had we been so far. Never as a fan, let alone as chairman, had I ever considered Leeds being in this dream-like position.

When those shaven heads walked out on that pitch on a balmy evening on 8 May, my veins itched with the adrenalin of the pre-match build-up. Apparently, I kept saying over and over, 'Fan-tas-tic! . . . Fan-tas-tic!' Because it was: the waves of noise that kept sweeping over us were something else. I looked to a corner of the stadium where our away support was gathered. 'Look at them all – fan-tas-tic!'

But the atmosphere was all we enjoyed that evening. We'd suffered a body blow with UEFA's late suspension of our mid-field linchpin Lee Bowyer, punished by video evidence for a 'stamp' they'd detected in the first leg. It was, perhaps, an omen.

Our European dream ended with a 3–0 defeat. Gaizka Mendieta was the star of their victory on a night which saw Alan Smith red-carded for a two-footed challenge that illustrated a collective frustration. But it had been an historic, unforgettable journey that had taken us into wonderland football stadiums, lasted an intoxicating nine months, and sent us 17,000 miles around Europe.

I returned home to the calculator and some number crunching. We'd finished fourth in the Premiership, just one point behind Liverpool. Our poor start to the season had cost us. We were back in the UEFA Cup but two things happened: we'd lost between £15m and £20m for missing out on the Champions League, and TV had lost interest in the initial rounds of the UEFA Cup, meaning the income from that tournament had been reduced from £7m to around half that. It was then that we felt the first strains of the financial pressures upon us; the club bowed ever so slightly under the weight. But financial pressures and balancing losses and profits in a volatile industry like football are not unusual; calculators and dreams fill the heads of chairmen.

Look at the facts we were playing with: in June 1998, at the end of my first season as chairman, our turnover was £28.5m. At the end of my third season, as shown in the annual report for 2001, it was £86.25m, before buying and selling players. This gave us a £10m operating profit. Once our transfers in and out were included into the mathematics, we'd made a loss of £7m. But, at the same time, and people forget this, an independent valuation carried out that year had priced our playing squad at £198m. Yet no one felt it necessary to offload players at that juncture. Why would we carve up a winning squad? We had a strong asset base, and a team that had just proved its worth in the semi-finals of the Champions League.

And, on the plus side, it was announced that qualification to the Champions League was being extended to fourth place in the Premiership for the 2001–02 season. In the previous three seasons, Leeds United hadn't finished out of the top four. There was absolutely no reason to panic, and we were all looking ahead and confidently mapping out requalification to the Champions League.

All we had to do was finish fourth, and that hardly seemed a tall order in the scheme of things. We may have been feeling a new financial strain, but there were no klaxons going off, no red lights flashing, and no one was putting their heads in the sand. The future remained positive and exciting.

•

Back at Hull Crown Court, two of our players had walked free. Hackworth was acquitted on the judge's direction because there was no evidence that placed him at the scene. And Duberry was found not guilty when it emerged he had done nothing to pervert the course of justice. What he did do, he admitted, was lie to police during interviews to cover for his friend Woody. But under the weight of his conscience and fear for his own future, he testified *against* his team-mate.

Michael had ferried some defendants away from the crime scene and, referring to a conversation he'd had with Woody, he said: 'I asked where he had been, and he said they had just had a fight with some Asians.' It was a sensational moment in the trial, according to those who witnessed the testimony, as a defender incriminated his fellow defender.

Duberry was photographed walking free, giving the thumbs-up. I was delighted for him. He'd been both brave and true, and, together with Hackworth, should never have suffered the humiliation of being in that dock in the first place.

What the jury *didn't* hear was that the victim Sarfraz Najeib heard someone shout, 'Do you want some, Paki?' He couldn't be sure who shouted it – a defendant or a bystander – and no other witnesses heard it. On those grounds, it couldn't be presented in evidence and the CPS eliminated race as a motive. It was imperative, therefore, that the jury didn't think racism was an issue in the case. So much so that the trial judge, Mr Justice Poole, said in his summing up that the suggested motive was 'group retaliation', and this was a decision taken after 'a painstaking examination of all evidence'.

But in the tenth week of the trial – 'the fag end of proceedings' as one barrister called it – and with the jury on its third day of deliberating its verdict, an article in the *Sunday Mirror* on 8 April 2001 spectacularly undid all those efforts to eradicate race as an issue. For some inexplicable reason, the paper published an interview with the victim's father in which he said he felt the attack on his son *was* racially motivated. The father no doubt believed this to be the case, but why the paper ran the story after all the judge had said I will never understand. It beggared belief.

It was enough for Mr Justice Poole to abort the trial and discharge the jury, which had 'striven for the past ten weeks to do justice in this case'. A multimillion-pound trial had collapsed because of one reckless decision. It meant enduring a rerun of the whole trial, and another season would be spent in the shadow of a trial hanging over us.

What I didn't realize was that David O'Leary had already started penning his book *Leeds United on Trial* – and the dressing room would find itself fair game.

FALL FROM GRACE

I wouldn't discover the manager had 'lost' the dressing room until much further down the line. And nor would he, and then he'd still deny it.

But, looking back, perhaps the first fissure had already appeared on 27 January 2001, before the FA Cup fourth round match against Liverpool. As the team left the Malmaison Hotel for the short trip by coach to Elland Road, I saw keeper Paul Robinson looking thunderous, and close to tears. I hurried up to him, and tried grabbing his arm to ask what was wrong.

'Don't talk to me now,' he said, 'but I'll tell you this – I'll never play for that bastard again!'

I looked at David O'Leary, in his own world, all stern-looking in pre-match concentration. Robbo had been playing out of his skin. His shot-stopping against Barcelona and AC Milan told only half the story of his six games in Europe and sixteen in the Premiership as deputy to Nigel Martyn, out injured since the October. Robbo had been much more than a stand-in, though; he'd surpassed himself, and put himself in the England Under-21s line-up. In such outstanding form, and having made a resounding case for Nigel to fight for his jersey back, you'd have thought it would have taken a brave manager to remove him from the middle of goal. Competition for places is what football is all about, to make the other person keep looking over his shoulder, to raise his game, and, if you happen to get injured and your deputy sets the world on fire, it then becomes *your* job to dispossess him. At least, that's how some people – Paul Robinson included – would view it.

After a week of training, and on the back of a 2–1 away win at Aston Villa, he'd psyched himself up for the FA Cup. Only David had decided to reinstate Nigel Martyn, as was his prerogative. Doubtless he had good reasons, maybe he thought the youngster needed a rest. It was the manner in which Robbo had been told that upset him.

Tough decisions certainly have to be taken in football, and managers sometimes have to break hearts but, after the performances he'd put it in, surely a young keeper like Paul deserved an explanation; to be braced for the fall. In the business world, they call it good man-management. In anyone's world, they call it not breaking the spirit of the young.

But, as the story was later told to me, it transpired that Robbo had been sitting in the regular team meeting that lunchtime waiting for the manager to turn over the flip-chart to reveal the starting line-up. Robbo hadn't thought twice about his name not being up there, in the penalty box. That's when David flipped the sheet to show 'Nigel Martyn' in goal.

Robbo was understandably gutted. But being the true pro that he is, he bit his lip, got on the coach, and sat on the bench. I later reassured him that the No.1 jersey would soon be his, that an international career was already on the cards with the Under-21s and that a lot of people, the manager included, did have faith in him. To demonstrate that faith, we'd immediately renegotiate his contract (it was due for renewal) and reward him for his recent performances. But I got the impression that while Robbo loved everything about Leeds United, he'd find it hard to forgive David O'Leary. He was young and still learning but one thing was true – Paul never did play for the manager again.

I didn't think, at the time, to register that episode as anything significant. Managers often have spats with players but, in such a closely knit dressing room, and involving such a popular young member of the squad, this seemed like the first red flag being raised from a spirited dressing room.

•

Since leaving Leeds, I've heard the urban myths about my time as chairman; the Chinese whispers that have become written in stone. In 2005, even Crystal Palace chairman Simon Jordan waded in, writing in the *Guardian* about agents, and why he'd never 'do a Peter Ridsdale and let them take me as a patsy, as a mug', and added: 'Agents made a fortune out of Ridsdale, and almost destroyed Leeds.'

It is sad to see another chairman jump on the bandwagon and speak without knowledge of the facts, suggesting I was some kind of Father Christmas to the agents who sat on my knee, as opposed to being a responsible chairman whose plc board scrutinized every expenditure and examined the minutiae of every transfer. But the greatest myth of all goes something like this:

> As a player, you could almost walk into Peter Ridsdale's office and name your price. He was absolutely throwing money at players. Take the Seth Johnson transfer. He walked in, expecting around £20,000 a week and, before he could say a word, guess what? Ridsdale offers £38,000!

Unfortunately, football doesn't work that way. Players don't walk in and talk salaries – I only wish they did! Agents negotiate *everything* on their behalf: the salary, the bonuses, the personal terms. Normally the only time you see the player is when it's time to come in and sign contracts. Seth Johnson joined Leeds from Derby County in a £7m deal, one of two players recruited for the 2001–02 season after being identified by the manager as an essential component for our renewed push towards the Champions League. David Batty was struggling with injury, Eirik Bakke was injury-prone and Seth had just broken into the England squad.

Throughout all negotiations in that October 2001, I dealt

with his agent, Leon Angel. But before I did anything, I found out what Seth was earning – roughly speaking – at Derby County. With that in mind, I entered negotiations fully clued up, and was prepared to offer £2,000 a week extra. But, to my surprise, Leon walked in with his requests – 'proposed contract points', he called them – on letter-headed paper from his company, Base Soccer Agency. And guess what? His proposal was just £1,000 a week shy of my written suggestion, and that's how we agreed an opening weekly salary of £29,000-a-week. Then again, hard facts, when supported by documentary evidence, tend to spoil the telling of a great myth so I'm sure the story will remain as Seth Johnson walking into my office, doing an Oliver Twist, asking for more, and then walking out with his trouser pockets stuffed with cash and coins falling out of his boots.

The second incoming player that season was twenty-six-year-old Robbie Fowler – 'always my number one choice', in the words of David O'Leary. He approached me in the September and said, 'I think Fowler is maybe "gettable" at the right price.' Word had leaked out that the striker was unhappy at Anfield following a series of spats with Gerard Houllier.

It was made clear to the manager that if we landed his latest target, he'd have to offload one striker because Fowler represented a non-budgeted player; and it placed even more onus on us – and more pressure on the manager – to qualify for the Champions League. David agreed and was bullish, and he persuaded the board that we couldn't afford to pass over someone of his pedigree, and that Fowler would make all the difference not just to sustain but enhance our league form. David actually said in the press that he would be judged that season on whether he qualified for the Champions League.

What's worth remembering here is that Robbie Fowler was like rocking horse shit at the time – unique; he had a lethal instinct for goal, and was a striker in a class of his own. Leeds were flying high in the Premiership, unbeaten in the first eleven matches.

In hindsight, the Fowler transfer would seem to be one deal too many. People have since said that we should have had the foresight to predict that at the time. Maybe they are right. Because, in my mind today, if I had my time again, I would have stood up to David O'Leary, said no, and not purchased either Fowler or Johnson. But I believed in David and the team, and when the manager approaches you and says can he buy the best striker around, and it will reinforce a team that is in great form, you don't sit there and say, 'Hang on a minute, what happens if all this falls apart?' Besides, when you look at the team's consistency over the previous three seasons, the thought of finishing out of the top four places hadn't entered anyone's heads. We were aiming for the Premiership title, never mind the Champions League places. I had a manager who felt the same way. Our strategy was based on the drive for success, not the fear of failure. And we were not building castles in the sky either – every target was realistic and under our very noses at the Premiership summit.

In Robbie's book, *Fowler – My Autobiography*, he wrote that 'what happened [with his transfer] perhaps suggests why Leeds got into such a state financially'; that I allowed 'the fee to rise and rise until it got to £12m' (it was actually £11m) and added, 'It was crazy, and maybe typical of what was going on at Elland Road around that time.'

It does amuse me when players attempt to give an insight on protracted transfer negotiations to which they weren't party but I suppose that's why Robbie was brilliant with a ball but not so hot with facts. The first he would have known – *should have known* – of any deal was when negotiations had already been finalized with Rick Parry, chief executive at Liverpool, so I fail to understand how Robbie can comment on the mechanics of private phone calls and negotiations up to that juncture.

My first dilemma had nothing to do with negotiations and more to do with a question which vexed both the manager and me: 'How the hell are we going to ask for Robbie Fowler without Liverpool realizing the interest is from Leeds United?'

Liverpool were our biggest rivals, having pipped us to the third Champions League spot in 2000–01 after we'd denied them the same qualification place the previous season. There was little between us. My fear was that the moment they got a sniff that Leeds wanted their man, increasing our firepower, the price would double.

So, as clubs are allowed to do, I employed agent Colin Gordon as an intermediary because of his strong links with Anfield. This was one 'middle-man' I had no problem in author-izing because the 3 per cent he would earn in commission would be more than paid for out of the money he saved us. Had Rick Parry dealt direct with me, I feared he'd be asking for around £16m. But the price he quoted Colin was £13m. That's because Colin's approach was along the lines of: 'Rick, I can get Robbie out, there is a club interested but we need to know the price you're looking at.'

Colin kept his inquiries going, facilitating our interest, making all the right noises. Then, with a price on the table, Leeds could reveal itself and step into negotiations. I offered £10m. Liverpool stuck to £13m. There was a lengthy stand-off. In his book, Robbie suggests Liverpool 'would have cracked and let me go for whatever Ridsdale was proposing' but he forgets that such poker-like posturing had a lot more to do with the wider Premiership picture; it wasn't all about Robbie Fowler.

In the end, both clubs, appreciating that he only had eighteen months left on his contract, compromised somewhere in the middle at £11m. Again, Robbie felt Leeds could have got him for half that sum, but there was no way that any club was selling a striker of his calibre, at that time, for less then £10m. Anyone who thinks we could have got him on the cheap misunderstands the nuances and intricacies of the transfer market; viewing it with the same simplistic eyes as some sports journalists do for the sake of an easy headline, or pithy phrase. Doubtless, Robbie felt that Houllier wanted him out and would let him go for almost nothing but the Liverpool board knew his value.

With the deal done, we were given permission to meet Robbie and, for reasons of secrecy, we met at my Leeds flat. In walked the player with his dad, Bobby, and accountant/agent George Stott. What was hilarious was that they all turned up to seal this multimillion-pound deal in a battered Montego car that must have struggled to make it across the M62! The paradox of seeing our new £11m striker clambering out of such a rust-bucket was a sight that made us all have a laugh.

Another peculiar sight that day was seeing *Daily Mirror* journalist David Maddock trailing in behind father, son and agent. What's he doing here? I thought, as we all shook hands. It's fair to say that I've never before gone into a meeting to discuss a player's personal terms with a tabloid reporter in the same room but I clearly didn't understand the special relationship. As Maddock quietly explained to me when I dared ask what his role was, 'We have a great friendship. If I tell Robbie to come to Leeds, don't worry, he'll come to Leeds.' It was as if the journalist was painting himself out to be some sort of indispensable figure for the deal. It was a very odd set of circumstances. Thankfully, after pleasantries were exchanged, Robbie went to his medical accompanied by David Maddock, who, the next morning, published his transfer 'exclusive', leaving his accountant and me to finalize the personal terms, and turn Fowler from a red to a white.

In his first few games, our latest acquisition soon began to pay rich dividends, although he did not find the net until scoring two against Everton in his fourth game; a week later he netted a hat-trick against Bolton, then one against West Ham – six goals in eight matches.

Robbie Keane was another striker finding the net, including a hat-trick in a 6–0 League Cup demolition of Leicester City back in October. We'd made his loan spell from Inter Milan permanent at the end of the previous season in an £11m deal –

but we could have had him for half that price before. It was to be another maddening example of my forays into the transfer market.

We'd paid £12m for Keane (£1m for his loan spell and then the £11m when the move was made permanent) but we'd had the chance to buy him at £6m from Wolverhampton Wanderers in 1999. I'd taken a call from his agent at Sfx sports management saying they were lining up suitors for Keane, it looked like a sale was going to go through and if Leeds was interested, we should step in immediately. I went to David O'Leary. He shook his head. He had no interest in the boy whatsoever. Then, two years later, he's begging me to sign the same player from Inter Milan! Of course, Robbie had developed as a player and other factors may have influenced David's change of heart, but I could not help thinking. Robbie on English soil? Not interested. Robbie on Italian soil? David couldn't sign him quickly enough. That delay cost us £6m!

In hindsight, we should have offloaded Keane the moment Fowler arrived, as had been agreed in principle with the manager because, as I told him, we couldn't afford both. But the minute Fowler arrived, O'Leary did nothing to help us get Keane out. I should have been firmer with him but, to my regret, I allowed the situation to linger on, increasing a needless cost to the club. I was restrained by a fear that if I tampered with the manager's squad-building, it could have disrupted everything at a time when we were in such a commanding position. Maybe also, in the back of my mind, I didn't want to hand the manager another excuse if it all went wrong. In that respect, I was a coward.

One player we allowed to slip through the net was current England international Jermaine Jenas, now, ironically, a team-mate of Keane's at Tottenham. Jermaine, then only seventeen, was at Nottingham Forest, and our former youth-team coach, Paul Hart, had alerted us to his talent. Our scouts looked at him on fourteen separate occasions and were impressed. Based on those impressive scouting reports, I thought it wise to sanction a deal. I presumed the manager would be all for it.

'If you sign him, I'll just stick him in the juniors!' he said.

The team was doing all right without the likes of Jermaine Jenas, to be fair. Leeds were virtually unstoppable in the first half of the 2001–02 season, a season that saw the name of the company change from Leeds Sporting plc to Leeds United plc. Of the twenty-one league games up to and including New Year's Day, we lost only two, and we were top of the Premiership with 41 points, two points clear of Arsenal and Newcastle. The press were beginning to believe we could stay there.

The road ahead would provide a stern test of our nerve and true spirit but from everything we had witnessed throughout 2001, and the confidence we had garnered, our strengthened squad was more than ready for the challenge. The team spirit was second to none. Surely nothing could get in our way.

But then David O'Leary's book hit the stands, and hit the headlines . . .

•

The sequel to 'The Queen v Woodgate & Others' ran from 15 October to 14 December 2001. A fresh jury at Hull Crown Court heard the evidence in a case which, second time around, saw Michael Duberry forced to become a prosecution witness. It all seemed unsavoury from a distance: two players from the same dressing room pitted against each other in a court room – Duberry saying Woodgate told him he'd been in a fight; Woodgate saying Duberry only said that to save himself 'because he did not want to go to prison for twenty months'.

The jury started its deliberations on Monday 10 December. As a club, we braced ourselves for verdicts, waiting on each hour. Outside the court room, people had told me that Woodgate leaned into his dad on a sofa, cuddling him. Two days went by without news. Then, late at night, after the team's fancy dress

Christmas party, I received a phone call: Robbie Fowler had been arrested . . . wearing full commando gear, with camouflage paint smeared on his face.

How much worse could things get!

Fowler and a friend had got into a spat with freelance photographer Ben Lack on a petrol station forecourt, and a camera was smashed. Our new striker, 'the Toxteth prowler', was arrested on suspicion of causing criminal damage. He'd been an innocent party in a something-and-nothing incident, and was soon released without charge. But it meant 'Leeds Star Arrested' made banner headlines, at a time when two other players were standing in the dock, awaiting their fate.

The timing was awful, and the press went to town, saying the incident illustrated all that was wrong about the club's image, and the irresponsibility of our players. Actually, it said a lot more about the pressure and scrutiny the trial had placed the club under because our lads couldn't even let their hair down at Christmas.

To compound matters further, there was real concern that Fowler's arrest could actually affect the outcome of the trial in Hull. Bowyer's barrister, Desmond de Silva QC, spoke for all defence counsel when he brought the matter to the attention of the judge, Mr Justice Henriques. There was deep concern, said the barrister, that reports in the *Daily Mirror* and *The Times* could infect jury deliberations, and jurors could conclude that 'this is just typical of Leeds'.

He said, 'The Leeds United squad had a Christmas party and the antics of some of the players left a good deal to be desired. The incident has made the press . . . and it concerns us. There are elements of ugliness about this incident.'

It led to Mr Justice Henriques reconvening the jurors and telling them, 'It's only fair and correct that you should be told that neither Jonathan Woodgate nor Lee Bowyer were present or part of that squad that night. You will put the event completely out of your minds . . .'

I confess that the extra publicity surrounding Fowler's arrest made me more nervous about our two players, regardless of the judge's direction. Human nature is a capricious animal, and I felt I was chairman of the most hated club in the world. Why would five men and seven women in Hull be any more sympathetic to us? Such irrational thinking doesn't contemplate evidence. It thinks crazy thoughts such as 'Will the mass of publicity and controversy have stayed in the jury's subconscious?' or 'Are there are any Manchester United fans on the jury?'

The jury spent a further two days reviewing the evidence, and deciding its verdicts. Just before noon the next day, I was sitting on the top table at the annual Variety Club lunch at the Queens Hotel, Leeds, when I received the phone call I'd been anticipating. 'The jury's come back in,' said Mark Castle from the other end of the line. I excused myself from the table. As I stood with the phone to my ear, in a city which knew verdicts were imminent, around 600 heads turned my way; they sensed a decision, and I could hear the intrigued chatter rising as I walked out of the room. 'I'll relay the verdicts as they come in,' said Mark. Every vein in my body was pounding. God knows what Woodgate and Bowyer were going through as they stood to meet the jury foreman's words.

'What's happening?' I whispered loudly into the phone. Six months, two trials, and jury deliberations that had lasted five days had left me on edge, and with a wafer-thin patience.

'Woodgate, guilty of affray . . . Bowyer, not guilty of grievous bodily harm with intent.'

But that was it. The jury hadn't decided all verdicts. It would take another agonizing hour before the phone rang again.

'Woodgate, not guilty of grievous bodily harm with intent . . . Bowyer, not guilty of affray.'

In all the outcomes I'd considered, I'd not prepared a statement for that one. It meant scribbling out new words on a scrap of paper before heading, in a daze, to Elland Road. The saga was over in one sense, but wasn't over in another – there was going to be an intense press conference, days of media analysis, and our own disciplinary procedures against the players for bringing the club into disrepute, regardless of the verdicts.

Those present in court told how Bowyer knocked his head back, closed his eyes and blew out his cheeks. Woodgate, visibly shaking, stood to receive his sentence. Mr Justice Henriques told him he could have gone to prison for three years but said, 'It has been obvious to everyone that you have suffered agonies during this trial. That's etched upon your face.' He received 100 hours' community service.

His friend Neale Caveney was also convicted of affray, and received the same sentence but Paul Clifford was found guilty of grievous bodily harm with intent and was jailed for six years. As the jury had seen it, Woodgate, Caveney and Clifford had all chased the Asian group for 300 yards and 'caused [them] sheer terror, running for their lives', but Clifford was the only one to go down that side street.

Witnesses saw five white men attacking Sarfraz Najeib but the 'other four remain unidentified', said the judge.

In the car on the short journey to the stadium, news was breaking on the radio and my mobile phone was melting with calls. I ignored them, choosing to phone all members of the plc board. I had mixed feelings in the madness of that journey: a certain elation that our stance to support the players, and not suspend them, was vindicated; at the same time I felt a sense of overwhelming sadness that the whole episode had happened at all. I just remember feeling completely deflated and reflective.

The television trucks were already outside Elland Road when I arrived; the club's reaction was almost as imperative as the players' reaction in Hull. As I saw the satellite dishes and monster aerials pointing skywards, I knew how big the moment was. *Got to get this right . . . Got to get this spot on*, I kept thinking.

Normally, I never prepare a formal statement ahead of a press conference. But, on that occasion, I wasn't going to risk busking it. David Walker, director of communications, ensured that I wrote down the words 'Leeds United were not on trial, two of our employees were'; *that* was the key message we needed to convey, and they became the first words I uttered in front of the live microphones and TV cameras.

Then, when the conference turned to questions from the floor, one television reporter stood up and asked: 'If Leeds United were not on trial, then why is that the title of David O'Leary's forthcoming book?'

I'm not normally lost for words or easily thrown off guard but at that moment I was floored. The cameras were rolling, and the media pack was hanging on my answer. I looked at David Walker. He was wincing. I turned to the media, and offered the most pathetic but honest reply: 'I had no idea that was the title of his book.'

I felt anger burning beneath the calm front I had to portray.

Leeds United were *not* on trial, and we'd made that clear from the outset and it was imperative that no one deviated from that line in the interests of the club. I was fuming. Suddenly, the trauma of the trial had become a commercial opportunity, and the media were laughing at us.

I went wild with David on the phone later. He was at Thorp Arch at the time. 'I can't believe you allowed that title on your book! You've undermined all that we've been saying from day one!'

He sounded unconcerned, and denied knowing the title of the book. He said it was a matter for his editor, not him, which I felt was odd. He knew he'd pissed me off but, then again, why should he care? It's very easy for a manager to swat away criticism, to be supremely confident, when he's sitting atop the Premiership.

As Leeds became more successful, I felt his self-importance seemed to inflate. I didn't sense a partnership between chairman and manager any more, and the cracks began to appear in our togetherness. He was off on his own, talking up how he still had to turn silver into gold, and turn boys into men; a manager painting a mountain for him still to climb when he was already near its summit. David, in my eyes, began to see himself as this indispensable manager, the man with the golden touch. The truth, as history would ultimately prove, was far different. I felt he'd started to believe in his own publicity, and the book was another example of his love for the spotlight.

It galled me, in the weeks afterwards, to see the book being promoted and David being photographed holding *Leeds United on Trial* with one hand, and brushing off criticism with the other. The press had a go at him for 'profiteering, insensitivity and crass timing' and it was difficult to defend him. David attempted to sidestep reporters' questions by saying he wasn't responsible for or consulted about the title (he must have had a very strange relationship with his editor). But he *was* responsible for the book's content. When I read his work, I realized it shone a light on the players, their strengths and weaknesses; he had harsh words for some individuals, and shared with us his private, and to my mind, patronizing thoughts about others. The sacrosanct code of the dressing room had been broken by the reigning manager.

I wondered what he'd have done had a player broken ranks and told the inside story from the dressing room? The very manager who had complained publicly about the inconvenience, disruption and distraction caused by the trial was suddenly dredging up a whole new focus, and creating yet more headlines from the book's serialization – and then wondered what all the fuss was about from his chairman! It was rank hypocrisy in my eyes, and I began to seriously question his judgement and wisdom.

For once, I found myself unable to defend the manager when newspaper columnist Sue Carroll wrote in the *Daily Mirror*: 'Well done, Leeds United, on achieving the double so early in the season. Double standards that is.' A *Mirror* editorial then thundered: 'Leeds, its manager and players have carried on regardless. They are a disgrace to the game of football.'

However keen David was to wash his hands of the book's title, he couldn't sidestep the further damage his book was inflicting. Suddenly, the players were being referred to as a 'disgrace' because of his book.

From my chairman's office, I could almost hear the team's respect breaking up and tinkling on to the tiled dressing-room floor. And for those unable to hear it, the ensuing results would be sufficient proof of something being wrong in the camp.

•

Lee Bowyer screamed his obscenities down the phone.

'You have no right! You have no fucking right to treat me like this!' he raged.

The cool and calm front displayed throughout a public trial suddenly cracked wide open. I'd been explaining to him over the phone that we were fining him four weeks' wages under our own disciplinary code for bringing the name of Leeds United into disrepute. At the time of the original arrests, I'd made a public statement that irrespective of the outcome, we'd administer our own disciplinary action, and it was time to deliver on that promise. Whatever the view of the jury, the good name of Leeds United had been destroyed in one night of drunkenness and, on that charge, Bowyer and Woodgate were as guilty as sin.

I'd earlier talked with Woody's agent and it was agreed he would be fined eight weeks' wages, and the fine was duly paid. The player displayed grace in his shame, and apologized for the problems he'd caused. But Lee clearly felt his acquittal had left him with a shining halo, and regarded our sanction as an insult to his good name.

'I was found not guilty on all charges – how the fuck can you charge me with anything!' he shouted.

I tried to explain but he wasn't in the mood for listening, or backing down. He just kept ranting about 'victimization' and he refused point blank to accept a disciplinary charge, let alone pay the £60,000 fine.

Afterwards, I spoke with the manager and it was agreed to suspend him until such time as the fine was paid. David was adamant that Lee should pay the fine. In private he was 100 per cent behind us. This stance backfired on me personally when Lee was left out of the team for the home match against Everton on 19 December. I took my seat in the directors' box. Lee took his seat in the gods of the stadium, sitting in a chair on the television and radio broadcast gantry directly above me. When Leeds scored, all the players turned to the stand, looked up to the gantry and saluted their suspended colleague. Those fists of defiance twisted my stomach into knots. Sections of the crowd chanted his name '*Lee Bow-ya . . . Lee Bow-ya!*'

Later, the manager was reported as saying the fine and suspension were nothing to do with him, they were a matter for the board.

Then Lee issued a statement: 'The club appears to be victimizing me and forcing me out, having attempted to impose an unfair penalty.' He also said there had been a complete breakdown in relations between him and me.

Privately, he made it clear he would never sign a new contract at Leeds while I was still in charge, and the episode also wrecked his relationship with the manager. It's why we ultimately released the £15m-rated midfielder to West Ham, six months before his contract expired, for £100,000, an effect of the Bosman ruling.

Many fans backed Lee and blamed the club but I still feel the decision to fine him was the correct one. I don't regret the stance we adopted. My only regret was that Lee didn't show more remorse for the damage his drunken night out had caused the club. He was still pie-eyed beyond midnight and behaving in a manner not appropriate for a professional footballer.

Our stance against Bowyer did nothing to stem the tide of hate that swelled even more after the verdicts were given. From the day both players walked free from court, the postbag bulged even more with hate mail. I'd estimate that we were receiving thousands of letters a week, most deciding that the jury had got it wrong, and that it was our fault. It was almost as if the consensus was 'If the lads can't be found guilty, then the club will.'

●

Everything began to fall apart on the pitch in the first week of 2002. The ensuing four months was like witnessing a car crash as a helpless spectator, watching a vehicle that had been cruising in front suddenly suffer a blowout, and lose control – and all in slow motion.

Our unfathomable and spectacular fall from grace began when we travelled to South Wales to play Cardiff City in the third round of the FA Cup. David had asked for the fixture to be switched from Ninian Park to the Millennium Stadium. His request was declined, of course, but the manager set himself up for a fall when he quipped, 'I'm disappointed. It would have proved excellent preparation for us if we go back there in May. We're well capable of starting and finishing our FA Cup campaign in Cardiff.' For a man more known for playing down his hand, this uncharacteristic boasting would come back to haunt him.

The omens were never good, even before leaving for Cardiff. There were loud murmurings of unrest in the camp over travel arrangements. It all began after David had insisted the team fly to Cardiff because he didn't want an arduous coach journey ahead of a cup tie, and on the back of the midweek New Year's Day fixture versus West Ham. So we spent the money on a plane, a cost that was becoming par for the course during our European run. But Viduka, Batty, Harte and Kelly all refused to fly; it was, in hindsight, the first signs of a mini-rebellion against the manager's wishes. Had David shown leadership, he'd have told them it was the plane or they don't travel. Instead, he caved in, and laid on two cars to drive the rebellious foursome to Wales, while the rest of the squad boarded the team plane at

Leeds-Bradford airport. That decision put a few noses out of joint when the other players realized what had happened. 'If we have to fly down, why aren't they flying down?' I heard one player ask. It stank of special favours.

So much for your ideal match preparation, David, I thought. It was a masterstroke in promoting disunity ahead of a big match.

Prior to the game, and in response to David's taunts about the Millennium Stadium, Cardiff's then chairman, Sam Hammam, spoke about the 'Bluebirds' being a bigger club than Leeds; a sleeping giant in what is now known as League One, and a club not intimidated by its Premiership rivals.

In this psychological warfare, Sam's mind games won out because we had a shocker of a match. Rio was scythed down and taken off injured, and Alan Smith was sent off before half-time. The atmosphere was already hostile inside the ground when Sam Hammam intensified emotions with a walk around the edge of the pitch during play, rousing the Cardiff fans and goading the away support; an over-zealous mascot in a cashmere coat. It was an irresponsible thing to do, and it led to violence in the stands as police dogs were brought in to restore order.

You can imagine how much Ninian Park went wild when Cardiff nicked the tie 2–1 with an 86th-minute winner. David looked ashen in the dug-out, and you could tell he was seething over the shock defeat.

As we traipsed out of the ground, crossing the tiny directors' car park to the coach, which was parked in the main road directly outside the stadium to return us to the airport, Sam stood at the main entrance, still intent on chipping away at David.

'I told you we were a bigger club!' he shouted, clearly intending it for our ears. David stopped in his tracks, simmering.

'Well, you were right about one thing,' Sam continued, laughing. 'Your FA Cup started and finished in Cardiff!!!'

David went for him, rushing like a bull towards a red flag.

Sam bleated as David grabbed him by the lapels of his jacket. I dived in, dragging him away. Sam – who had it coming to him with all his provocation – still says to this day that I stopped him from being punched. I'm not sure about that. All I was sure about was that our manager had lost his cool, and I'd never before seen David get so riled. He was clearly feeling the pinching pressure of expectation. Not that any of us knew that the Cardiff defeat would be the start of an inexorable decline. But, somewhere around that time, the backbone of the soaraway Leeds United team suddenly snapped in half.

We went two months without winning a single match, and were dumped out of the UEFA Cup by PSV Eindhoven. By the start of March, we'd plunged from top of the Premiership on New Year's Day to fifth place, ten points adrift of the leaders. There were no excuses. David had built his dream team. He'd been in top spot. There was no long list of suspensions or injuries. Indeed, we had strengthened the team with Fowler and Johnson. Yet we found ourselves playing like relegation candidates.

Contrary to popular opinion, this slide had nothing to do with the fall-out of the Woodgate–Bowyer court case. If any-thing, the trials had somehow galvanized the team, and brought the lads closer together. It's an inescapable fact that in 2001 – the year of both trials and Brian Kidd's appointment as coach – we scored more points than any other Premiership team in that twelve-month period; it was the form of champions if you took the back end of the 2000–01 season and the front end of the 2001–02 campaign. The evidence does not support the theory that the trial derailed Leeds United. I still don't know what the hell went wrong. I mean, what team at the top of the Premiership goes from 1 January to 3 March without winning a match, *and* gets knocked out of the UEFA Cup and FA Cup?

For me, the tipping point was that first week of January – the week when David's book was published and promoted. It would be some weeks later before a spokesman from the dressing room would make clear the team's feelings about the manager's literary contribution at such a delicately balanced stage of the season.

It was in early February, after a 4–0 home defeat by Liverpool, that we held our first 'crisis meeting' with the manager in the relaxed surroundings of the Malmaison Hotel, Leeds; the usual venue for the team's pre-match meals. He sat down in a private lounge area with me and David Walker. The meeting was primarily arranged to 'discuss the consequences if we don't qualify for the Champions League'. I was alarmed by our slide down the table. Suddenly, it had all started going wrong and we needed to stop the bleeding otherwise we'd need to administer some major financial surgery.

'If we don't qualify, and recent results are giving us cause for concern, then it would require a mass clearout in the summer to raise revenue,' I told O'Leary in a relaxed but business-like meeting.

I left him under no illusions about the financial implications on his shoulders should he fail in his and the club's objective. He said he felt Champions League qualification was still achievable, and there was nothing to worry about. But, in the event of needing to offload players, he was prepared to trade if we fell short, and he listed six players he was prepared to release. Number one on that list was Olivier Dacourt. He then mentioned four other players: a goalkeeper (he didn't mind which one), Gary Kelly, Ian Harte, and a striker (he didn't mind which one). I wrote down the players he'd dispense with as he spoke. Selling Dacourt was, he agreed, an option we could pursue anyway. From that moment on, I put out the tentacles to gauge interest in our French midfielder.

David had no other miracle cures for the decline in form but offered his reassurances that he was working hard, and everything was going to be all right. On first impressions, he didn't seem unduly concerned. Not even when I reminded him: 'We spent extra money on Fowler and Johnson on your guarantee to get us there.' But, as cool as he appeared, it became clear that he felt the dreams of Leeds United resting on his shoulders. He suddenly *had* to deliver. There was no more wriggle room, no more excuses. He'd been given the managerial genie's lamp, had every wish granted, and been backed to the hilt by the board with his own £97m dream team.

Even the media tired of his excuses. Brian Reade in the *Daily Mirror* wrote on 2 March: 'Excuses excuses: Only one man is to blame for Leeds' mess, and that's you O'Leary.' He listed the excuses that had been trotted out: that one boozy night had destroyed three years' good work; that people forget the trauma the team has been under; that Leeds were suffering as the most hated team in the country; that there were injuries and suspensions; that players with big reputations had failed to stand up and be counted; that luck comes around and balances itself out – 'but I'm still lighting my candles and it's not enough'.

'So, ultimately it's God's fault. Anyone's but yours, eh, Dave?' wrote the columnist, and added: 'O'Leary's initial use of amateur psychology was amusing. We enjoyed all that psychobabble about his team being little babies. But now, like the Pampers he claimed he had to change, it stinks.'

As the media and the board cranked up the pressure, I think David started to sweat for the first time.

I felt our meeting had been a watershed moment. From then on, his relationship changed with me. He put distance between us, and I felt he took our warnings about a dire future as a personal slight, as if we were seeking a scapegoat. Maybe he felt it was me doubting him for the first time? Maybe he'd viewed it as us putting him on notice?

Whatever it was, he bristled with me, and suddenly started getting closer to Allan Leighton, as if he needed to seek a new ally. I thought it ironic that he sided with the one director who needed the most persuasion about his appointment in the first place. David has a natural knack of gravitating towards the seat of power and he always believed that Allan was the power behind the throne, if you like. He was trying to align himself with the perceived power-broker in the hope it would save his skin.

Just before the Tottenham game on 1 April at White Hart Lane, David spent a long time chatting with Allan by the tunnel, prior to kick-off. It was clear that the manager was feeling the pressure.

•

I went to Lazio to sell Olivier Dacourt in the last week of March 2002, and returned with a signed agreement for £14m. I was over the moon. In one fell swoop, our short-term financial pressures would be alleviated, and that came as a relief to a board getting increasingly tetchy about results on the pitch. On returning to the UK, I went to the training ground, together with David Walker, to inform the manager. I beckoned David over from the pitch to tell him the good news.

I was stunned at his response: 'We can't sell him! How can I let him go when we've Manchester United this weekend?

'Hang on a second,' I said, 'he was top of your list to sell, and we've got £14 million and doubled our money.'

He seemed unconcerned. 'I'm not even sure he'd want to go to Lazio. If he goes anywhere, he'd want to go to Juventus,' he said.

I pointed out that we'd had no contact whatsoever with Juventus and yet we did have a written agreement from the president of Lazio for a price not even I could believe we had achieved.

David seemed irritated by my persistence. He said he'd talk to Dacourt. 'Just leave it with me, Peter.'

Later, I spoke to him, and he insisted the player wasn't going anywhere. Next thing I know, Dacourt had issued a press statement saying we were treating him like a piece of meat, and he was happy to stay at Leeds United. A player I'd been told was for sale suddenly wasn't for sale . . .

Over the coming weeks, there was increased speculation about Dacourt being linked with Juventus. Paper talk, I assumed. But Lazio ran out of patience and withdrew their offer. Then, just before the last game of the season at home to Middlesbrough, David informed me that Juventus had asked *him* to meet in Monaco.

That's fishy, I thought, why on earth would Juventus contact the manager and not me? So I asked him. 'Why do they want to meet you?'

'I know their coach very well,' he replied. What's more, he then explained, they'd asked to meet him on that match-day Saturday, and he was prepared to miss the Middlesbrough game 'because there was nothing to play for and this could be good business for the club'. Our UEFA Cup spot was already assured, and so he felt he didn't need to be at Elland Road. He said David Walker could accompany him to Monaco. The manager knew I never missed a game, and so it seemed to me to be a blatant attempt to keep me out of transfer negotiations. I'd learned the hard way about what I felt was David's interference in this process when we first brought Dacourt to Leeds. Here he was again, on another deal involving Dacourt, attempting to wield his influence.

This time, I stood firm. 'I'm sorry, David, but there is no way you're missing the last game. Tell them, we'll meet in Monaco on the Sunday, and there's no way you're going without me.' I then rang Dacourt's agent, Bruno Satin, who seemed a little flustered over my involvement. I made the position clear to him, too. A few hours later, he rang back to say the meeting had been cancelled. I was later informed that Juventus had suddenly lost interest in Dacourt. But there was still a lot more yet to emerge about David's involvement with Juventus.

•

Sometime towards the end of the season, one of the senior players asked to see me in my office. It was a day off from training and he arrived in casual dress, jangling his car keys as he sat down, his knee bouncing restlessly on the spot. It was clear something was bothering him the moment he walked in, and he said he was concerned about the team's performances. Then he got to the point.

'Mr Ridsdale, unless you change the manager, I want out this close season and won't be signing a new contract. I also feel I'm representing the mood of most of the dressing room – the lads have lost it with the gaffer,' he said.

It was explained to me that the moment David published his book, many players felt 'he stopped being one of us', and many had lost respect for him and would not forgive him. This player said he felt recent results, and the decline in form, could all be pinned on a broken spirit caused by *Leeds United on Trial*.

'I don't understand him – I don't understand why he had to do that,' he said.

I had been warned early on in my chairmanship to treat with extreme caution any complaints from players because it could merely be someone with an axe to grind. But this player was emphatically telling me that the manager had lost the majority of the dressing room. So, to test the temperature, I decided to speak to a number of our players' agents to determine whether the manager's position was as dire as this one senior player had suggested. The feedback, and strength of feeling against David, shocked me. TEN players, either directly or indirectly through their agents, said they would be looking to move elsewhere if David O'Leary remained as manager for the 2002–03 season. While I'm not going to name names, these players were, without exception, international footballers who are still playing the game at the top level today.

All of a sudden, it made sense why the team had been in rapid decline, and why results had been so poor. Almost half the squad was being led by a manager they didn't respect any more. Here was the cause and effect of the crisis that sent the club over the edge; the manager's book had caused the destruction of a winning team spirit, and the effect was a virtual collapse in form on the pitch.

That season, in the remaining games, David failed to clinch a Champions League spot for the second consecutive season, which meant another £20m hit we couldn't afford. Poor results then had a domino effect on the club's finances. In the countless inquests held into the demise of Leeds United, all the microscopes have focused on the finances. The board and its chairman accept the blame. We took a calculated gamble. But we lost not because we were reckless but because a strategy that had hitherto proved effective suddenly unravelled as a direct result of the manager's failure to deliver on his promises. I'm not passing the buck. I'm just saying that David O'Leary, and other managers who succeeded him, must also accept their share of the blame – and yet the managers, and especially David, seem to have walked away scot-free from blame.

The bottom line is this: on New Year's Day 2002, Leeds United were top of the Premiership, looking strong, and no one had even considered not qualifying for the Champions League. Had we done so, the £20m would have been assured and a crisis would have been averted. Instead, O'Leary chose to sanction his book and, in doing so, pressed the self-destruct button as far as I'm concerned. And that's the moment the dream started to implode. As a board, we had to start thinking about radical measures to stave off a financial crisis, and find consolidation.

The future of the club and manager would be decided at a board meeting held at Elland Road on 31 May 2002. And, for the first time, David O'Leary asked to attend so that he could address the board in person.

TRANSFER MERRY-GO-ROUND

I couldn't believe what I was hearing.

I looked at the other four incredulous-looking directors sat around the boardroom table, and their eyes darted towards me with equal urgency as David O'Leary, sat to my left, outlined his proposed strategy for the future.

And there he was, in full flow, explaining how he needed another £23m for new players.

As he spoke, fixing his gaze on anyone but me, it was clear he was deadly serious, stating that he needed three more players 'to get us back to where we need to be'. It was an incredible managerial suicide to witness as he walked into his first ever board meeting, at a club with its back against the wall, to ask for a further £23m on top of the bounty he'd already been gifted, and ultimately failed with. 'Failure' is, of course, an odd word to use against a manager who had taken us so far into the high echelons of the Premiership. But David had always said he'd be judged on whether we qualified for the Champions League and so, by his own high standards, he had failed. He also failed to understand, or turned a blind eye to, the predicament such an under-performance had placed us in, if his inexplicable request for more money was anything to go by. Then again, it was to be a morning of surprising revelations and comments.

David had known, ever since our meeting at the Malmaison in the February, that non-qualification for the Champions League for a second consecutive season would mean a radical financial review, and force a clearout of players; to sell, sell, sell not buy, buy, buy. We needed to reduce the wage bill and make savings of £30–40m. We suffered a £28.2m operating loss in 2002 – £23m worse than the previous year – and so we urgently needed to return the club to an acceptable financial position. This in itself was not an issue because we'd built up a squad valued at £200m, and Manchester United were already hovering with their interest in Rio Ferdinand, a player we valued at £30m. We were hardly in dire straits but, nevertheless, our situation required sensible management action to reduce our debt, and we needed a willing and co-operative manager to work with us to make those savings. Instead, David asked for more money to invest in new players, as if we had Monopoly money to throw about. It was a reckless position to adopt before a board that was expecting a manager to talk the language of prudence, and to earmark players to be sold.

The rest of the board – Stephen Harrison, Allan Leighton, Richard North and David Spencer – looked at me as if to say, 'I thought you'd briefed him about the situation. What *is* going on?' I think some of them wondered whether I'd told him the full story.

But David had all the facts. No one knew better than he did that the heat was on and yet inexplicably he attempted to deflect the blame for the team's poor performances elsewhere. He said comments made by me in the chairman's statement in the interim report regarding player sales 'destabilized the season' and 'unsettled the players'. Presumably he was referring to my mentioning how 'we would expect a net income from transfers this coming summer' because nothing else of note was mentioned. Whatever the reason, the blame for causing disruption within the dressing room was being laid at my door. It was all the chairman's fault. I bit my lip and said nothing.

What David had overlooked was that the poor run of form which ultimately killed our Champions League hopes occurred between 1 January and 6 March. The interim results were published on 8 March, following which only three games were lost between then and the end of the season. By then, though, the damage had already been done to our league position.

In my view, David decided to adopt an aggressive strategy: asking for more money and deflecting the blame for the season's decline. I also felt he was challenging the board with a subtle message that suggested 'It's either the chairman or me – who are you going to back?'

Tracksuits never belong in a room full of suits at times when business decisions need to be made. Asking for £23m from a club with no more money was a joke, and his refusal to accept responsibility was almost embarrassing. In recent years, fans and critics have accused myself and the Leeds board of being financially reckless. I, for one, have always owned up to the mistakes that we made. But not one of us was ever as reckless as O'Leary was asking us to be that day. He seemed blind to both the balance sheet and his own culpability as manager.

When David left the room midway through the meeting, there was a disbelieving silence. 'We thought that he knew the situation we're in here,' said non-executive director Richard North.

'He absolutely does. I'm speechless,' I said, wondering if someone who looked the spitting image of David O'Leary had just masqueraded as the manager, and hoaxed us; that the real, sensible, wise David O'Leary was elsewhere, unable to attend. I'd expected him to enter that meeting and be contrite. I thought he'd asked to attend so that he could essentially save his job by saying all the right things. Instead, he walked in, put the revolver to his head and pulled the trigger.

Another worrying discrepancy had emerged during his address to the board. He said he'd been to the European Under-21 championship in Switzerland. This was news to me because I, too, had attended the same competition to watch England's Under 21s, in my capacity as a member of the FA International Committee, until they were knocked out in the quarter-finals. David, who loved the city of Zurich, confidently told the board that he'd been scouting, thereby justifying the cost of his trip to Switzerland. I'm assuming it also explained why his itemized telephone bill (paid for by the club) was peppered with calls to a Zurich-based mobile. David reassured us that he was on legitimate business, and he'd watched both semi-finals on Saturday 25 May. This puzzled me greatly, so when he left the room, I voiced my doubts.

'He says he's scouted at both semi-finals,' I explained, 'but there's something not right because one was in Basel, and the other in Zurich – and they both kicked off at the same time.'

Maybe I should have challenged David when he was sat there but I didn't need to make more of a fool of him than he'd managed to achieve on his own. In explaining this inconsistency, it became absolutely clear that the relationship of trust between the manager and me had broken down, beyond repair. Whatever he was doing in Basel or Zurich was his business but I wasn't going to have him mislead the board, and treat us like idiots.

'We need a manager who we can trust and who understands the financial position of this club, and I need a manager I can work with,' I said.

Also swimming around in my mind were those representations from the ten disaffected players. The board meeting was told about the Lee Bowyer situation – that he refused to sign a new contract 'because his relationship with the manager had broken down', as well as with me. Full-back Danny Mills had also come out and criticized the manager for speaking ill of his disciplinary record in a newspaper column. Danny said O'Leary should learn from the likes of Arsène Wenger and Alex Ferguson, who support players in public and keep criticisms internal. Rio Ferdinand has also come out since to say that David's book washed too much dirty linen in public and wrote in his autobiography, *Rio: My Story*: 'A lot of us felt he should have left it alone and not aired his views in public. It just alienated the team.'

David has since denied he lost the dressing room, suggesting such a claim was part of a smear campaign. One of his 'closest friends' was quoted in the press saying: 'David is horrified by the suggestion that there was a dressing room revolt. You can't get four top-five finishes out of players who don't respect you or aren't with you.' His 'close friend' clearly failed to recognize the timing of the damage caused by David's book – because *that* was when the rot set in. Even if impartial observers were overly kind to him, they could do no better than conclude he'd split the dressing room down the middle with his opinions in a book and newspaper columns.

To my mind, the scale of the player revolt was impossible to ignore, and it was crystal clear that his position was untenable on many fronts; he'd lost the respect of many players, lost trust in the boardroom and lost the backing of fans. And our once sound relationship was deeply fractured. Allan Leighton's view was that 'when there is a breakdown in relations between the chairman and manager, it's time for a change', and David O'Leary was virtually friendless by the end of that meeting.

It was then that the unanimous decision was taken to terminate the manager's contract and draw up a list of candidates. When the name of Celtic boss Martin O'Neill topped that wishlist, we were presented with an awkward problem: David was due to be a pundit alongside Martin for the BBC's coverage of that summer's World Cup in Japan and South Korea. None of us wished to cause Martin – who I was convinced would join us – the embarrassment of having to sit next to his predecessor in a television studio for four weeks, so we decided not to sack the manager until after the tournament. This was a sign of weakness, in hindsight. We should have ruthlessly pursued our man from the off.

Nevertheless, as soon as we wrapped up that May board meeting, I put the wheels in motion. I phoned Celtic's majority shareholder Dermot Desmond to fix a meeting. At our subsequent dinner in London, he gave me permission to approach Martin but added, 'I don't think he'll have any interest but you can try.'

I knew that when a club signs Martin O'Neill, he comes with

his own backroom staff as part of the deal; recruiting Steve Walford and John Robertson is a prerequisite to signing a perfectionist of a manager who is a stickler for the team he works with. But far from being a problem, that prospect added to the excitement of his appointment. Such a trio would work wonders for Leeds, I thought, especially with the calibre of squad they'd inherit. Martin O'Neill and his team – first choice, remember, when George Graham left – were always the dream ticket in my eyes.

I ultimately had three meetings with Martin, usually held at the headquarters of Bass plc in North Audley Street, London – the offices of Richard North – and we hammered out a deal. He said he always felt that, when things didn't work out following the departure of George Graham, 'we were destined to work together'. But he seemed caught between his contractual obligations with Celtic and the opportunity at Leeds. He seemed spooked that Dermot had granted permission but added, 'He's always said that if I wanted to leave, then I could. If I can be sure he's given permission, I'll be happy to talk terms.'

It was *the* big job in football management at the time. Leeds were one of the 'Big Five' and I sensed Martin hungered for the challenge, with all its attached prospects of European football. Martin never once asked about how much money he had to spend. He didn't need millions to spend. Each time we met, his animated vision of the future and his passionate ambition for success merely confirmed to me why this master tactician was the man to steer Leeds United through its financial challenge. He was supremely confident in his own capabilities without relying on the chequebook as part of his tactical plan. He developed winning teams with the tools he inherited, in a manner very much in the Brian Clough mould.

We were always a long way from agreeing a deal but Martin took a draft contract, and seemed to spend an age reading it as we sat there. Or maybe he was pretending to read it. I could see him agonizing, stalling for time. One minute, he was talking excitedly about the opportunity, the next, he was asking if it would be wiser to wait a year. But he said he would discuss the contract with someone he knew, and confirm Dermot's position. We shook hands, and despite seeing how torn he was between his Celtic obligations and Leeds ambitions, I felt he was within touching distance of Elland Road. I was over the moon. I was convinced we'd landed our man.

●

I was apprehensive summoning David O'Leary to Elland Road in the final week of June. I had never had to fire a manager before and, although relations had all but broken down, I felt sad because it meant the end of a memorable journey of many highs, domestically and in Europe. But, in the end, he was the nearly man, never the ultimate winner. 'David O'Nearly', as one newspaper columnist called him. Leeds needed to push on to the next level, pursue the championship, and the Champions League. David had taken us as far as he could go.

I didn't mess around as he sat down. I didn't feel the need to soft-soap him.

'David, the board has decided it's time to make a change. I think for everyone's sake, you should move on and we should find a new manager.'

His immediate reaction was to disagree with our decision. He felt he had much more to offer. Nor did he agree when I told him that he didn't have the support of the dressing room: he scoffed at that one and said, 'If every chairman listened to the dressing room, there'd be a management change every week. Football is not a popularity contest!'

'I agree,' I said, 'but it *is* about respect, and I believe you've lost the respect of the dressing room.' The tension bristled between us across the table but there were no signs of anger from him. He took it like someone who had been expecting it. But I felt that a quiet resentment was shielding his bruised ego, a resentment that would later show its face in his weekly column in the *People* newspaper.

'Can I use your phone?' he asked, calmly. He called his solicitor Michael Kennedy with me still in the room. He handed me the phone after about thirty seconds of brief, to-the-point conversation. We shook hands, like old associates tend to do when parting ways, and he was gone.

I sat back in my chair that afternoon, and didn't take many calls. I reflected on David's time, both the successes and failures. I wondered if we'd given him all the money in the world, whether he'd have been capable of taking us to the very top. I remembered jumping into his arms in the San Siro in November 2000 when our 1–1 draw sent us through to the second group stage of the Champions League.

Times never felt better than that. Yet there I was, sitting in my office eighteen months later, reviewing these scenes in my mind, like a depressive nostalgic, yearning for the good times to return. People talk about the trial and Galatasaray and the combined impact of those two extraordinary episodes but, throughout it all, Leeds were in blinding form; if anything, they were a team inspired in crisis. If there was one event I wanted to turn back, it was David writing his book.

I sat there for hours, reflecting on the madness and stupidity of it all. It just seemed such a pointless own goal. I'm sure David was reflecting, too, in his private moments, even if he hasn't made himself publicly accountable for the team's under-performance, or acknowledged that when the media started talking about his greatness, he buckled. But the man who was paid a fortune and commanded around £3m in compensation from his dismissal can't just walk away and say, 'Nothing to do with me, guv.'

Let's be quite clear: when you provide a manager with the calibre of squad that David was blessed with, and then he doesn't win, there can be no excuses. He squandered a golden opportunity for silverware, and that will be his legacy: the man who gave us one hell of a ride but won us nothing. I don't think David ever fully appreciated how lucky he was. He'd inherited a wealth of talent from the youth academy, and was given a financial clout that made him a heavyweight in the transfer market. In the end, he was punching above his weight.

Of course, the board and myself must also carry the can – we allowed him to spend way too much money. We made the mistake of putting our money where his mouth was. The business minds on the plc board had been swayed by the convincing arguments of the man with the footballing brain. And the more we sniffed the Champions League, and remembered the taste of our semi-final experience against Valencia, the more intoxicated we became in our belief. But I think he made the mistake of amassing too many quality players who couldn't get into the squad. At one stage, we had twenty-four full and Under-21 internationals on our books, all competing for a place. Inevitably that led to an excess of talent that became disgruntled or disillusioned sat on the sidelines.

Should we have signed all the players we did? No. Did we build too big a squad? Yes. And I accept that we should never have signed Fowler or Johnson. We should have told David that enough was enough. It now seems clear that the sheer size of the squad exacerbated the break-up in team spirit because the dressing room lost its small, tight-knit, cohesive feel. We gorged ourselves on football talent and it made us ill.

The prescribed cure was Martin O'Neill, and I'd been eagerly anticipating his call. On Thursday 4 July, while I was at the FA's summer conference in London, I started to get fidgety, checking my phone every five or ten minutes for a text message or missed call, desperate to know how his resignation from Celtic had gone. But Martin suddenly became elusive. I started bombarding his mobile with calls, and it took me until long after lunch to contact him.

'Martin! How did it go?' I asked, when I finally got through.

His hesitating despondency made me inwardly groan. 'It's been very difficult for me,' he said, 'but Des has persuaded me that I've still got a year to run on my contract and I've always honoured contracts. I'm ever so sorry, but my contractual obligations here prevent from me taking up the appointment at Leeds. I'm sorry, Peter.'

I felt all the energy drain out of me. At no stage had I anticipated him *not* becoming our next manager. Martin is an honourable man and loathes being perceived as someone who would dishonour an agreement, and I respect that, but I couldn't help but feel let down. I couldn't help but feel that the croupier had just swiped away all the chips I'd placed on red – after it came up black.

I had no back-up plan, just a crumpled old list of discarded names and next-best options: Steve McClaren, Guus Hiddink and Terry Venables. I was left scrambling around for second-best options with people I didn't believe in as much as Martin, and with a board looking to me to find the right man.

In a strange way, I felt completely isolated. The truth is that I didn't enjoy a single day at Leeds from the moment David O'Leary walked out of the ground. Looking back, I should have quit as soon as Martin O'Neill said no because it never went right from this point on. I also felt the board's eyes were on me; an unspoken pressure to 'get us out of this mess'. Rightly or wrongly, I truly felt that the musketeer spirit of the board had turned into a reliance on me to find the managerial solution, and then put the big name forward for rubber-stamping approval.

From the summer of 2002, I had no sense that we were in it together. It suddenly felt like we had a mountain to climb but everyone else was sat at the bottom, watching me struggle to the top, waiting for me to fall. And then, even when I made my next-best recommendation, it wasn't good enough. The plc board would overrule me, and make a decision that would take matters from bad to worse.

•

If Martin O'Neill was the heir apparent who'd skipped the throne, then Steve McClaren was, to my mind, 'the spare' who

was next in line. I had a good working relationship with his
agent, Colin Gordon. He told me that Steve – seemingly treading
water at Middlesbrough – would love the Leeds United job.
'He'd be very interested if I were to approach him,' were his
exact words. Some weeks later, Boro chairman Steve Gibson
apparently went ballistic when he felt there was more to the
McClaren–Leeds link than mere press speculation.

'Have you been tapping up my manager?' he demanded to
know in a phone call. 'I'd like to know what the hell's been
going on!' He said he was concerned about Steve's loyalty to
Middlesbrough and, as a fellow chairman, he deserved an explanation.

I confirmed we had spoken to Colin Gordon, 'but at no stage
have we ever had direct contact with Steve,' I said. 'I'm not even
sure if he was aware of our interest.'

It was all immaterial anyway. I wanted Steve and made a
strong case for him to be manager. But I was outvoted by the
board, which favoured Terry Venables instead. In Allan Leighton's opinion, the plc couldn't afford the slightest risk of a
second manager rejecting the post. Venables was available.
McClaren was not. And, essentially, that's what nailed it for
Terry, who, ironically, has since ended up as McClaren's right-
hand man at England. I could see the wisdom in opting for the
candidate who was available but I couldn't get excited about
Venables. Yet I was persuaded that he was a steady pair of
hands with a proven track record of bringing home the trophies
at Barcelona and Tottenham, and taking England to the semi-
finals of Euro '96. Also, Viduka and Kewell had made it known
via their agents that they 'would welcome the appointment of
Terry Venables', having been impressed by him during his stint
as coach to Australia. Crucially, Venables had also proved he
could handle vice-like pressure, on and off the field.

All these factors led to a decision that sent me on a flight to
Spain on 6 July to meet 'El Tel' and sell him the job. He and his
wife picked me up at the airport in a Mercedes ML, greeted by

that trademark cheeky smile, and his bundle of contagious energy. In the hour-long drive to his villa in Alicante, I plastered an artificial smile on my face, determined to be positive for business reasons, but still feeling gutted about Martin O'Neill. I was sat with a man I'd never wanted as manager, trying to convince him that he was the man for the job. It was like wanting the Aston Martin but being asked to settle for a Mercedes.

Back at his villa, Venables was clearly interested in the job, and he was intent on finding out whether Rio Ferdinand could be saved from joining Manchester United. It was the most speculated-upon transfer of the summer after a superb showing from Rio in the World Cup for England, and the manager-elect felt he could persuade Rio to stay because they had a special relationship; it was Venables who'd introduced the central defender into his Euro '96 squad. When he asked what our intentions were for the player, I told him the bottom line: that we wouldn't lose Rio until someone met our £30m valuation. As outlandish as that might have sounded in football in 2002, I truly believed Rio was worth it.

As for Venables' spending power, I told him that he had none until we qualified for the Champions League. Until that moment, he was joining a tight ship. If he won that coveted trophy, we'd pay him a £1m bonus, I told him. He smiled. And if he could win us the Premiership title as well, he'd receive another £1m bonus. He laughed. I think we both found each other's ambition infectious, and I warmed to him the more we spoke about the way ahead.

The club still had the squad capable of winning trophies. We needed to raise money urgently but that was never a real concern because, at that time, we were calculating £14m for the imminent sale of Dacourt, £30m for Ferdinand, possibly £6m for Robbie Keane and Liverpool were making strong noises about Lee Bowyer, a player we valued at £12m. The *Evening Post* newspaper in Leeds headlined such transfer prospects as '£60M IN

ONE DAY' and predicted 'the transfer bonanza . . . was set to have the Elland Road cash tills rattling'. It wasn't just paper talk, it was a distinct possibility and, with that kind of money, we could have used up to £20m to reinvest in the squad.

Our critics have said we should have foreseen financial disaster in that summer of 2002 but they forget that those deals would have turned the situation around, and solved all our problems – the hair's breadth difference between success and failure. Those deals, seemingly imminent at the time, answered all our prayers, and would have secured our future. That is what we were working towards that summer.

Also, by this time, we'd raised a further £60m via a bond scheme, borrowed over twenty-five years (payable in annual lump sums), in an arrangement with three separate American pension funds, and secured by future gate receipts. The sole purpose of this 'loan' was to pay off existing bank debts of £25m and leave sufficient funds to invest in the squad to keep us up there with the elite – hence the signings of Ferdinand, Keane, Fowler and Johnson. Until then our borrowings had been through HSBC and the Ray Ranson scheme, but that had left us exposed to having to repay on an immediate recall basis.

You can't build the long-term future of a business like that. So we announced our intention to launch the £60m bond scheme publicly. We went to the shareholders for approval, and received unequivocal backing. It allowed us to refinance our bank debt and was masterminded by a man called Stephen Schechter, an experienced financial whizz from Wall Street who'd master-minded a similar scheme with Newcastle United. For people who have criticized such borrowing, it is no more than millions of people do each day when they take out a mortage. Our 'mortgage' was £60m for a team independently valued in excess of £200m. If that were a house, it would represent an equity of around £140m so it made absolute sense. Despite much com-mentary since, this borrowing was not based on having to qualify for the Champions League but assumed that out of every five years, we would be in the UEFA Cup every three years and the Champions League once.

All this I explained to Terry. 'You'll be inheriting a squad that has been a top five team in the previous four seasons and, despite the fact that we'll have to sell some players, we've got a steady ship that's still on course.'

Even if we lost Rio Ferdinand, I said, we still had the world-class Jonathan Woodgate, available for his first full season since being arrested. We had no plans to sell him. And that was the truth at the time. No one, let alone me, foresaw the disastrous season that lay ahead. We recruited Terry as a manager to keep us among 'the Big Five', fighting for a Champions League place. Just like today's Liverpool and Arsenal, a top-four finish was our realistic aim, and finishing out of the top six was unthinkable – as were the ramifications of such an outcome. But Terry was confident, as he indicated to the BBC: 'We have the drive in the squad and club to go right to the very top.'

He was appointed manager on a two-year contract on 8 July 2002, with a one-year notice period that freed us to pursue Martin O'Neill when the time was right. In the press, I said Terry was 'the best man for the job'. I suppose it's what you'd call the chairman's vote of confidence.

•

Italian agent Pino Pagliari had phoned to say Juventus managing director Luciano Moggi wanted to meet to discuss the Olivier Dacourt transfer. It was the day after Terry's appointment, and I flew direct to Turin with Stephen Harrison, and headed to an upstairs restaurant for our fine dining rendezvous.

We waited and waited for three hours, nursing one bottle of white wine and countless glasses of still water. Moggi had been delayed at a Serie-A meeting, Pino reassured us, as the evening turned to night. Shortly before 11.30 p.m., in walked the man himself, looking supremely confident, and flanked by two body-guards. As he sat, they stood like pillars to the temple. I swear it was like we'd just walked into a scene from *The Godfather*. No wonder they call him 'Lucky Luciano', I thought.

There was no apology for being late. Nor was he in the mood for small talk. He said nothing for a few long seconds and then, suddenly, he started gesticulating towards Pino, rambling in angry Italian, his words firing with the speed of a machine gun. I didn't need to understand a word to know that he was clearly upset about something. Pino acted as interpreter. 'He says that before he can discuss the Dacourt transfer, he wants an explanation as to why you sent your coach, David O'Leary, to discuss this transfer with Juventus . . .' And then Moggi started pointing at me, then looking at Pino, then looking at me. '. . . but you, the chairman of Leeds United, went to meet the president of Lazio,' continued the translation, 'and he wants to know why he was not good enough to discuss business with you, and why you gave that privilege to Lazio instead?'

Moggi sat back in his seat, deeply offended, waiting for my explanation. But I didn't have one because I didn't have a clue what he was talking about. My genuine surprise was viewed as a further insult, as if I was making an even bigger fool of him, explained Pino.

'I'm being honest! The only meeting I was ever aware of with Juventus was due to be held in Monaco, and that was cancelled,' I said. I'm not sure whether Moggi truly believed me but his manner eventually mellowed. What transpired, as Pino told the story, shocked me: David O'Leary, he said, had visited Juventus in person to discuss the Dacourt deal. It was a deal I'd neither known about nor authorized.

I was given the precise date of the meeting. If all this were true then to my mind it would make some sense of his opposition to the £14m Lazio deal, and his determination to head to Monaco without me. I apologized profusely to Moggi. He accepted – reluctantly, grudgingly – and then spent the next twenty minutes explaining his interest in Dacourt, a target he'd only pursue if they managed to sell Edgar Davids, he said. Then, after saying his piece, he left.

'What the hell was going on with David, Pino?' I asked, as soon as the big man had disappeared down the stairs.

'You *must* have known ... you *must* have known!' he pleaded with me. It was clear that both he and Moggi were claiming to be under the impression that David had authority to be acting on behalf of the club.

When I returned to Leeds and checked David's movements via his expenses, I found air tickets paid by Leeds United for him and Manchester-based Pino to travel to Milan around the date I'd been given – a date that had coincided with the Milan derby. I'd assumed that was the purpose of his visit when he'd submitted his expenses.

What confused me was why would David fly to Milan if he was meant to be meeting Moggi in Turin?

None of it made sense. Not even David's later claim, many weeks down the line, when he said he was met at Milan and driven to Turin because it was 'the most convenient flight'. This one issue became a huge sticking point between the manager and me. All dialogue passed through his solicitor and, for a time, we stalled on paying his compensation and the matter ended up in arbitration. I didn't want to pay him; that £3m compensation stuck in my throat. But we were forced to back down because he hit us with a claim for punitive damages in addition to his compensation that, had we lost, could have cost us a further £9m. The vagaries of the legal arbitration system meant that, as a plc, we had to adopt a risk assessment and, in our financial position, the mere prospect of worsening our debt led us to the reluctant calculation that we'd be wiser to settle at £3m.

Why £3m? Because he was on twelve months' notice and his contract stated that he was entitled to twelve months' pay as compensation; his lawyers argued that in his previous twelve months his pay included a £1m bonus for reaching the Champions League semi-final, and that this payment structure was the basis for compensation due. To say that was outside the spirit of his agreement was an understatement. This, of course, was my fault for not making clear in one of the contract clauses that the compensation should be based on his normal salary, not extra-ordinary bonuses – a costly mistake I will never make again.

David's eventual argument was that we knew about his trip to Juventus; that he *was* authorized. But if I knew about it, why didn't we receive a crumb of feedback on the meeting and the possibility of any offer? To this day, I've never been able to satisfactorily resolve in my own mind why he would get involved in a potential transfer like that. But one thing it did prove was that we were absolutely right to sack him when we did.

As for the Dacourt deal, interest from Juventus soon waned, and a possible revenue-raiser of £14m fell away. *That* was a setback. As for Moggi, he's since become infamous after being banned from the game for five years in 2006 after being linked to a match-fixing scandal.

•

I suppose none of us notices the effect that work has on us; we feel the pressure tighten in the head, and sense we're becoming more irritable at times but, if you're like me, you'll convince yourself that you're coping, and that's what I was telling myself in that summer of 2002. My wife, Sophie, saw it differently, though. In her eyes, I'd started drinking too much and, she said, I was turning into a horrible person. I'd saved all my diplomacy, pleasantries and smiles for Elland Road, and was returning home and closing down; I was irascible when my quiet contemplation in the conservatory was disrupted.

'You're just not a very nice person to be around, right now,' said Sophie, 'and this isn't you. I'm worried about you.'

My days involved leaving the house at 6.30 a.m. to be in my office for 8 a.m., and there I'd stay until 7 p.m., arriving home – if we weren't away on club business or matches – at 8.30 p.m.

And even then, the phone wouldn't stop ringing until around 10 p.m. I'd arrive home, wolf down a dinner, then pour myself a white wine, quickly followed by a second, a third and a fourth. I'd sit on the sofa in the conservatory, looking out into the darkness of the fields that stretch out from our house, with a wine bottle in one hand, and a glass in the other; bottle to glass, glass down neck. I think it helped me sleep more than anything else. Sophie felt I was working too many hours, working too hard, taking too much on my own shoulders. She was right, of course. I was becoming remote from everything and anything other than Leeds United.

That conservatory, by night or day whenever I was at home, became a sort of refuge from the madness. Sophie said she watched and worried as I sat there, staring out at the field for hours on end. But on those fields, split by the River Greta, I was building thousands of scenarios around players, results, finances and transfers; or projecting the triumphant nights in Europe, and imagining the inches and points we were away from the Premier-ship title and the Champions League. I'd lose myself in a world of 'if only'.

I probably cared too much for a football chairman. It had nothing to do with the investment I'd made, or money I'd stand to lose. This was about a lifetime invested in Leeds United, and how desperate I was to get the show back on the road for me, the players, the fans. I was impatient for success, and started to worry about the Champions League hurdle we hadn't cleared for two seasons. I'd said during an interview with a local radio station that 'I didn't expect to finish out of the top six', and then I started worrying about what would happen if we did. I was worrying about scenarios that hadn't even materialized.

In my mind, the sacking of David O'Leary made Leeds United imperfect; a sign that we had somehow failed, that a memorable journey had taken a turn for the worse. I had wanted Leeds United to be perfect, to be among the greatest, to be spoken about around the world in the same terms as Manchester United, Liverpool and Arsenal. I felt an immediate pressure to stop us falling behind. It was a non-stop pressure, applied under the spotlight of intense media scrutiny, every single day and, on some deep level, it was clearly getting to me. But I'm someone who bottles everything up and deals with it all in the privacy of my own mind. I never blow, and so I became silent and moody. I can't have been easy to live with. I've kicked myself countless times for becoming so distant from my wife and girls as I allowed an all-consuming job and passion to overwhelm me. But Sophie's observations and concerns helped to snap me out of it – and I gave up drinking. So much so that I became known as 'the lime cordial kid' by fellow director David Spencer.

A few weeks later, all of Sophie's worries were realized. I was driving back from Elland Road, via the A65 through the Wharfedale corridor, and had just pulled up at some traffic lights in the town of Ilkley. It was then I noticed a tingling sensation in my chest, followed by mild pains in the rib-cage. By the time I'd driven through the neighbouring village of Addingham and approached Skipton, I'd convinced myself I was about to have a heart attack. I found myself driving slowly across the A65's chain of by-passes, reduced to a crawling pace by the fear that I was about to collapse imminently on the outskirts of the York-shire Dales, miles from the nearest city hospital. I rang Sophie on the mobile, she phoned the local ambulance station and paramedics met me at the roundabout in Settle.

I was taken by ambulance to hospital, leaving one paramedic to drive behind in my BMW. I found myself in accident and emergency at Lancaster Infirmary, wired up to an ECG machine, and attached to a drip, as they took blood tests. It's fair to say that I'd terrified myself with self-diagnosis, and lay there moni-toring every breath, every twitch, every tingle.

I was then made to feel like the silliest hypochondriac ever when they diagnosed a hiatus hernia. The doctors said that under acute stress, the reflux action can induce a tingling sensation to the chest. I was so relieved that the embarrassment of fearing a heart attack didn't even register, but it was enough of a red flashing light for Sophie.

'That was your warning call,' she said. 'You either do something about all this or, next time, it will be more serious. Football might be more than a game – but it's not worth killing yourself over!'

•

Manchester United had inquired about Rio Ferdinand at the end of the season. United chief executive Peter Kenyon had pulled me to one side at the FA Premier League summer meeting, and asked if we'd be interested in selling. Absolutely not, I told him. But when Rio impressed everyone in Japan and South Korea, I knew the phone would soon be ringing again.

The board had already anticipated this move, and we'd discussed Rio's future at the May meeting when David O'Leary was sat around the table, and we *all* agreed a valuation of £30m. Of course, that was the private situation. In public, David much preferred to distance himself from such reality, describing the proposed sale as 'criminal'. As his column in the *Sunday People* made clear, he wrote, 'I don't want Rio to go. I am against the transfer ... and demanding £30m or more won't be much of a consolation. The decision rests with the Leeds plc. They'll ask my advice and I'll tell them we shouldn't sell.'

But the truth was that, however reluctantly, David had backed the sale of Rio, as the board minutes illustrate. For when he addressed the board, he said that while he 'didn't want to sell Rio, he would recommend we accept any offer in excess of £30m because no player is worth that sort of money'. He finished by stressing that, whatever decision was taken, 'it was vital that the board and manager were seen to be showing a common approach to the media'. That determination to pursue 'a common approach' clearly ended when he was sacked.

In relation to that dismissal, the *Sunday People* followed up with an article that was almost laughable. It read:

> David O'Leary was sacked as Leeds manager for telling the truth. O'Leary, who was ordered to toe the party line by the plc on the proposed £30 million sale of Rio Ferdinand to Manchester United, defied their demands and spoke out in his People Sport column.
>
> O'Leary believes he was fired on Thursday for refusing to be silenced. Last night, speaking from his holiday base in Sardinia, he told us: 'I stand by everything I said in the *Sunday People*.'

It beggared belief.

Meanwhile Rio, who was getting used to the heat of constant back-page speculation, came to see me on 30 June, three days after the manager's dismissal. That morning, he'd done an exclusive interview with the *Sun* newspaper, saying how he was torn, and how much he didn't want to leave Leeds. Even his agent, Pini Zahavi, had contributed reassurances some days earlier, saying, 'If Leeds say no, then Rio will stay. He is a loyal soldier.'

As we shook hands in my office that day, I told Rio I was delighted to read in the paper that he was happy to stay. He was unable to contain a spontaneous burst of laughter. He sat there in his jeans, and white T-shirt beneath V-neck sweater and then smiled.

'You *know* that was for the supporters . . . me and you both know I'm off!' he said.

Maybe the man who had succeeded Lucas Radebe as captain was not such a loyal soldier but someone who was media-savvy, sensible enough to know when to protect his own image with the fans, knowing the vitriol that Eric Cantona's defection across the Pennines had caused. Maybe he just saw the writing on the wall, but as he walked into my office that day, I think his mind was made up. In fact, it's my opinion that his mind was made up in the Far East, surrounded by the lure of Manchester United players in the England squad.

At least I got honesty from Rio in the office, even if the fans didn't. I like him. He's a great lad, and I couldn't begrudge him the move, or deny that we needed the money – at the right price. But until we received that price, I was going to fight like hell to keep him. So I told him the truth from my side: 'Well, Rio, we want you to stay. I would sell at the right price but, at the moment, we've had no offer for you.'

That soon stopped him smiling. 'You must have done,' he queried.

'We've had no contact from anyone whatsoever . . . unless you know something?'

'No, no, no . . . I've just read the papers, haven't I, so I thought there'd been contact.'

Within forty-eight hours, after we'd both made our positions clear, a fax arrived from Manchester United, offering £20m. My faxed reply to Peter Kenyon was short but to the point two days later: 'Sorry for the delay in responding, but only just stopped laughing. How much are you offering for his other leg?'

Two weeks passed before Rio, frustrated at the lack of progress, insisted he wanted to go.

'If you want to leave that badly, I must ask you to put in a written transfer request,' I said. Rio had been 'spinning' his message in the media, looking to shift blame on to the board, so I wasn't taking any chances. I wanted back-up if the fans accused us of selling the crown jewels.

It was 17 July when his handwritten note was faxed through. 'The media is full of speculation that Manchester United FC is interested in signing me and I would like the opportunity to follow up that potential interest,' he wrote, adding that he found the publicity 'unsettling'.

That request sent me on a plane – from my family holiday

in the south of France – back to England to join Stephen Harrison in a meeting with Peter Kenyon and fellow United director David Gill at Peter's house, between Stoke-on-Trent and Manchester.

'If your new offer doesn't start with a "three", we've no interest whatsoever,' I said. Peter increased his offer to £22m, and he 'might be prepared to improve the add-ons [the perform- ance- and goal-related bonuses] to take it to around £26m'.

'Sorry, Peter, but it has to be £30m. I think this is a wasted trip,' I said. There was an awkward impasse, and he tried tell- ing me that no one spent £30m on a player, and I wasn't being realistic.

'We all know Rio wants to join us and that it represents good business for Leeds United,' he argued. And I knew he was right, but something told me to hang out for more. We were, admittedly, sat around the poker table. No one truly knew the state of our finances back then so he could never have known that I was countering his straight flush with a two-of-a-kind hand, but that didn't stop me calling his bluff. I was going to push this deal – and my luck – to the absolute max.

So, as part of that staged bravado, Stephen and I decided it was time to leave. As we walked down the driveway, I whispered to him: 'Don't look back. Just keep on walking.' Once we were in the car and driving away, I looked at him, blew out my cheeks and said: 'I hope to God we're doing the right thing here because if they walk away now, we're fucked.'

Manchester United knew their offer represented a £4m profit for us, that Rio wanted to leave, that we ideally wanted to sell, and that no one else was bidding. It was hardly a seller's market. We returned to Elland Road and spoke with Rio, who was itching to know about progress, and that's when I told him, 'I'm sorry but the offer wasn't good enough. You can only go if we get the £30m.'

That same day, we issued a statement to the press. It was our turn to be strong.

I met Rio Ferdinand and we had amicable and constructive talks about his future. I stressed that we do not wish to sell Rio under any circumstances . . . I also stressed that Leeds United have not received a bid from any club that would come anywhere near meeting the valuation we put on a player we believe to be the world's best defender.

Our hardball strategy had the desired effect. The next day, at 8.36 a.m., Manchester United faxed a renewed offer of £26m plus £4m add-ons, and saying the offer was valid only until 5 p.m. that day. Our £30m valuation had been reached. But I wanted as much money up front and early as possible, so I hung out for the £4m bonus structure to be improved. I told Rio the offer was not quite acceptable and he should report to Leeds-Bradford airport the following morning to leave with the squad, as captain, for the pre-season tour of Australia and Thailand. He wasn't happy, to say the least. I think he felt we were trying to sabotage the transfer, and force him to stay at Leeds.

That night, after I'd returned to the south of France, I got a message from Rio saying he wouldn't be travelling because the whole saga had affected his psychological well-being, and he was feeling ill. In any other industry, it was an employee crying 'stress'. Not surprisingly, he didn't show at the airport, and all hell broke loose in the press, and I knew then that the game was up. We had no option but to let Rio go. But we did so as Manchester United strengthened their offer with improved add-ons in a deal finalized over the phone. We had – somehow – sold our £18m purchase for £30m eighteen months later. I breathed a massive sigh of relief, feeling the pressure lift from my own board. That £12m profit suddenly provided the breathing space we needed to restructure our debt.

We'd also struck a deal with Liverpool, who agreed to buy Lee Bowyer for £12m. He travelled to Anfield to discuss personal terms but, basically, dicked them around for a fortnight, dithering over his decision, torn between the opportunity and his clear desire to return to London. His heart was never in it, and that made the Merseyside giants withdraw. As Liverpool's chief executive, Rick Parry, said to me, 'Normally, if a player comes for talks to Liverpool, and a deal is done with the club, it doesn't take them two weeks to make up their mind! When we realized he wasn't that keen to join us, we lost interest.'

That was a further £12m gone begging, in addition to the £14m we'd anticipated from the sale of Olivier Dacourt. But there was still Robbie Keane, and a price tag of £7m still attracting interest in the shop window.

There was a new arrival at Elland Road that summer – a bespectacled, white-haired professor of economics called John McKenzie turned up out of the blue, offering his support. He rang me, saying he was a significant shareholder, and was keen to get involved with the club he'd supported since moving to Yorkshire in the 1970s. We met for lunch at a club in Berkeley Square, London. Bizarrely, to prove his shareholdings, he fished from his pockets some scraps of paper with numbers and dates on; this, as opposed to a share certificate, was his 'book' of stock. He didn't strike me as a wealthy man on first appearances. His shoes were scuffed, and had seen better days. Later, I'd visit his house in a village outside Ilkley, West Yorkshire, and it was a modest bungalow, nothing special. And yet, over lunch, he pointed to his scrap of paper to pinpoint the days when he'd bought a significant number of shares in the club, and said he was deliberately keeping his stock under 3 per cent (at 3 per cent he'd be obliged to inform the Stock Exchange) because he didn't want his wife to know how much he'd spent. He laughed as I continued to weigh him up. All I kept thinking was that he'd need to have about £1m of net income floating around to afford such a portfolio, and yet there was nothing about him that suggested any wealth.

I didn't know where this academic had come from, with his business-rescuing experience rooted in the education sector. And it crossed my mind that he might be a stooge, funded by someone else to enter the equation at Leeds United. But his support and enthusiasm soon drowned out that niggling question, and his background in business and finance would prove helpful, I decided. Later that year, he was appointed to the football club board, that band of appointees who sit beneath the plc in the club structure. But it was clear John wasn't there just to make up the numbers.

•

On 29 August 2002 – two days before the transfer window shut with a clank for the very first time in English football – I got a call from agent Pino Pagliari to return to Juventus because, he felt, the Dacourt deal could be back on.

I flew to Turin – en route to the UEFA Cup draw in Monaco – with club secretary Ian Sylvester, and we went directly to the club's headquarters in Corso Galileo Ferraris. It's not like walking into football theatres such as Old Trafford, Anfield or Elland Road. Its cold, marble-floored entrance reminded me of a bank building more than anything else; the only hint that this nondescript building was a footballing headquarters was a small plaque on the wall that read 'Juventus FC'. But it might as well have been the upstairs restaurant where we'd all met on the previous occasion because it turned out to be a *Groundhog Day* experience – arriving on time, and waiting two hours for Moggi to turn up. When he arrived, we went into his office, joined by Pino, and I sensed there was some bemusement as to why we were there. Moggi spoke in Italian, busying himself with other things. Pino explained that the sale of Edgar Davids – the precondition to their being free to buying Dacourt – had not happened and so the trip was a wasted journey, and he apologized profusely. I was livid but somehow kept my cool. Part of me even felt that we were being toyed with as continued punishment for Moggi's lack of forgiveness over the David O'Leary situation.

As Ian and I stood to leave, the bald-headed Pino asked if he could have a quick word, and the three of us disappeared into another management suite. Pino always seems in a rush, is always on the phone, and always hunting the next deal. He is the kind of man who can never sit still, and he seemed to have lots of nervous energy buzzing around him that day. After some hurried small talk, he asked to see just me outside the room, in the corridor.

He asked if it was true we were going to sell Robbie Keane to Tottenham, and I confirmed that we hoped to finalize the deal within the next twenty-four hours. That's when Pino asked if I'd be willing for him to submit an invoice for 'agent services' in connection with that £7m transaction.

I immediately sensed where the chat was heading, so I asked, 'Why would you submit an invoice? The negotiations have not had anything to do with you!'

'But Peter, if I bill you for £600,000, we split the commission fifty-fifty,' he said. 'You're the chairman – no one needs to know that I *wasn't* involved.'

There he was, in the corridors of Juventus FC, attempting to entice me with a £300,000 bung, asking me to invent his role. It was the most blatant attempt to pocket a bung. He stood opposite me, his eyes alive with greed and hope. I wondered whether this was the reason for our trip to Juventus, and that there had never been any hope of resurrecting the Dacourt deal.

'Pino, wrong man,' I said, 'I've never taken a bung or been party to such a suggestion and I'm now going to need to report this conversation to my board.' The hope drained from his face. He protested, asking me not to do that, and he apologized for offending me but I immediately went back into the room to tell Ian what had taken place, and phoned finance director Stephen Harrison on my mobile, there and then. I asked him to ensure the phone call was minuted at the board meeting the following week. Pino had left me in an impossible position. I didn't like making it official but if I'd said nothing, there was the danger that he could make mischief for me in the future. I had to protect myself.

I returned home and Robbie Keane was sold for £7m five minutes before the transfer deadline. Terry Venables was more than happy to release him because he'd inherited five quality strikers, and he didn't figure in his immediate plans. It meant that we'd raised a total of £37m to ease the cashflow situation, not the £60m I'd been looking to raise. It wasn't the definitive cure it could have been but, nevertheless, the prognosis was much healthier, and allowed us to spend £2.75m on signing Nick Barmby from Liverpool, and we loaned in Swedish international Teddy Lucic. Going into the 2002–03 season, all we needed to do was maintain our status as a top-five club and aim for the Champions League. The foundations had been reinforced.

This was the core of the squad Terry inherited: Nigel Martyn, Paul Robinson or Scott Carson in goal; Danny Mills, Gary Kelly, Lucas Radebe, Jonathan Woodgate, Michael Duberry, Dominic Matteo, Ian Harte, Teddy Lucic, Matthew Kilgallon and Raul Bravo in defence; Lee Bowyer, Eirik Bakke, Paul Okon, Nick Barmby, David Batty, Seth Johnson, Stephen McPhail, Jason Wilcox, Harry Kewell, James Milner, Olivier Dacourt and Simon Walton in midfield; and Alan Smith, Mark Viduka and Robbie Fowler up front – with the exciting Aaron Lennon bursting through from the youth academy.

After the first game of the season, beating Manchester City at home 3–0, an upbeat Terry Venables turned to me and said, 'I think we've got a really good chance this season. With this team, we can go all the way.'

And, looking at that squad of full-international and Under-21 international caps, few would have disagreed with him.

DODGY BUSINESS

At the next board meeting, four games into the new season on 5 September, Leeds directors convened in the offices of Bass in London, and 'the bung' was discussed. I'd already verbally placed it on record but wanted the matter engraved in stone within the plc's minutes:

> Peter Ridsdale informed the board that, during a visit to Juventus Football Club in Italy, he had been made an offer by Pino Pagliari, an agent associated with Juventus, to receive £300,000 personally in return for approving a £600,000 invoice in respect of assistance with Robbie Keane's transfer to Tottenham Hotspur. Peter had informed the agent that neither he, nor the club, do business in such a manner, and had declined the offer.

It was now a matter of public record, and there was no way it could back-fire.

I've known only too well what it feels like to be viewed with suspicion over transfer deals. The Rio Ferdinand–Rune Hauge £1.7m commission episode was a smear against my reputation. It made good sense to cover my back in relation to the Pino offer.

With the matter recorded in the board minutes, I felt cleansed after that dirty episode in the offices of Juventus. I don't think anyone in the board meeting believed the audacity of Pino, looking to make money out of a deal when he was a million miles away from any involvement. Richard North, the finance director, found it particularly odious. Then again, no one in that meeting fell off their chairs with shock either, because most people in football know the uncomfortable truth: that a bung culture exists somewhere and somehow in football; a whispered knowledge shared over Cuban cigars and late-night whiskies among a tiny network of individuals. Should anyone dare say it too loudly or, God forbid, come out in public and even talk about such dodgy business, the PR stampede from agents, lawyers and advisers – screaming that the game is clean – smacks of an industry that doth protest too much. To emerge from football's bubble and speak of bungs is like emerging from a Masonic lodge, and breaking the code of silence.

Look, bungs happen. In the same way that players are tapped up by other clubs. In the same way that many people suspect that the randomness of cup draws might not always be as it seems on the television. These are the ugly truths of football and to suggest otherwise is dishonesty in itself. My transformation from fan to chairman was an eye-opening experience in many respects.

'The bung culture' is a much more commonly debated controversy, and there is almost an ambivalence to its existence within the game. Personally, I think the whole issue needs to be placed into context. I'd confidently say that 98 per cent of the industry is clean but there is an undeniable 2 per cent stain on the game's back, caused by people driven by greed, eager to cream off the odd £250,000 or £500,000 here and there, believing such amounts to be 'peanuts' in the context of £10m deals. But don't even begin to tell me that this murky side of football's business doesn't also exist within the bad-egg minorities of other industries such as the City and showbusiness. Wherever there are vasts amounts of wealth, there are people on the take saying, 'That's the business.' In my view, even if one bung exists, it's one too many and unacceptable, and I won't be personally satisfied until it's all completely eradicated, though I suspect that's a naive hope. But it's a practice that is nowhere near as rife as headlines would suggest.

In my time as chairman at Leeds, I was offered a bung on two other occasions aside from the Juventus episode. I'm not talking about sports-bags or brown envelopes stuffed with money, and dodgy offers in dark alleyways. The days of money in brown envelopes – à la Brian Clough and George Graham – are now redundant clichés that merely help dramatize the myths. It's a lot more sophisticated than that, and there is no such thing as a paper trail. On those two other occasions when I was 'sounded out' about whether I'd be interested in making some money, the approaches were so subtle that the enticements hid behind their own ambiguity.

'So, Peter,' said one individual involved with me in negotiations, 'just so that we are clear. Will you be taking any commission?' was how he put his toe in the water with me. When I made it clear that I don't do business like that, the matter was never raised again. I wasn't one of 'them', he wasn't one of 'us' and you turn a blind eye because you know there's little point in kicking up a fuss. What was the crime? Being asked if I took commission? That's hardly damning evidence.

But that hasn't stopped someone calling in the police.

That's why Lord Stevens, the former Metropolitan Police Commissioner, arrived with his team of twenty investigators on football's doorstep in March 2006 with a warrant to search for evidence of corruption and financial irregularities. It's the equivalent of some suspicious neighbours calling in the police because they're convinced something dodgy has been going on next door, and the police rush in, with blue lights flashing, hoping to find the 'culprits' red-handed – and yet they find nothing but a bad smell. Lord Stevens' nostrils may well twitch but I'm not sure he'll detect the source. Personally, I think he's expecting to scratch the surface and find hard evidence but it will never be that easy. If the football authorities *really* want to aggressively pursue this issue and not just undertake a face-saving inquiry that goes through the motions to placate the supporters, Stevens needs to continue treating it like the most complex of serious fraud cases.

Lord Stevens' efforts seem to be a repeat of the FA's previous efforts to investigate sleaze and corruption in 1999, when it appointed ex-police officer Graham Bean as its compliance officer with a brief to go forth and expose the wrong-doers. The only difference is that Lord Stevens is now supported by twenty investigators whereas Graham was a one-man band. He became friendless, clubs were uncooperative and, in my opinion, he wasn't given enough support or resources by the FA to assist him. He was put up as the lip-service investigator and Graham, without realizing it at first, was the FA's answer to smother the controversy which followed the George Graham bung scandal: big headlines to begin with as proof that 'something' is being done, then all is allowed to peter out until the problem has been forgotten.

I believe there has never been any real impetus behind serious financial regulation of the Premiership or Football League. As a result people like Graham Bean find themselves being blocked and frustrated within a bureaucratic spider's web. Graham was a competent investigator whose cutting edge was blunted by politics. I co-operated fully with him over the Rune Hauge payment which brought him to my door. This was his conclusion about that whole saga: 'People were wrong to point the finger at Peter Ridsdale over that deal. We did all the necessary inquiries, and there was nothing there; not even a suggestion of any impropriety. Why was Peter smeared with innuendo over that transfer? Because people had it in for him at the time,' he said.

Graham's earnest investigations yielded no major revelations or significant scalps. It's hard with both hands tied behind your back. It was only in 2006 when the then Luton Town manager Mike Newell said 'football is full of people taking back-handers and yet nothing is ever done about it', and when the then

England coach Sven Göran Eriksson was reportedly caught on tape by the *News of the World* saying how he knew three Premiership managers had received bribes, that the FA decided to bring in Lord Stevens for a second, more serious sweep of club corridors. All this took place against the backdrop of Italian football being busted for its own widespread corruption in 2006. Was it only a matter of time before the English game suffered the same fate?

Lord Stevens' 'Quest' inquiry finally published its results in June 2007. Out of the 362 transfers he investigated, he has found seventeen deals that contain inconsistencies, and named fifteen agents and three managers whom he believes deserve further scrutiny. In short, he hasn't nailed one bung. As far as I can see, all he's achieved to date is to make a number of recommendations of ethics, principle and fairness to improve compliance within the game. So what his inquiry has proved to date is that corruption is not endemic within football, and the focus is on a minority of agents, based mainly overseas. If anything, Lord Stevens has managed to uncover the true scale of the problem, and detach the exaggeration and media hype once and for all.

One thing is for sure – the fans are not waiting with bated breath for his final outcome.

As a fan, I remember being horrified when the revered Don Revie's reputation was tarnished with allegations in the *Daily Mirror* in 1977 that he attempted to fix matches by bribing players with payments of £500 while manager of Leeds. I didn't want to believe it; I didn't think it really mattered. By hook or by crook, he had turned my team into giants and that's all that mattered to me back then. Indeed, such a mindset makes me even wonder whether fans of today really care whether an agent or a fixer pockets £250,000 from a transfer that brings a potentially title-winning striker or midfielder to their club in a world where the cream of Premiership players are commanding in excess of £100,000 a week. As much as supporters talk about greed and obscene money in football, they still cheer and chant these immensely well-paid heroes on to the pitch, applauding their celebrity contribution to the dreams that surround each club. I don't see unions of supporters waving placards outside the stadiums, protesting about capitalism. Which is why Brian Clough remained a hero at Nottingham Forest despite a well-documented fondness for pocketing almost £1m in kick-backs from the transfers he personally oversaw. It seems that only George Graham was coated in shame, to be made an example of, when he was caught taking back-handers while manager of Arsenal.

But, in the present day, when the current media hysteria dies down, the police go away and the politicians find their next drum to bang, I think you'll find that a bad refereeing decision causes more rancour among the fans than a 'bung culture' that seems to be accepted as a necessary evil of a commercial world already swamped by the riches of television rights, merchandising deals and multimillionaires investing in clubs. Only when there is evidence of match-fixing – therefore cheating fans out of points, titles and trophies – will there be real uproar.

•

If I was Lord Stevens, I'd have known exactly where to shine my torch. I'd simply follow the smell surrounding the relatively unknown foreign imports that have flooded the British game, and then never made an impact. I'm not talking about players of the calibre of Cantona, Zola, Vieira, Kuyt or Ronaldo. I'm talking about the players with names and reputations that few of us know much about, and yet they show up as impressive stars flashing on the radar, commanding stupendous fees and wages. These are the players who seem to arrive from the corner of a different continent, with massive price-tags, play a few games and then disappear out of the English game in a relatively short time-scale, at a massive loss to the club involved. *These* are the deals deserving of the scrutiny of Lord Stevens.

In theory, the mechanics of the dodgy deal goes something like this. Player X appears on the British transfer grapevine with a 'talked-up' reputation. He's the hot new thing, has been impressing scouts in Outer Mongolia and is going to set the British game alight. He just needs his chance. Invariably, this reputation comes not from scouting reports or video evidence but from the mouths of agents or advisers with contacts or associates in the far-flung region. Player X is being touted around for £5m when his real value is probably more like £2m and yet no one in England or Wales can take a view on that valuation because little is known about his standard or quality. It's not a Mark Viduka or Olivier Dacourt, where their reputations and skills went before them, and everyone knew their market value was spot on. With Player X, it's an assessment in the dark.

Suddenly, Player X has travelled to the UK and been signed by Z-FC. Because it's a foreign deal, the transfer fee does not have to be paid through the FA clearing house (as with domestic deals) so no one is quite sure where all the money goes or how it is divided, but it is paid overseas; there is no checking system, no accountability. But you can bet your bottom dollar that not all the £5m has been received by Outer Mongolia's football executives.

Then, within a matter of months, Player X doesn't live up to either his reputation or his price-tag, melts back into the reserves, gets homesick and a deal is done with another club in Europe. The man from Outer Mongolia is now a movable commodity, with a price enhanced by the word 'Premiership' stamped into his CV.

Do I have any first-hand knowledge of such deals going down in the English Premiership? No. Have I heard such scenarios being discussed? Yes. And I'm hoping Lords Stevens is already on the scent, and that the authorities, like me, have pointed him in the right direction, because he's pretty much wasting his time looking too exhaustively at domestic deals.

●

No agent in Britain is going to take too kindly to his or her work being scrutinized by the football authorities. There is a defensive mechanism within the agent that rides up each time any hint of suspicion is laid at their door. I, for one, am a big fan of the British football agent and I think they receive a harsh press; they've become convenient fall-guys for all that is perceived as greedy about the game.

Agents are the essential cogs within the transfer machinery. Of course, some players dispense with them and opt for lawyers or accountants to represent them instead. But all clubs need third parties to negotiate with, on behalf of a player. Or a club needs to retain an agent to act on its behalf to facilitate a transfer, such as Leeds' recruitment of Colin Gordon over the Robbie Fowler transfer. Then it's up to individual clubs and board directors to determine what an agent is worth. But for the majority of transfers, the usual percentage commission is around 5 per cent of the total fee.

It is wrong to suggest that all agents are bent. In Britain, the vast majority of agents are professionals representing a player's commercial interests, contract negotiations, legal issues and accounting files. Agent services today are more like lifestyle management, in the same way managers control all the minutiae of life for pop stars; it's the element of showbusiness and celebrity that has invaded football. In some ways, I think it's worrying because it promotes in the footballer a sort of parental dependency on the agent, and that can't be healthy for their personal development as human beings. Most footballers are known for their talented feet, not their razor-sharp minds.

Jonathan Woodgate is a world-class defender but could never be described as a mastermind. On one occasion, he'd been told to look after his own passport, and had specifically been told 'to keep it somewhere safe'. On one European trip to Madeira, soon after 9/11, the squad arrived at Leeds-Bradford airport and the players were asked for their passports at the check-in. Jonathan hadn't brought his.

'Where is it?' I asked him.

'You told me to put it somewhere safe so I did. It's in the safe at home!'

This moment of hilarity forced the Leeds United plane to take off and make an unscheduled diversion north to Teesside airport where we'd arranged for his passport to be delivered from his house. He got some stick for that afterwards but it supports my point that players get used to not thinking for themselves. Agents are on hand to answer their every query, respond to their every whim, and iron out any problem in their life. Find a footballer in the middle of a crisis and I know the first person he'll call – his agent.

Agents are wrongly seen as parasites, undeserving of their commission. But players cannot represent themselves, and I'd dread to take a player through every complicated clause within a contract. Agents ensure that the game runs smoothly and, in my view, their round-the-clock work ethic makes them worthy of the fees they command. They are professionals in a commercial world, and it's their job to drive a hard bargain in the interests of their client, and to obtain the maximum fee. As chairman, it was always my job to stand firm in the interests of the plc and buy a player for the lowest possible price.

I'd much prefer to deal with British-based agents because, despite coming across the odd unsavoury character, the majority of them are straight, fair and good people. It's the few dodgy deal-doers, rather than the player representatives, who I don't like dealing with; these brokers of spurious involvement who think they can make a few calls, or send a few faxes, and then submit invoices for ridiculous amounts of money. Give me an agent who actually represents a player any day of the week.

The only real gripe I have about the world of players and agents is the aspect of player contracts. I don't like the hypocrisy of certain players who, when they put pen to paper with their signature, expect the club to honour that contract. But if they want to leave in mid-contract, they've already inserted a clause allowing them an escape route. Player contracts at the highest levels are one-way streets, and it's the same for managers as well. If I had my way with the football regulations, I'd ensure that a player who leaves mid-contract forfeits his payments due under the existing contract. Currently, the system is stacked way too much in favour of the player.

●

My automatic wariness about foreign imports with little reputation reared its head when Terry Venables, looking ahead to the January 2003 transfer window, suggested that we consider Brazilian midfielder José Kléberson. Now, I'm not for one minute saying there was anything dodgy about this potential deal but it did make me uneasy, and my caution over spending money on a relatively unknown quantity soon overrode Terry's advice, which was presented in good faith.

Kléberson, who played for Atlético Paranaense, had just turned twenty-three and was being talked about as an exciting player. But he'd only made his international debut in the February of 2002, and was restricted to a few cameo performances from the bench during the World Cup. Oddly, Brazil manager Luiz Felipe Scolari still described his midfielder as 'the driving force behind the team'.

Terry Venables said he had a friend who had contacts in South America who could make a deal happen and bring him to Leeds United. So I rang this friend, and he told me that Kléberson was on the market for $10m (about £5.5m). This seemed a staggering amount of money but perhaps, I reasoned with myself, it was all to do with Brazil becoming world champions that year; clearly such a medal added value. But I had zero experience of the South American market, and no videos to watch. I wasn't prepared to do business until we'd investigated further so I sent communications director David Walker and FIFA-licensed agent and fluent Portuguese-speaker Mickey Walsh to Brazil to check it out, and have a face-to-face meeting with the Atlético president. When David reported back, it was a different story.

'They're willing to sell him, they say he's a World Cup winner and they want $6m [£3.3m],' explained David.

'But I was told they wanted $10m,' I said.

'Well, they've told us $6m – and they think they're driving a hard bargain with that!'

As I said, I have a natural aversion to these deals and felt that even £3.3m was over the top. Besides, we were hardly in a financial position to proceed. So it was an inquiry that led nowhere. Some months later, Kléberson joined our rivals Manchester United for a reputed £6.5m, so, if true, Atlético had pushed the deal further. He dislocated his shoulder in only his second start, and was a mere fringe player after that, making just twenty-eight appearances before being transferred to Turkish side Besiktas. I blew a sigh of relief and thanked my lucky stars over that one because that's the risk of taking on unknown quantities.

Not that our luck was in when it came down to team performances. We'd been turned over by Sunderland – stealing their first win at Elland Road in forty years – and then Birmingham City and Blackburn Rovers, then a 4–1 home defeat by Arsenal, followed by a 1–0 reverse in front of our fans by Liverpool. Bolton and Charlton added to our humiliations at home. We'd slipped to sixteenth in the table by the start of December, and been unceremoniously turfed out of the Worthington Cup by Sheffield United, squandering a 1–0 lead by letting in two goals in the final minute. Terry Venables was proving to be a disastrous choice, and the sound of booing filled Elland Road for the first time in my chairmanship. 'Venables out! ... Time to go!' I heard pockets of fans chanting, and suddenly the smile had been wiped from the manager's face.

And then, at a match I can no longer pinpoint, I remember hearing the tide turning.

It sounded like this: 'Ridsdale, Ridsdale ... full of shit, Ridsdale ... full of shit!'

It came from the Kop. It stung. I remember driving home that night, feeling like shit, and feeling a panic rise inside me, like someone facing impending doom.

CROWN JEWELS FOR SALE

In early December 2002 Martin O'Neill and his wife drove south from Glasgow down the M6, and took the winding roads through the Lake District to my house. I hoped that he was going to become the next manager of Leeds United, succeeding Terry Venables.

When he stepped out of his car in my driveway, I knew that I had to persuade him to join Leeds, miles away from both Celtic Park and Elland Road, in the tranquillity of the countryside. Discussions over the phone had led to this meeting. He had come down to discuss terms to become manager when his Celtic contract ran out at the end of May.

I handed him a copy of a proposed contract. It was similar in terms to the deal that I had offered him the previous summer. He said he had come to listen to the terms I could offer and asked for assurances about the club's financial position and the attitude of Terry Venables to being replaced. He also told me that his joining Leeds was dependent upon any new deal that Celtic might put forward.

He agreed to take the contract away with him and to look it over. He understood that as he had turned us down on two previous occasions, the last time six months earlier, I needed from him a statement of intent that he was seriously interested in the position. I quickly drafted a document that I felt would demonstrate to the board that I was close to having a successor to Terry Venables lined up. At long last, I thought that I was on the way to getting the manager that I had wanted for so long;

the man I'd wanted before David O'Leary; the man I'd wanted since George Graham's reign.

I looked out across those fields which had become such a depressing outlook in previous months, and suddenly the future seemed brighter. I was able to give Martin the assurances that he was seeking. I thought if I could land him this would be a management coup I couldn't wait to announce; a manager I couldn't wait to have sitting in the home dug-out. Or, more typically in Martin O'Neill's case, pacing the touchline in his tracksuit. At the third attempt, the deal to bring Martin to Leeds United seemed to have a chance of being achieved. I'd worked tirelessly to persuade him to come and meet me. On the phone, I'd urged him to take up the challenge. I told him that at some stage I thought that we would work together and that this was a golden opportunity. 'You can see by the results that things aren't working out with Terry,' I said.

Martin said he was excited by the prospect, and felt it was a more attractive opportunity third time around because 'you are clearly struggling and I feel it gives me a chance to turn things around'.

'The only way is up, Martin!' I laughed.

Business continued during the meal. Now, Martin doesn't do small talk because all he talks about is football – non-stop. Excited and animated, restless even in his chair, he spoke about the strengths and weaknesses of each Leeds player; he aired his thoughts about which players he'd like to bring in; and he was adamant that he could deliver that much longed-for silverware. In the presence of that man, you just want to get cracking and work with him.

That day, I said that we would pay him £2m a year to become the new manager. He left me with a signed document which I could take to my board as evidence that he was serious about becoming our manager, and it read:

> This document states that I will enter a pre-contract agreement with Leeds United AFC on Monday 6 January 2003

to become their football manager when my present contract
expires on 30 June 2003 with Celtic FC. I will come earlier
if Celtic agrees to release me from my contract. I am happy
for Leeds United to publicly announce the above statement
on 6 January.

    Yours sincerely

              Martin O'Neill

No one has ever known about this document before; in my
mind, we'd every chance of gaining a top-class manager, who'd
solve all our problems, return us to winning ways and, consequently, bring us the success that would steer us out of financial
trouble.

Five weeks earlier, at the annual general meeting in November, I'd been re-elected as a director and won a vote of confidence
to be kept on as chairman. The institutional shareholders later
told me they thought it wise that I remain and fix the problems
rather than have someone start afresh. Martin was going to be
that fresh start, ushering in a new era.

On 4 January, I sat back and watched us ease past Scun-
thorpe United in the FA Cup third round, looking at Terry in the
dug-out, knowing his days were numbered, knowing in my mind
that this 'marriage made in hell' (as one reporter would later
describe it) was over. In six months' time, come June 2003, I
believed that the Messiah would arrive when he was contractu-
ally free to do so. He told me that he would be happy to work
alongside me as chairman. If we can just hang on till then,
everything will be fine, I kept telling myself.

Unbeknown to me, time was something I didn't have on my
side.

•

The decision to sack Terry Venables had been taken in mid-
December 2002, the day after Malaga had beaten us 2–1 at
home, dumping us out of the UEFA Cup. We'd also slid to
sixteenth in the league and, during matches, the fans would

chant the name of his predecessor: 'O'Leary . . . O'Leary . . . O'Leary!'

I couldn't wait for the board meeting next day to bring the issue to a head. 'Not only is this our worst run in Europe and our worst run in the league, but if Terry stays, we're in real danger of being relegated,' I said. It was agreed unanimously to terminate his contract and seek out Martin O'Neill for an arrival in the June. Until that time we'd appoint a caretaker manager as a short-term, stop-gap measure; a trouble-shooter to keep us in the Premiership and pave the way for Martin's real work to begin.

It had all gone wrong under Terry. In fact, it had never gone right. There was a lot of talk in the newspapers about him tinkering around with the squad but what really disturbed me was the confused feedback from the players. They really respected him but, from what I was told by a number of senior squad members, he was constantly adjusting tactics for every match, based on the strengths or weaknesses of the opponents. The Leeds players found the chopping and changing – sometimes in the middle of the matches – hard to cope with. 'His systems change like the wind!' one player said to me. We'd had injuries, of course, but that alone didn't justify our free-fall out of the top five.

So it was agreed we'd inform Terry of our decision to sack him after the away game at Bolton, televised on Sky the following Monday, 16 December. But sod's law dictated that Leeds turned on the style to win 3–0 in a live, televised thriller. Terry was beaming afterwards, unaware of the axe above his head.

I rang each director from the Reebok afterwards and asked, 'Are we still sacking him?'

We decided to defer his dismissal until our next defeat because we'd look like idiots sacking a manager after such a comprehensive victory. It's when I look back at such a decision that I realize we made some bizarre judgements under pressure; far too concerned with our appearance and 'how things would look' as a plc. We knew the decision to sack him was right, and we should have been ruthless and done it there and then. Instead, we procrastinated, and it was a spineless mistake.

Terry, typically, went on a mini good run, losing just one out of his next seven games. I found myself in a strange position because we desperately needed the points and yet with each game we won, or each draw he scraped, his stay of execution was prolonged. There I was, applauding the man I couldn't wait to remove. The dead man walking just carried on walking. And it felt like the club was walking a tightrope. Each game felt like a must-win. The fate of Terry Venables was secondary to the urgent need for points to clamber back up the table. With each goal I recalculated our position; each set of three points – or even a point – could be enough to lift us one more place in the table, earning us £500,000 with each new position; conversely, each position slipped lost us the same amount. Every roll of the dice left me fretting from kick-off through to the final whistle.

By the start of the January transfer window, our football position had eased and we'd climbed five places to eleventh. I never thought I'd feel so relieved to find breathing space in the mid-table . . .

Unfortunately, our financial forecasts were not so comfortable. Upward graphs that had once reflected income-streams had suddenly turned into a dive, and the debt graph was shooting through the roof. Our strategy required success to feed the finances, and mid-table mediocrity wasn't going to be good enough. So with the transfer market open again, our focus became consumed not with the search for a stop-gap manager but with balancing the books; the decision to sack Terry therefore became driftwood.

One thing needs to be explained in relation to the transfer window. Had Terry been able to stick to his brief and maintain the momentum of previous seasons and keep us in the top five, there would have been no need whatsoever to raise cash by releasing player assets. But our world had been turned on its head in January 2003 – out of the UEFA Cup and not looking at all likely to qualify for Europe the following season. We were forecasting a £13m reduction in television and broadcasting income as a result.

Come January, Stephen Harrison and I held a meeting with the manager to outline exactly how much money we needed to raise, and by how much we needed to reduce the wage bill. We calculated savings of around £15m in total. This was not a position we'd foreseen at the start of the season. It was the position resulting from recent form. I explained all this to Terry but he stubbornly questioned whether it was the right thing to do. Whether it was right or wrong, the team's performance left us with little choice. But he, like most managers to be fair, was arguing to keep his squad together.

I tried to explain that, without such action, the club's future could be at risk, but he turned to me and said: 'Clubs like Leeds United don't go bust – they just merely change chairman. You're just trying to save your own skin here, and you're putting my job at risk!'

One thing I've learned in football is that business and managers don't necessarily mix that well.

Terry felt we were pulling the rug from beneath him. Indeed, this would be an excuse he'd rely on further down the road. But he failed to see that Leeds United had gone into reverse under his stewardship. He also failed to remember a meeting we'd had in November, after the 2–0 defeat at Tottenham – and one month *before* we'd decided to sack him – when I agreed to meet him and his agent Leon Angel in his favourite hotel, the Carlton Tower, in Knightsbridge, London. That defeat at Spurs had left us in fourteenth position, and Terry called that meeting, in my opinion, to try to extricate himself from a pressured situation that wasn't reflecting well on him. He was making all the right noises to find the exit door, saying how we both knew it wasn't working, that it wasn't the job he'd been sold, and that he didn't have the money he needed.

I sensed what he was trying to do and told him: 'If you want to go, then you can quit but I'm not prepared to sack you so that you can walk away with £2m compensation.' It was, like most of our meetings, businesslike and to the point.

If the Leeds job was, as some newspapers had said, a last chance for Terry to restore his reputation, then it was going horrendously wrong for him, so I could understand why he'd want out.

Grudgingly, on both our parts, he stayed and things went from bad to worse, leading to that emergency meeting in January. It was then that the enforced sale of Jonathan Woodgate was first mooted around the boardroom as an option that might have to be considered, and Newcastle United were already hovering with interest.

'You assured me that you wouldn't be selling Woodgate!' Terry protested, angrily.

'Yes, I did,' I agreed, 'but that was when neither of us had anticipated being this low down the league and out of Europe.'

I calmed the situation by saying Woodgate would be sold only as a 'last resort' in the options available to us. Our sales targets were Dacourt (£14m), Fowler (£7m), Johnson (£5m) and Bowyer for whatever price we could get for a player threatening to 'do a Bosman' as he neared the end of his contract. But I felt others on the board believed transferring Woodgate would need to happen, regardless of my clearly stated reluctance.

We were a club in distress, selling players to balance the books; talk of our financial weakness was filling the rumour mill of football and Fleet Street. We were being reported in the newspapers as 'cash-strapped'; that we needed to administer 'brutal cost-cutting', knowledge of which our rivals were going to exploit in the market place. As the *Sunday People* described it, 'Premiership vultures are looking at Leeds stars regarded as the "crown jewels".' And Woodgate was the diamond tiara.

In the end, our intended transactions didn't go as planned. All we managed to do was ship out Dacourt on loan to Roma (saving £1m in wages); Bowyer to West Ham for a paltry £100,000; and Fowler to Manchester City for £7m on the condition we subsidized his salary by a fifth of his earnings for the balance of his contract. We got a lot of stick over that from the fans but this arrangement is a common feature within football. Besides, in our position, it was far better to save four-fifths of his earnings and receive £7m as our best offer than not do the deal at all. Johnson had looked certain to move to Middlesbrough but everything fell through when he failed a medical. I was suddenly some £7m short on my target savings, with the transfer deadline looming. The rest of the board looked to me to execute the 'last resort' and sell Woodgate. I felt the expectation heaped upon me, as the fan within wrestled with the burden.

That same week, and unbeknown to me at the time, Alan Woodgate, Jonathan's father, received a telephone call out of the blue. The call, which lasted no more than a minute, was from an anonymous man who told him: 'Newcastle United want Jonathan. If you want him away from Leeds United, he'll have to ask for a transfer.' Alan made it clear, apparently, that there was no way Jonathan would hand in his ticket at Leeds, and then demanded the caller's identity. 'Maybe he should consider it,' said the caller, 'but that's all he has to do. The rest will happen.' And then the line went dead. Jonathan's father immediately phoned his son's agent and said: 'I've had the most bizarre call. I think we've just been propositioned to get Jonathan away from Leeds.' Alan was rightly told to ignore the call.

Back at Leeds, we couldn't ignore reality. As directors of a plc, we had a fiduciary duty to take the right decisions, irrespective of the emotions of the fans or manager. I tried explaining this to Terry but he wasn't in the mood for listening. He was in denial and already preparing to deflect the blame, in my view kicking up fury over Woodgate's sale so as to create a cloud that his own failings as manager. He was reported as being 'heart-broken' over Woodgate's sale and I found that incredible; the definition of 'heartbreak' is to watch a manager take your team from top-five performers to sixteenth in the table, out of Europe, and out of the League Cup, in the space of four months.

I spent days and sleepless nights wondering how to keep Woodgate. At one point, as a last-ditch alternative measure, I started a dialogue with Liverpool about the sale of Harry Kewell. Rick Parry was definitely interested and, in principle, he agreed a £10m fee, or thereabouts, with negotiations still to be finalized. For a couple of days, this deal seemed destined to happen. I actually remember praying for it to happen. Harry would have been a great loss but it was better than losing Woodgate.

But it soon became clear we couldn't tie the deal up in time, and Liverpool preferred to wait until the summer. I waited and Liverpool stalled. As I waited, Alan Woodgate received a second mystery phone call, reminding him that Jonathan could still hand in a transfer request, and Newcastle would take him. Who and where were these calls coming from? He'd later ask me, but I didn't have any answers. When the Liverpool–Kewell deal wasn't happening, Woodgate's transfer was accelerated. I'd done all I could to find an alternative, and failed. Selling the family silver became the only option. I sat in my office, near the phone, knowing I'd have to ring Newcastle United. As I doodled and scribbled in the notepad of paper, I could only imagine the backlash from the Leeds fans, who viewed Woodgate not only as a son but as the future of the club.

They're going to hate me for this, I thought, as I picked up the receiver to dial Newcastle's chairman, Freddy Shepherd.

I'd publicly stated that would we sell him 'over my dead body', and I'd meant it. I strongly believed that our other sales targets would be met. It was another mistake to misunderstand the capricious nature of fate within football's markets.

I'd taken calls from Freddy throughout January, always resisting his bid of £6m, hanging on for the Seth Johnson deal to go through. Now, I had to place my sentimentality in a drawer, and put my business head back on.

Newcastle increased their bid to £8m with a £1m add-on if the Magpies won the UEFA Cup during the term of his five-year contract. I travelled to St James' Park in the day before the transfer deadline, armed with an urgency to sell that must have appeared like begging bowl thrust under the nose of a rich man. But this was a matter of survival.

I shook Freddy Shepherd's hand and said, 'You know this deal is going to cost me my job!'

Freddy winced, and sympathized. In his thick Geordie accent, he said, 'I feel for you, son. I know it must be difficult. I know you don't want to do this,' and he put out his hand to shake mine, and ordered two cups of tea to warm us from the snow outside. I tried improving the deal but Newcastle didn't budge. Whatever argument I tried, whatever negotiating lever I pulled, Freddy was intransigent. He was highly confident in his strategy. I had been reliably informed that there were suspicions that I'd 'bottle it' and not do the right thing for Leeds United. This left me feeling that Freddy had already discussed the Woodgate transfer with someone else.

But, despite the fact that this single decision lost me the confidence of the supporters, I'm proud that I found the backbone 'to do the right thing' and finalize a deal which the board was going to steamroller through, regardless.

It would later become clear that someone had undermined my authority and intercepted negotiations just in case I wobbled in my convictions – and there it was: the first neon sign that I no longer had the 100 per cent belief of everyone around me. As things began to fall apart, I sensed there was an increasing loss of confidence in me from some quarters.

What the fans must understand is that the board was dead set on steering the Woodgate deal through, with or without me. I was damned if I did, and damned if I didn't. As I told Leeds fans in an open letter published in the *Yorkshire Evening Post*: 'If someone else had been chairman . . . it's no good believing decisions would have been different.'

On the day we finalized the deal, I'd never felt so depressed. I rang Woodgate and wished him all the best, and told him that his departure was the last thing I'd wanted. He was as stunned as I was at the speed of the transfer but he was a true gent. 'I know you didn't want to sell me,' he said, 'and I'll never blame you. I want to thank you for standing by me like you did last year.' I ended the call and felt like someone had winded me.

It felt hard, on an emotional level, to justify the Woodgate sale. Given what we'd all lived through – seeing him make his debut and develop into a world-class defender, knowing his trauma through the trials and then seeing his rehabilitation – it was the most painful decision I'd had to sanction. The fan within me sat on my shoulder, hissing and spitting in my face; this alter-ego that loathed me for the transaction I'd overseen.

As I pulled up outside the Thorp Arch training ground to confirm the news that Terry Venables must have expected, I sat looking out across the pitches, worried sick about the ramifications. After much paranoid rumination, I rang Allan Leighton and told him my credibility with the fans was shot and it would be best if I tendered my resignation as chairman.

Allan talked me down, and said: 'You shouldn't be quitting your post for being seen to do the right thing, and it was a collective decision to sell Jonathan Woodgate. It is the right thing to do for the club, Peter, and you're the only person who has sufficient rapport with the supporters to communicate this to them. You can't quit now.'

Back then, I felt boosted by his words, and supported to the hilt. But I would learn of an oddity within the Woodgate transfer process that would make me view Allan in a completely different light. But that insight would only be delivered to me in the days following my departure.

At the time, I was focussed on announcing the Woodgate transfer to the fans, dealing with an upset manager and walking the plank from the great ship LUFC. What infuriated me more than anything was seeing Terry Venables reacting to the news like someone whose soul was tied to Elland Road, implying that we'd just made his task ten times harder by selling Woodgate, and he was going to milk this opportunity for all its worth when we held a press conference to announce the transfer.

That day, Friday 31 January, was my toughest ever media experience. I'd grabbed a piece of paper and scribbled the message I wanted to convey to the fans: 'Should we have spent so heavily in the past? No. But we lived the dream. We all enjoyed the dream. By making the right decision today, we can rekindle that dream in the future. This will make us stronger.'

I felt like a guilty man rehearsing a plea of innocence, and it was clear I was out there on my own. When I tried running those words by Terry before we faced the cameras, he didn't want to listen. 'It's up to you what you say,' he said, 'this has nothing to do with me.'

For a minute I wondered whether it was wise to have him alongside me in front of the bank of TV crews, microphones, photographers and reporters. I was nervous enough without having to contemplate the reactions of the man beside me.

Reluctantly, for the sake of keeping up appearances for the plc, I decided that chairman and manager should at least attempt a united front. But I hadn't reckoned on his performance at the conference. As soon as I sat down and started to speak amid exploding flashguns and live microphones, I noticed Terry sitting back, arms folded, staring at the ceiling, as thunderous and sullen as you could imagine. For me it was a show of defiance that put a thousand miles between himself and the decision to sell the club's prized asset.

I was furious deep down. There he was, on live television, reminding the media that he'd been promised Woodgate wouldn't be sold; portraying himself as the pure football man 'adrift in a sea of business-suits', as one newspaper put it. There he was, coming up smelling of roses. I found his behaviour unbelievable. He knew the situation we were in and knew the hard choices we had to make. Instead of us all pulling together as a club I felt that the manager was more interested in making out that he was in an impossible situation and that he would need to be a miracle worker to make a fist of this job.

One newspaper described that press conference as 'an all-time tragedy classic' – to me it was more like a farce. The petulance of the manager had drowned out the message, and he was able to walk away to headlines such as 'Furious Venables Considers His Position'. He told the press he needed time to think about his future. How I wished we'd sacked him in the December when we'd already decided his future, I thought.

Meanwhile, a storm was breaking around me. Fans gathered outside Elland Road, chanting for the board to be sacked, and shouting about treachery and lies. A poster was strapped to the hand of the Billy Bremmer statue and read: 'JANUARY SALE – 1 SET OF LOYAL FANS (worth nowt to a plc)'. That afternoon, the club was bombarded by abusive emails and phone-calls.

Over the coming weeks, the postbag would bulge with more hate mail. As I'd predicted, I was the hero turned villain; the 'traitor', the 'Judas', the 'scum'. As much as Allan Leighton had reminded me it was a 'collective decision', it all felt personal. And I didn't see him or anyone else riding to my public rescue. I also suspected that I knew what Terry had been doing – leave me high and dry without managerial support which, in turn, would get the fans on his side and be the beginning of the end for me. Terry may well have lost his managerial touch but he remained expert at pulling off a PR master-stroke. He'd out-manoeuvred me.

As an article in the *Guardian* observed: 'The bond between Venables and Ridsdale has been irreparably broken by the sale of Jonathan Woodgate to Newcastle about which the manager says he was misled and kept in the dark. Either he or the chairman must go to ease the disunity on a sinking ship.'

Over my dead body will I be going first, I thought. Whatever the public perceptions, he was the one hanging on by his fingertips, and only the distraction of the transfer window and a good run in the FA Cup had saved him. The board's mind was already made up in regard to his fate. It was just a matter of time. To my great disappointment, in mid January, I heard from Martin O'Neill that he had decided to stay with Celtic and had signed a twelve month rolling contract which was announced at a press conference on 22 January.

I even had support from a Leeds United legend, Peter Lorimer. He wrote in the local newspaper:

> We're now paying the penalty for trying to match the big boys like Manchester United and Arsenal. A lot of people have said it was a gamble that shouldn't have been taken but when we were trying it, everyone thought it was brilliant. I honestly think it was a gamble worth taking and, if it had come off, there would be no complaints . . . and if you can't sell the players you want to, then you've got to sell the ones you can – it's simple as that.

I just needed to hang on for a few more months. In a few more months, we'd get the show back on the road.

•

'We can't guarantee your safety at Goodison Park,' said one of the security advisors at Leeds. In the space of twenty-four hours since Woodgate's sale the reaction had been venomous. Hatemail arrived the next day, emails poured in and the local radio phone-ins were crammed with irate callers. Overnight, I was 'Public Enemy No.1'.

One letter, delivered by hand to Elland Road, simply said, 'Keep looking over your shoulder, Ridsdale – we'll get you for this.' One crude note was pinned beneath the windscreen wipers on my car: 'We hope you die for selling Woodie.' In the coming weeks, the threats would escalate to the point where I needed to bring in West Yorkshire Police. Detectives tried reassuring me that would-be assassins never inform their target of imminent danger and that such threats could never be serious. But one letter, using letters cut out from a magazine and newspaper, simply said, 'YOU ARE DEAD.' It was a bloody frightening time, regardless of the police reassurances. While I never actually believed anyone would set out to kill me, I did think some idiot might have a pop at me.

This hate built into hundreds of letters a week, using the most foul and horrific language and threats. One day, I opened the gates at the end of the driveway to my house and found a note, pinned to the wood, which said: '*We know where you live.*'

I'd become almost accustomed to receiving hate-mail over the Woodgate–Bowyer trial but that was different because I always knew the abuse was coming from non-Leeds fans. This time, the hate *was* coming from our supporters.

For that Everton match, both clubs had to take seriously such targeted hate, and so, on the safety advice issued, Everton kindly sent a club minibus to collect me at a lay-by somewhere ear Aintree. It had been decided that I'd need shepherding into Goodison to protect me from my own fans, like a 'scab' being driven past the picket-line.

I'd driven to the lay-by with Professor John McKenzie, newly arrived on the football club board. Ever since his appointment, he'd made a big play of the fact that he'd been a supporter of mine and reiterated, 'You're going to need allies like me with the transfer window coming up.' As a financial adviser who'd done work in the Far East, he soon became a wise sounding board and, ultimately, by the March of 2003, he would become a director of the plc, recommended by me, and with the enthusi-astic backing of Allan Leighton.

So John McKenzie suddenly found himself not just in the back of a minibus with me but in an influential position as the club entered its storm. He travelled with me to Everton, he said, 'to show me some solidarity'. John was always there through those tough weeks but I've since wondered whether he was sticking close in order to learn the ropes, intentionally or subconsciously.

The minibus transported us both to Goodison Park and dropped us *inside*, not outside, the ground, driving us through the emergency exit gates and directly into the stadium, pitch-side. It felt ridiculous to be sneaked into a ground but I genuinely felt it was a temporary precaution, and that emotions would die down within a week or two. I can't say that I settled during the match, which we lost 2–0, because I was distracted by the constant abuse from the Leeds support, finding its voice to berate me: 'We thought you were Leeds, we were wrong ... We thought you were Leeds, we were wrong. *Ridsdale out! Ridsdale out!*' they chanted, for the full ninety minutes. It was relentless. I knew there and then that I'd never survive. I'd been the sup-porters' chairman – their representative on the board – and had been proud of that unique relationship. But at Goodison that day, I knew I'd lost them.

I sat there watching the game, feeling numb; watching the game on auto-pilot, unable to avoid focusing on the hatred I'd never wanted to know. Each time I heard them sing, over and over, 'We thought you were Leeds, we were wrong', it was like torture; as if I was tied to that chair in the director's box to take a beating in public.

It's a mortifying experience to be sat among fellow directors and wives, and having your name ridiculed at such volume; everyone pretends not to hear, but they're all cringing for you. It was the start of a weekly drip, drip, drip of hate and humilia-tion. I sat there and contemplated the next home match. If this is how loud it gets away from home, what will it be like at Elland Road? I thought.

I wouldn't need to wait long for the sledgehammer to land.

Gillingham in the FA Cup fourth round replay provided the answer. I walked into the directors' box, ignoring the insults shouted up from the seats below, and looked to my left towards

the Kop. 'Lies United – Ridsdale Out' read one massive banner.
'Judas' read another. Then they started singing in support of
Venables. I felt sick over the collective amnesia that meant people
chanted for this manager whose legacy was to take us from a
top-five team to sixteenth, facing relegation.

Let me tell you now, if Arsenal or Liverpool suddenly found
themselves out of Europe and four places from the bottom, they,
too, would face major problems. And does anyone really believe
that Chelsea, with its dreams financially supported by a lone
Russian billionaire, is a triumph built on sturdy foundations?

'Do you have *any* fucking idea what you are doing?' a fan
screamed towards me, reminding me to focus on who was *really*
to blame.

'You're wrecking our club, Ridsdale!' bellowed someone else.

Thankfully, a 2–1 victory over Gillingham sucked the sting
out of the encounter. But when Newcastle came to Elland Road
eighteen days later, and we lost 3–0, it felt like 40,000 were
calling for my head. Woodgate didn't play that day so the salt
wasn't rubbed into the wound but, nevertheless, that defeat
heightened the hostility against me.

As my name was abused in a cacophony of noise from each
side of the stadium, I wished to be one of the fans again. I
wanted to be Mr Nobody, not Mr Chairman. It pained me
acutely to be the man they blamed and loathed. I wanted them
to realize I was still one of them but they'd cut me loose. I was
no longer worth believing, and not worth listening to. I was the
man who had the dreams of 40,000 people littered at my feet,
and I felt that huge responsibility and guilt. I'd let them down,
despite the fact I'd done my best. I'd bust a gut to make the
grand plan work and, for an unforgettable time, it had. But it
was falling to pieces, and I couldn't seem to do right for doing
wrong.

'Sack the board, support the team ... Sack the board,
support the team!' they chanted in wave after wave. 'Who's the
bastard in the boardroom?!' they sang over and over again. I

looked down to the dug-out and saw Terry Venables, master-minding yet another inept performance, and wondered how on earth he was managing to get away with it.

It was around this time that *Broken Dreams*, the book written by journalist Tom Bower, was serialized in the *Daily Mail*, and 'the scandal' of the £1.75m Rune Hauge commission for the Rio Ferdinand transfer was pinned on me. The word 'scandal' suddenly smeared me, and added to the impression that I'd been frittering away the club's money. 'Heat Turned Up On Ridsdale' said the London *Evening Standard*, which wrote, 'The Leeds chairman originally tried to blame former manager David O'Leary for Hauge's involvement but it emerged today that he was responsible for the payment . . . it was a letter signed by Ridsdale that authorized the £1.75m fee.'

Despite the fact that it was David O'Leary's signature all over the authorization form, the truth mattered not. The weight of the publicity meant that the plc board felt obligated to hold its own internal investigation into the Hauge saga. Suddenly, I felt eyed with suspicion from within. But I understood that the transaction had to be seen to be clean, so I cooperated fully, and provided complete transparency. I kept my dignity in the safe knowledge that the truth would emerge in the end; that one day I'd be able to have my say in public. But at the time, the damage was being done to my reputation.

'Where, where, where has our money gone?!' chanted the Leeds fans, pointing out with banners that they supported 'LUFC not PLC'. The hate-mail also intensified. Suddenly, for the first time in my life, Elland Road became a place I dreaded.

'I just don't want to go in,' I kept telling Sophie when I left the house each morning. Leaving her and the girls at home had become a worry because, ever since the sale of Woodgate, security guards had been posted at our house on both police and club advice. The note pinned to the gate had to be taken seriously, and we had to instruct the local school that nobody other than Sophie and I would collect our girls at the end of the classes. Charlotte and Olivia could sense the tension around the house, and there were some upsetting nights.

Sophie was worried sick half the time, especially at night. It's one thing feeling a siege mentality at a football stadium but to wonder whether anyone is watching your home is another thing entirely. You're not reassured by the presence of security guards – they act as a permanent reminder of the perceived danger, and it leaves you constantly on edge.

'We can't live like this, Peter, and I can't see you take much more of it,' Sophie kept telling me, and I knew the situation, in both my worlds, was becoming intolerable. 'This isn't about football anymore,' she added.

She knew, as much as I was hating every second of the experience, that part of me was still determined to regain control, and turn things around. But it had reached the stage where David Mellor had suggested I go into a darkened room with a gun and do the decent thing.

'Is it really worth all this suffering?' she implored. And it wasn't. I knew it wasn't. But I couldn't bear the fact that to back down would be a white flag of surrender, of failure. I believed then – as I still believe now – that I could have turned things around; that, had my plans come to fruition, we'd have ridden the financial storm and found a stronger, brighter future.

Then came the Middlesbrough game at home on 15 March 2003. Sophie came with me, as she did for every home match. We entered a boardroom mixed with support and sympathy. It was almost as if everyone else sensed the end was near.

As kick-off approached, I walked into the director's box, walking down the side of the enclosure that boarded the seats in the main stand. For the first time, the corporate fans sat nearby in the main stand turned on me. I was used to abuse from the Kop but not from the suited supporters sat around me. It seemed the anger and hatred were creeping to more and more parts of the ground, closing in on me. And I don't mind admitting it – it made me feel slightly claustrophobic.

The abuse was shocking as Sophie walked in front of me. I kept my head down, taking in each step, eager to reach our seats in the front row. Someone, leaning over into the directors' box, prodded me in the chest and screamed his thoughts in my face. I was jostled then pushed; hands were waving in front of me, gesturing obscenities. In the distance, I heard the Kop sing for my sacking. I heard one man expectorate violently, and his spit landed on the right lapel of my suit: 'You're not fit to be chairman!' he screamed.

I sat down, shaking. Sophie gripped my hand and I smiled, knowing the photographers' cameras were trained on me from pitch-side.

Something broke inside me that afternoon in regard to my relationship with Leeds. The fans had lost their respect for me, and I was fast losing all respect for them, and falling out of love with a club that I'd adored since childhood. I sat there, watching another defeat unfold, and thought about it all: the manager who'd briefed against me over Woodgate, a board no longer fully behind me and shuffling John McKenzie into position, a fan-base which sounded more like a lynch mob, and press coverage that suggested I was out of control and, as one columnist said, had 'lost the plot'. Elland Road – this house of dreams for so much of my life – had become a place of personal hell.

That afternoon, I started to emotionally detach from a life-long experience because the memories were turning ugly. I wasn't regretting becoming chairman but I knew the time had come to step down. The dream was over, for me and the club.

After half-time, as I walked back up the steps to the board-room, the ritual abuse continued. Then one of the corporate supporters – this hooligan in a suit – screamed another obscenity, and spat at my feet. That was the final straw. I looked at the distress on Sophie's face.

'Come on,' I said, 'we're going.' For the first time in my life, I walked out of a Leeds United match, and drove home.

It proved to be my last home match as chairman; the spitting, the abuse, the banners, and the booing became my good-rid-dance farewell.

I listened to BBC Radio Leeds in the car on the way home, and heard us lose 3–2. The sombre voice of the commentator couldn't hide the deafening boos behind him. Leeds, inexplic-ably, were fifteenth with 34 points and in danger of relegation; the same form that had plagued us since before December had returned to haunt us. I felt as helpless as everyone else, and yet responsible for the appointment of Venables, even though he hadn't received my vote. There was no way I was going to walk out without addressing that issue. If it was my last act as chairman, Venables had to be sacked if Leeds were to stand a chance of staying up. Regardless of my fate, I couldn't see my club get relegated after all that we'd achieved.

And so, with board approval, I was commissioned to ring former Sunderland and Manchester City manager Peter Reid. I'd identified him as the man to rescue us from the Venables predicament. Peter was holidaying in North Wales, and we agreed to meet discreetly, on Tuesday 18 March, at the Carden Park Hotel, outside Chester.

I booked a private room using a pseudonym so that no one could spot us, and offered him the job for eight matches only, with a basic retainer and a cash incentive for each point earned. It basically worked out as a total package worth £500,000 but did not, as has been wrongly reported, a bonus for Premiership survival.

'The more points you win, the more money you earn, the more we stay in the Premiership!' I told him. 'But whatever happens, this job is for eight matches. Even if you win all eight remaining games, I cannot guarantee you the job for the next season,' I told him.

Peter knew the score, and was happy to take up the chal-lenge. He seemed the ideal stop-gap candidate; a manager the plc board felt met our requirements to find someone with a track record for 'immediate impact results'. The long-term picture was a different story, and the plc board never had Peter Reid in mind for the 2003–04 season. That was agreed unanimously because he was not regarded as a long-term solution. But, for the short term, he was ideal.

As we walked out of Carden Park from our clandestine meeting, a young lad came up to me and said, 'Hey! You're that Peter Ridsdale. What you doing here, then?' So much for trying our hardest not to get spotted. I think they call it infamy.

The press were told that I'd got Peter Reid out of bed with a phone call to offer him the job after Venables had been sacked. But that wasn't the case. Peter was in the bag before then.

Two days later, I called Venables to my office at Elland Road. As soon as he sat down, exuding this air of defiance, it was obvious we could no longer work together. There was no respect from either side – more like barely concealed resentment. I explained to him that results weren't good and it was time for a change in the interests of Leeds United.

'That's your call,' he said, but then questioned whether I had the authority to make the change, suggesting I'd lost my power base. I think Terry perceived Allan Leighton as the real power-broker calling the shots on the plc, the real wisdom behind the chairman.

'I don't think you could sack me even if you personally wanted to,' he said. Politely, I reminded him that I was still the chairman, and could readily dismiss him.

'Well go on, then ... sack me,' he said. So, with board approval up my sleeve, I did. The look on Terry's face suggested that he didn't know whether to believe me or not.

'I'm serious,' I said, 'and I can confirm that the board has agreed to terminate your contract with immediate effect.'

Afterwards, Terry came out and defended himself by saying, 'As the squad grew weaker we had to fight harder and harder. Then the chairman says the results aren't good enough as if the two things [selling the club's best players and losing matches] are unrelated!'

With his rose-tinted spectacles on, he'd forgotten to look at the first half of the season which had left us, pre-transfer window, in the Premiership basement. Even with Jonathan Woodgate, he'd been failing. As for the players sold 'from underneath him', the Keane transfer was at his behest because he had a surplus of strikers; he'd fallen out with Dacourt and wasn't playing him, and Lee Bowyer had to go because he was threatening to do a Bosman. And he chose not to pick David Batty. Without Dacourt and Batty, he'd removed two-thirds of the midfield engine that had been part of the Champions League semi-final team.

Venables didn't mention the players that he *did* have at his disposal, such as the exciting James Milner. He emerged as a sixteen-year-old 'teen sensation' capable of deflecting the attention away from a certain Wayne Rooney, whose talents were causing a buzz on Merseyside. James, a product of the youth academy, became the youngest player to score in the Premiership in a 2–1 win over Sunderland, and then added to his tally with a goal in a 2–0 victory over Claudio Ranieri's Chelsea. Terry still had the options of Smith, Viduka and Kewell up front, with the likes of Wilcox, Johnson, Bakke, Milner, Lennon, Barmby and Okon in midfield. For central defenders he still had Matteo, Radebe, Duberry and his own import, Teddy Lucic, to choose from, with the likes of Mills, Kelly and Harte as full-backs, and Paul Robinson, Nigel Martyn or Scott Carson in goal. Venables was hardly left with a team worthy of his Premiership sob story.

But we didn't have time to reflect on the what-might-have-beens because his successor had eight games to restore some belated dignity to an abysmal season. The former high expectations at Elland Road had been replaced by a desperation to survive in the Premiership in both footballing and economic terms.

Peter Reid's first match was at Anfield forty-eight hours later on Sunday 23 March. We lost 3–1, and we dropped a further place in the league. Once again, I got hammered by the Leeds

CROWN JEWELS FOR SALE

fans. But, as Liverpool coasted to victory, I looked to my right to the flags being waved in the Kop end and, instead of singing 'You'll Never Walk Alone', the mass choir of Reds started to sing, 'One Peter Ridsdale . . . there's only one Peter Ridsdale.'

Anfield was laughing at me. I was officially the laughing stock of English football, and my dignity could take no more.

Later that week, I went to see Allan Leighton at his office at Bhs in London to discuss my exit. In my mind, I'd arrested the decline by getting rid off Venables, had brought in the right man in Peter Reid, and had taken the right actions to prevent relegation. The next thing to do was to do the decent thing and step down. I knew by looking at Allan's face that he knew my time was up, too.

'I've lost the fans, and I've had enough,' I said, and we sat down and discussed the settlement package. He asked me to return at 6 p.m. to finalize discussions, and to give us both time to think it all through.

When I returned, Professor John McKenzie was sat there with him, having already accepted the chairmanship. It felt like a ruthlessly quick replacement but, then again, who was I to argue? I'd done exactly the same by replacing Terry Venables with Peter Reid. That's football.

To this day, I'm convinced Professor McKenzie was deliberately drafted in with an eye on the top job. He came from nowhere and, as history would pan out, would disappear just as quickly, but not before sticking in the boot to my tenure.

I left London for the refuge of my sister-in-law's house on the Suffolk–Essex border, holding an agreement that I'd remain at Leeds as non-executive director, a move which, I was told, had the backing of the institutional shareholders. A board meeting ratified that decision, and installed Professor McKenzie as non-executive chairman.

I don't necessarily like the word 'resignation' because it sounds like I jumped ship; a more accurate phrase would be 'hounded to hand in my resignation'. As much as I wasn't enjoying life as chairman, I still felt there was a job for me to do to correct the mess, but in the panic to find a solution, my exit had been demanded and granted. But that's football. When the team is doing well, the manager is a hero. When the team is doing badly, the chairman needs to be sacked.

Allan Leighton and his new chairman John McKenzie clearly felt matters were in control, and redeemable. At the 27 March board meeting, which I attended to confirm my resignation, the plc board agreed that it could fund and manage the debt of £78.9m. It was *not* considered to be in the grip of a major financial crisis. Indeed the plc felt it was capable of funding an ongoing debt of £65m despite missing out on European football. The goal stated at the meeting was to reduce the £78.9m debt to £65m through management and staff cost-cutting that summer. No one was panicking. There was not even a murmur about 'largesse'. There was no mention of club spending being 'irresponsible and indulgent', as John McKenzie would later say. What's more, I was asked that day, together with Stephen Harrison, to help 'manage' the debt and draw up measures to bring about necessary savings in my capacity as non-executive director.

But Allan Leighton and John McKenzie must have had second thoughts in the days that followed the publication of the interim results that revealed the extent of the £78.9m debt. I was clearing my desk on the Tuesday before the next league match away at Charlton when Allan rang, and said it would be best if I stayed away for a few days because the press were asking questions about whether I'd really quit (they'd have had a field day had they known I'd been asked to help manage the debts, I thought).

'I'm only clearing my desk, Allan. Allow me time to clear my desk, please,' I said. I wasn't in the mood for hanging around. With all the flak I'd faced, I just wanted to get in and out of that chairman's office as quickly as possible. I'm not one for moping around and getting nostalgic. I'd walked through many revolving doors in the world of business before, and I honestly felt nothing but relief as I drove away from the stadium, relieved of my duties as chairman.

I didn't say goodbye to the players because what do players care about chairmen who come and go? I'd phoned Peter Reid on the Sunday night to tell him what had unfolded and he was shocked. 'You've only just bloody hired me!' he said, in thick Scouse. I told him that the chairman didn't matter, the manager did.

'Just make sure you do the job I hired you to do,' I told him, 'keep them up.'

Two days later, I was back at the ground for a meeting with John McKenzie, and to provide notes on my thoughts about reducing the debt. John had previously said how he'd need to pick my brains to allow for a smooth transition, and I was happy to give such input. He'd also asked me to draw up a list of managerial candidates, knowing, as we'd all agreed, that Peter Reid was not a long-term option. So I supplied a list of names that included Gordon Strachan, Paul Hart, Micky Adams and Martin O'Neill, even though I knew the latter would be an impossibility in the circumstances.

I thought I was being helpful, and had perhaps deluded myself into thinking my advice would still be beneficial. But then, with some awkwardness, John McKenzie told me that he felt it would be in everyone's interests if I didn't attend any further games between then and the end of the season.

'It's felt that you would become a distraction,' he said.

'But you've appointed me a non-executive director,' I argued.

That's when he told me that, having reviewed the position with the institutional shareholders, it was felt I shouldn't have been offered that position in the first place because 'it's just not going to work and isn't practical after all that has happened.' I was sent away to consider ways in which 'both parties can amicably sever ties completely'.

He was right, of course. I was barmy to think of me, the ex-chairman the fans had blamed, sitting beside the man the fans regarded as 'Mr Fixit'. But the polite way of saying 'Can you please sod off now' still made me feel like the criminal banished from the kingdom.

In those initial days following my departure, the plc board felt like it was bumbling along, uncertain what to do for the best. With John McKenzie at the helm, it had a 'green', hesitant academic who seemed unsure of himself in the football world, and yet was portraying himself as this sage who had gripped the purse-strings in his iron fist.

One the surface, it seemed that control had been restored. The financial wisdom of the new chairman could not be doubted but, in my mind, his lack of football credentials would further handicap the progress that needed to be made. But my voice no longer mattered.

That weekend, I sat glued to Sky Sports, watching the goal-flashes constantly roll with the Charlton v Leeds latest score. In his second game in charge, Reid's Leeds United ran riot with a 6–1 victory, Viduka netting a hat-trick. It was almost comforting to witness such a magnificent result without fending off a barrage of abuse. From the safety of my own armchair, I sensed old emotions of excitement and pride return. I even found myself clenching a fist when the sixth goal went in.

Eleven days later, Leeds United plc formally announced that I'd severed all ties with the club. I was formally thanked for my contribution but I walked away knowing that I'd be remembered in club history as the man whose legacy was a £78.9m debt.

I only had lone voices like Ray Fell, chairman of the LUFC Supporters' Club, sticking up for me in the newspapers. He said, 'The feeling I have is one of regret that something that started so promisingly ended like this. What Peter did for this club should not be forgotten – in his own words, we lived the dream.'

As for me, the only quote I'd like to be remembered for, the one that best summed up how I felt as I walked away to reflect on the mistakes I'd made, is the one I gave to the *Yorkshire Evening Post*: 'My heart will always be in Leeds United.'

As a commentary in the same paper said:

It's time for previous disenchantment with a dream-maker to be shelved. Grudges and frustrations must be set aside if this once mighty club is to climb back to its rightful position and deserved success. Peter Ridsdale has been tardy in understanding the best thing he could do for Leeds was to walk away. But now that he has, the building must begin in earnest.

Just days after my resignation, England played Turkey at the Stadium of Light in a 2004 Championship Group Seven qualifier. Jonathan Woodgate was one of Sven-Göran Eriksson's substitutes, and his dad, Alan, was sat in the stands when, in that most unlikely of settings, he was able to shed new light on his son's transfer to Newcastle United just weeks earlier. It was half-time after a poor and goalless first forty-five minutes when Alan was suddenly approached by football agent Hayden Evans, someone I'd often had dealings with as the agent to David Batty. Hayden approached Alan Woodgate and explained that he'd been 'acting on behalf of Allan Leighton for Jonathan to go to Newcastle'. In Alan Woodgate's mind, the penny dropped. The mystery calls, reminding him that all his son had to do was submit a transfer request, suddenly made sense, whether Hayden was the actual caller or not.

Hayden Evans was acting on behalf of the non-executive director at Leeds United, and it seemed obvious to me that it was Allan Leighton who feared I'd never have the bottle to sell.

Alan Woodgate had some sympathy for my position. He picked up the phone one afternoon and said: 'Mr Ridsdale, there's been something weighing on my conscience ever since Jonathan was sold to Newcastle. Everyone I speak to blames you. But it wasn't just you making it happen – it was Allan Leighton.'

And that's when I learned of how my non-executive director was pulling the strings behind the scenes, engineering a contingency plan, for the good of the club, in case I buckled. What's puzzled me since is why Hayden Evans was ever involved. It was, ultimately, me who had finalized the £8m transfer without the need for an agent. Leeds United plc didn't retain, pay or employ Hayden Evans. So he must have been acting in a personal capacity for Allan Leighton, or doing it as a favour. Either way, it sticks in my throat to know that, while I was in angst about a way to keep Woodgate at the club, the levers for his departure were already being pulled. I just hope the fans can now take into account these other factors that have come to light.

Meanwhile, the new regime at Leeds United were determined I'd carry the can in many other respects, too.

THE BLAME GAME

Peter Reid did the job and kept Leeds United in the Premiership. The team finished five places from bottom in fifteenth, having won fourteen of its thirty-eight matches.

With the season over, the real inquest began into the dream that died as the fans demanded to know the full story behind what went wrong. With no figurehead as the focus of the fans' abuse any more, responsibility became the hot potato passed around the board – and kicked back to my front door.

That summer, John McKenzie gave an interview to the *Yorkshire Evening Post* which would cement public opinion against me, making it sound like the plc had just removed its blindfolds, had its hands untied from behind its back, and suddenly stumbled across the extent of the debt, suffering an amnesia about how everyone from Allan Leighton downwards had digested and approved every decision and strategy. But it's always easier for public relations to blame the man who went as opposed to those still present.

In what was described as 'a thinly veiled attack on Peter Ridsdale', the deliberate impression was given that I was this spendthrift who had somehow acted unilaterally, and gone unchecked – and that's a stigma which has stuck to this day.

John McKenzie was reported as saying that he'd carried out a review of the books and uncovered largesse of 'an irresponsible and indulgent nature'. His findings were listed thus, and my annotations follow in italics:

— The total compensation to David O'Leary and Terry Venables
  was £5.7m.
  *But the board collectively agreed to terminate these contracts
  in the footballing interests of the club, and agreed the exact
  amounts of compensation payments.*
— £600,000 was spent per year on a fleet of over seventy
  company cars, including £70,000 on one vehicle, and
  suggestions I lorded it around the city in a chauffeur-driven
  car.
  *The truth was that I always drove the fifty-five miles from
  home to work in my own BMW X5, and we had forty-two
  cars. Just about every plc in this country has a fleet of vehicles
  for management and senior staff. As for the £70,000 on one
  vehicle, that refers to a pooled Mercedes, and it was contract-
  hired on a monthly basis and was never bought.*
— £70,000 was spent in one year on private jets for directors and
  senior management.
  *Private jets were only hired for the team for European games,
  or for club transfer business when expediency in the deal was
  essential. Every club that competes in Europe charters a plane
  because it's the only way to take the shortest and easiest route
  for a squad worth millions. Take, for example, a match in the
  Ukraine. To travel there by normal scheduled airline would
  have meant a Leeds–Bradford shuttle to London Heathrow, on
  to Moscow or Kiev and then many hours on a coach. That's no
  match preparation. When you're earning £7m (UEFA) and
  £20m (Champions League) for being in Europe, chartering a
  plane is a justifiable cost of participation, and there's not a
  team in Britain that doesn't pursue that same policy.*
— £20-a-month rental on a tropical fish tank in the chairman's
  office.
  *John McKenzie forgot to mention the second fish tank – in
  the boardroom. Those tropical fish cost £280 a year in a
  company turning over more than £80 million, and I was half
  expecting him to detail what I'd spent on first-class stamps.
  Today, the Chinese whisper is that I spent 'thousands on*

*goldfish'!! In the Far East, many offices house fish tanks for
good luck so when the poor run started under Venables, I felt
the fish could do no harm, and ordered two tanks for Elland
Road. The irony is that those damn fish have brought me
nothing but bad luck and much grief, and became the symbol
of profligacy.*

When McKenzie started going on about the fish, I knew there
was clear desperation to deflect blame. All his claims were either
taken out of context, sensationalized or inaccurate but the world
of football believed them. Worse still for me, much of the Leeds
fan-base believed him.

Suddenly, the public message coming out of Leeds United
was one of shock-horror over the debt and scale of the 'crisis' –
completely at odds with the plc's private stance at the March
board meeting, which accepted the club was 'capable of funding
an ongoing debt of £65m'. One calm, manageable strategy in
private. One alarming discovery to spin in public, all designed to
make me look like the incompetent idiot, and everyone else as
the innocent bystanders saddled with the consequences of my
mistakes. After that article, the press turned on me. I became
the whipping boy for everything that had gone wrong at Leeds
United. Yes, I'd made mistakes, like everyone else; honest mistakes, which I wish I could take back and put right. But to be
held solely responsible was cheating the fans of the truth.

And the hypocrisy was this. There it was, this club in dire
financial straits, and yet it approved an upfront 'consultancy
payment' to John McKenzie – an estimated £200,000 lump sum
on top of his reputed £100,000 salary. When costs were being
cut, and non-executive directors had decided to forego their
£35,000-a-year salaries, it never made sense to sanction such a
payment. In my eyes, it was unjustifiable. But John McKenzie –
who ultimately became executive chairman – preferred to concentrate on 'my' expenditure, not his.

With the air of a man riding to a club's rescue, he predicted he could turn the club's finances around but warned: 'It's like an oil tanker that is heading straight for the rocks and the shareholders have put someone else on board to turn it around. The trouble with oil tankers is they're two miles long and they don't turn around in two minutes.'

It was a dramatically dark analogy to paint, yet there hadn't been talk of rocks ahead in board meetings, where the coast was clear, and the storm manageable. With lucrative assets in the squad and gate receipts still bringing in £10m from 35,000–40,000 home crowds, plus planned cost cutting in senior and middle management positions, the club had a positive prospect of turning things around, and emerging just as strong as before. Behind the scenes, the board knew what it had to do to reach its manageable debt goal of £65m. It needed to sell two or three key players to raise around £13.9m. It hardly amounted to turning around an oil tanker.

But maybe John McKenzie, an adviser to a number of Japanese and Chinese institutions, preferred to see himself heaving and sweating at the wheel of an oil tanker. That way, if the new strategies succeeded, he'd be a hero. If they failed, as they ultimately did, then he could rely on the oil tanker being just too heavy for him, despite his best efforts.

As chairman, I accept that I'd allowed expenditure to get out of hand, allowing it to run away with our dreams. At times, I was breathtakingly naive and didn't stand up enough to David O'Leary. Fowler and Johnson were two deals too many. We speculated when we should have been more cautious; we fantasized when we should have been more realistic. We banked on success being self-financing and, for a time it was.

But we were not wrong to link success on the pitch with increased profits and revenue. Nor were we wrong to invest in players to chase that success. Where we were wrong was in buying *too many* big-name players because that overloaded the wage structure, which buckled when we failed on the pitch. We didn't have a contingency plan for the team falling out of the top five. As a plc board, we believed in our own success too early, and too much. But we were never deliberately reckless, and nor were we intentionally careless with the club's money. Indeed, we had auditors check and double-check everything we did.

In the January of 2003, we'd brought in a team from Ernst & Young to advise us. Moreover, one of its advisers, Neil Robson, succeeded Stephen Harrison as finance director. The expert overview was that we had to be seen to be taking the tough but correct management action to control the debt. Selling players was the quickest way to get our finances under control, said Ernst & Young. Hence the sale of Jonathan Woodgate. A club that had finished fifteenth couldn't afford to maintain a squad that had been assembled to compete in the Champions League. But, if we cut our cloth accordingly and freed some key player assets, the future would hurt but we'd remain healthy, or as 'healthy' as any other Premiership club managing substantial debts.

But, with me gone, the plc board also had one fundamental decision to make that was crucial to Leeds' survival in the Premiership – it needed the right calibre of manager who could return success to the pitch, and revive the team's fortunes, with all the renewed financial upturns that would bring. It needed a manager capable of sending Leeds United back into the higher echelons of the Premiership. It needed, more than anything, to get that one decision right.

•

Three things staggered me as I watched events unfold as the deposed chairman. Peter Reid was appointed permanent manager, Harry Kewell was sold for a net £3m, and not a single other player was sold in that summer, when the club needed to realize savings of £13.9m to reach the 'manageable' debt goal of £65m.

The Peter Reid appointment was a crazy decision when you consider the plc had agreed during my tenure that he was only ever going to be a quick fix. But the directors performed a volte-face that sent the team backwards, not forwards. It made the mistake of believing that a man who could stave off relegation in eight games was good enough for an entire season of thirty-eight matches. It was like saying the winner of the Lincoln Handicap was good enough to win the Epsom Derby. Peter Reid was what Leeds needed to climb out of the basement. But a wholly different calibre of manager was required to push for the honours. They all knew that, but they ignored the form book. I despaired from the sidelines, knowing it was the wrong appoint-ment but knowing my opinion no longer mattered.

Peter, true to form in the transfer market, brought in *ten* new players, eight on loan, two on frees, including six from overseas. But none of them made a collective impact on the pitch – only on the wage bill. The club should have been selling two or three players, not adding to the squad.

Meanwhile, to compound matters, £10m-rated Harry Kewell was sold on the cheap. One of the biggest talents on the club's books was allowed to switch to Liverpool for a net £3m. This was the deal that made me itch to get back in there and scream, 'What the hell do you think you are doing?' But I'd only have been accused of throwing stones in glass houses. I'm not passing the buck here. I knew where I'd gone wrong. But I also had this strong sense of knowing what was required to put things right again. I knew that Harry had scored a wonder goal in the 3–2 victory over Arsenal in the penultimate game which had enhanced his value to around £10m. Leeds needed to maximize their asset at a time when Manchester United expressed interest and joined Liverpool at the table. In that position, a high-stakes auction was in the offing. Had John McKenzie had experience of wheeling and dealing in the transfer market, he might have known that.

Instead, Leeds mishandled a golden opportunity and virtu-ally gave Harry away in a deal which attracted the incredulity of BBC *Match of the Day* presenter Gary Lineker. Incredibly, on 9 July 2003, Leeds agreed a £5m deal with Liverpool, of which

£2m was paid in commission to the player's agent, Bernie Mandic. This was, apparently, a payment 'for work he had done in Australia for Leeds United', according to evidence given in the High Court of London when Gary Lineker's comments in the *Daily Telegraph* brought a libel action from Harry Kewell before the matter was settled out of court in 2005.

What had actually happened was that John McKenzie had written a letter to Harry's agent saying that, if he could get a bid of around £5m, he'd receive £2m commission.

Who in their right mind authorizes a commission that represents 40 per cent of a transfer deal? Did John somehow think that by offering that incentive, Kewell's agent would go out and seek a higher price? Indeed, Leeds would later go on record saying they expected the deal to fetch around £7m. But you can hardly blame Bernie Mandic for settling at £5m when he had a player that wanted to move to Liverpool and could turn to Rick Parry and say, 'I've got a letter here saying Leeds would accept £5m – let's do business.'

It was commercial madness in the strategy adopted, the fee that was obtained and the staggering commission that was given away.

The sweet irony was that the plc's internal investigators and the FA's 'sleaze-buster' Graham Bean had come knocking on my door over a £1.75m commission (on an £18m transfer) to Rune Hauge and yet the new regime of Leeds United was backing a bizarre £2m payment (on a £5m transfer) to Bernie Mandic!

But still, the world and his brother didn't bat an eyelid. Leeds slipped to eighteenth position by the end of September, and the supporters chanted: 'Ridsdale . . . are you happy now? Ridsdale . . . are you happy now?'

•

I despaired over the politics at Leeds United at times, but whatever differences of opinion were faced within the football club, the politics doesn't get in the way of one essential rule: the board's business was transparent and had to be approved collectively.

If only the same could be said for the Football Association.

I was part of the FA's International Committee which created a smaller subcommittee charged with appointing the next England coach after Kevin Keegan's abrupt departure in 2001. I was one of the 'seven guilty men' who appointed the Swede, Sven-Göran Eriksson, to the English post, and it was a decision which didn't win universal backing at first – not even on the FA's own subcommittee.

For Sven was not the members' first-choice coach, and I was one of the majority who voted for the then Newcastle United manager Sir Bobby Robson to be given his second stint in charge, and to appoint a younger coach alongside him. That way, we would have groomed the future manager alongside the wise owl.

Adam Crozier, the FA chief executive, was dead against this option but when it was put to a vote, he lost and the majority voice won. That decision sent him north to St James' Park to approach Newcastle chairman Freddy Shepherd. Not surprisingly, Freddy wasn't in the mood to lose his manager and he rejected the approach. This suited Adam. He wasn't going to argue too vehemently with that rejection. With his heart not in it, he was hardly going to spend time trying to prise Sir Bobby away. Both Adam and David Dein, the erstwhile vice-chairman of Arsenal, had been insistent that Sven-Göran Eriksson was the future.

For those of us who believed an English coach should be appointed to the England job, we were perceived internally as behind the times and lacking vision. Adam, who had set a six-year target to win the World Cup, was adamant that Sven was the right man. He couldn't have been happier when Newcastle blocked our approach because that freed him and David to meet Sven, our second choice, and do the deal.

At our next main board meeting, the appointment was

confirmed. Once Adam had expressed his delight, I asked to see the contract and paperwork, to examine the details. But he refused, and adopted a need-to-know attitude – and clearly the rest of the FA subcommittee, in his eyes, didn't need to know.

I was stunned. I asked why we were being denied such information. Adam expressed a fear that, if he told the meeting, one of us could leak it to the press. So we weren't allowed to see one document pertaining to our new employee's contract on the presumed scenario that it could lead to a leak to the media. It was farcical. But that was typical of Adam's classically secretive style. Whenever he was on weak ground, or challenged about 'sensitive' information, he'd retreat because he was, he said, fed up that details from meetings kept appearing in the Charlie Sale column in the *Daily Mail*. Here was the man charged with 'giving the FA the kind of direction and sense of purpose that used to be lacking in the moribund, arthritic organization' (as the *Guardian* put it) and yet he was acting like a furtive, over-paranoid political spin doctor, trusting no one but his inner circle. Until the day I left Leeds, I never did know a thing about Sven's contract, and that's the kind of situation which would never have been allowed to happen within a plc football club.

It wasn't so serious all the time, though. I remember the day when Sven was asked to attend the FA's international committee meeting to offer an explanation after his affair with Ulrika Jonsson was exposed in the *Daily Mirror*. A sheepish-looking Sven sat next to chairman Noel White, and launched into a rambling, long-winded apology. When he finished speaking, there was an embarrassing silence and most people, including Sven, stared down at the table, looking at their hands, wondering where to look and what to say. Not even Noel White could find the words that would break the ice. Then a broad Yorkshire accent broke the silence from beside me. It was the no-nonsense Barry Taylor, now chairman of the FA-Cup committee and director of Barnsley, and he said, just a little too loudly: 'Eeee, there's no need to be embarrassed, Sven – we're only fuckin' jealous!' And the room fell about laughing.

•

The goldfish-tank headlines had turned me into the walking legacy of LUFC; the legacy that had wrecked the club. No one would touch me in the business world, and headhunting firms suddenly had nothing to offer me. None of this helped a confidence which was already shattered.

In the introspection that comes with having time on your hands, even I questioned my judgement, and wondered whether I'd lost the business touch that had given me such a buzz, and such success, in the retail world before being tempted by the dreams of Leeds United. My self-doubt was beginning to feed on the headlines just like everyone else. But I knew that I needed to get back to work, earn a living, and restore my reputation. Even if no one else believed in me any more, I had to prove a thing or two to myself.

I'd not intended to return to football. Had someone said come and be the managing director of Marks & Spencer, I'd have jumped at the chance to return to my old world. Sophie, of course, tends to disagree – she's convinced I couldn't resist the drug that is football.

Funnily enough, she wasn't surprised when M&S didn't step forward.

Instead, I was invited into preliminary discussions with Oldham Athletic, Luton Town and Queens Park Rangers to talk about getting involved with new investors. Nothing came of those talks, except it tended to prove Sophie was right, as always. Then Barnsley Football Club, which had recently gone into administration, made an approach through Barry Taylor. Call me a glutton for punishment, but a light turned on within me, and the chance of getting involved with another Yorkshire club in the Second Division (now named League One) excited me. It also helped that I was being asked to work alongside lifelong

Barnsley fan Patrick Cryne, who was investing the lion's share of the £7.2m needed to rescue them from administration. I also agreed to invest my own money, a gamble placed on my own abilities. And so six months after leaving Leeds, I returned to the chairman's office as part of the takeover at Oakwell. I'd be lying if I said I had no motivational interest in proving people wrong. Whatever the reasons, I felt renewed by the experience.

By December 2003, we'd steered the club out of administration and reduced the wage bill, and we later replaced manager Gudjon Thordarson with Paul Hart (one of my recommendations for the Leeds job). He made the key signing of Stephen McPhail and loan signings of Ross Turnbull, from Middlesbrough, and Michael Chopra, from Newcastle, and the team mounted its serious challenge for promotion into the Championship.

Further up the M1, Leeds United was up for sale and facing administration. John McKenzie had stepped down as chairman, and the team propped up the Premiership under Eddie Gray, who'd succeeded Peter Reid when he was sacked in November after a 6–1 defeat at Portsmouth, the club's worst league defeat since 1959, leaving them rock bottom.

As for Leeds being on the brink of administration, I don't believe the debts from my tenure were wholly responsible. I've accepted responsibility for the errors I made but another key reason Leeds were facing insolvency was that the new management structure hadn't taken the necessary action to save more money.

John McKenzie later boasted in his 2003 yearly report about a £20m cost saving being made but such talk was all smoke and mirrors because such a saving was, in the main, the annualized impact of business already done in the January transfer window before I left, removing the wages of Dacourt, Fowler, Woodgate, Bowyer (and then Kewell) plus their transfer fees.

How I yearned to be putting right the wrongs at Leeds,

instead of Oakwell. But I was restoring my own confidence, and pleased to be part of a deal that saved Barnsley FC from extinction. I stepped down in December 2004, with the club well on its way to a healthy future, to allow Patrick and current chairman Gordon Shepherd to put in place their vision for the club. (Barnsley went on to secure promotion to the Championship at the end of the 2005–06 season.)

Ironically, the *Yorkshire Post* summed up my contribution with these words: 'In the last 14 months, Ridsdale has served Barnsley with genuine pride and put a ship that was sailing too close to the rocks back on a safer course.'

Meanwhile, John McKenzie's oil tanker had hit the rocks, and Leeds were relegated into the First Division (now the Championship), having won just eight games all season.

Once more, managerial appointments had been a major factor. The lunacy of appointing Peter Reid full-time had come home to roost, and then they'd compounded matters by making Eddie Gray his successor. I've nothing against Eddie as a person, and he was a legend as a Leeds player but he was never going to be the man who could stave off relegation. Far from making better decisions in my absence, the plc board seemed to be going from bad to worse. Once they were relegated, Kevin Blackwell was installed as manager but the loss of Premiership status led to an exodus of talent: Alan Smith, Paul Robinson, Ian Harte, David Batty, Jason Wilcox, James Milner, Mark Viduka, Aaron Lennon, Dominic Matteo, Scott Carson, Nigel Martyn and Michael Duberry.

It also meant the financial problems were multiplied tenfold, and the implications were massive. A mid-table Premiership club can expect to earn £25–30m in TV revenues, whereas a First Division club (excluding parachute payments) could expect around only £1m. Leeds had dropped into another planet.

The greatest myth is that they were relegated *because* of the debt. But debt doesn't relegate teams, especially when the squad had, while still in the Premiership, remained intact. The truth is that relegation was the result of the wrong managers being appointed.

Make no mistake, Leeds had the playing talent to survive. And I absolutely believe that with the calibre of that team, with the right manager, they would not have gone down. But no one is prepared to believe that. As one angry fan wrote to me, 'We were forever shackled by the decisions taken by you!'

I soon realized that whatever happens to Leeds, and whatever decisions were taken in the years that followed, I'd always be the one carrying the can. The PR hatchet job wielded by John McKenzie had proved his one effective decision.

Only striker Alan Smith tried to provide a balanced overview of the situation at Leeds before his enforced sale to Manchester United. In Phil Rostron's book *Leeds United: Trials and Tribulations*, Smithy gave his take on the demise in fortunes:

> Two or three years ago, no one would have expected Leeds to be in the First Division. You would just not have imagined it. In hindsight, maybe we could have taken a step back then but, when it's all happening, as it was then, you want to push forward and build because you are striving to win something. A lot of fingers have been pointed and a lot has been said but I'm not going to blame anyone for it because when we were in the semis of the Champions League no one was moaning about us buying players and paying big wages.

Alan was, like me, Leeds through, and through, but not to the point where he was blind to the errors made in the period that preceded the crisis. United we stood. United we fell. Marching On Together. But the blame-game had changed all that. Even Smithy got stick for crossing the Pennines because certain sections of the fans couldn't understand that Leeds just had to offload someone of his talents in order to survive. Leeds once attracted big-name stars because the strategies were working, and the club was flying in the right direction. Times had changed and, for his contribution to Leeds United, Smithy deserved gratitude and good wishes for his move to Old Trafford; a son moving on to better himself.

•

In March 2004, a Yorkshire-based consortium led by Gerald Krasner completed the purchase of Leeds United, allowing the club to avoid administration by taking over the assets and liabilities of Leeds United AFC, and ensuring £80m of debt was wiped away in a deal with three major creditors who accepted, instead, a percentage of monies owed.

This was only made possible after the sterling work of financial whizz Trevor Birch, who replaced John McKenzie as chairman in December 2003. He bought crucial time for Leeds, staved off the creditors and negotiated for the right consortium to come in. So the core debt was wiped away; they were no longer saddled with the debts we'd left behind.

So there was a clean slate; no crippling legacy for which I could be held responsible because that legacy had been dealt with. Leeds were back to where they were in the pre-Howard Wilkinson days but with new management in place, new strategies to follow, new people to take responsibility. Leeds were like any other relegated club: the likes of Sunderland, Birmingham City, Sheffield United or Leicester City. In their renewal, there was hope of returning to the Premiership – depending on the management decisions that were taken from that moment onwards. I fail to see how I could ever be held responsible for the future of Leeds. But, as the inexorable decline continued, that's exactly what would happen.

I had other things on my mind – such as clearing my name of wrong-going.

When Krasner took over, the plc arm of the club was wound up and that meant one thing – the Department of Trade & Industry's Insolvency Service was duty-bound to investigate the plc's financial activities. This exhaustive inquiry would take two years, and examine every cashflow forecast, every expenditure and every player transfer to determine, once and for all, whether there had been gross mismanagement or improper financial conduct.

•

In early 2005, I received a phone call from Sam Hammam, owner of Cardiff City, saying he was in trouble, and needed my advice.

When we met, he looked like a man with the world on his shoulders, and when he outlined the mammoth financial burden besetting his club, I could see why. If Leeds thought it was in dire straits, you should have seen Cardiff's figures. It had £30m of debt, compared to a turnover of £9m. It had seemingly no chance of finding air to breathe.

Compare that with Leeds, which, when I left, had a £78.9m debt and an £86m turnover with player assets to realize. Forget steering an oil tanker, saving Cardiff was like raising the *Titanic*. Suddenly, the grim realities of football around the country, and away from the higher reaches of the Premiership and its Sky TV jackpots, was plain to see. Here was the poverty that few in the Premiership get to grapple with.

I couldn't see a route to salvation for Sam, and he was no longer the same man who had happily taunted David O'Leary and the rest of us three years earlier when they dumped Leeds out of the FA Cup.

'I think it's an impossible situation,' I told him; 'if you're still in business in a few weeks' time, give me a call and I'll see what I can do.'

I walked away, honestly expecting Cardiff to have folded before the phone rang again.

But Sam somehow kept them going, and I relented to his constant pleas for help. Sam is tenacious, and won't stop until he gets what he wants. So on 1 April 2005, I agreed a three-day-a-week role to work as a consultant.

'You're basically here to advise me how to get out of the shit!' he said on day one.

My first job was to inject a dose of realism into his world. With £30m of debt and £1.7m owed to the Inland Revenue and with no means of paying it back, drastic action was needed. Creditors were threatening to close Ninian Park so the first thing we needed to do was buy time, and get those same people to trust in the club, to see that we were aggressively pursuing a route out of trouble. It wasn't easy. After the first three months, I felt we weren't going to achieve anything yet, in that time, I'd seen the passion and enthusiasm from everyone involved at the club, and I shared their determination to grind out a solution, and make the maths work. I also felt for Sam – he'd put his heart and soul into Cardiff. He'd made mistakes, he'd been over-ambitious at times, but he wanted the best for Cardiff City, and he had my empathy. All I could think was that if this was my club – if this was Leeds – I'd bust a gut to save it, for Sam, for the staff, for the fans. So that's what I stuck around to do.

The only way of keeping the club alive was to get investors to put money in. But I emerged from meeting after meeting with investors and the local council with the same message: 'We'll only invest money in Cardiff if there is a change of control.'

Informing Sam of this harsh reality was a tough task. His heart really was in the club, and to have to wrench it away from him was a bit like asking a parent to hand over their only child. But Sam knew his sacrifice would save Cardiff. As the majority shareholder, he selflessly voted in favour of a new regime. He saw the rope to pull him and Cardiff out of a hole, and he grabbed it. At an extraordinary general meeting, it was agreed to dilute the shares to authorize new sources of investment, and Sam's shareholding went from 82 per cent to less than 4 per cent in one fell swoop. Investors backed Cardiff with multimillion-pound cash injections, and financial stability was restored. I was installed as chairman, and it was agreed, as part of a package that was put together, that £9m of debt – and historic interest – would be off with a formula to write off the remaining balance. We had, by then, paid back the £1.7m to the Inland Revenue, and £2m of outstanding fees to architects who had drawn up plans for a new stadium that had been going nowhere.

But the bottom line with investors was that, if Sam didn't go, they wouldn't come in and the stadium project would have collapsed (the debt was restructured around the creation of a new stadium).

Those measures combined to save Cardiff City FC.

My only regret was that I'd never been given that same chance at Leeds but when you don't have the will of the people, it's impossible. At Cardiff, fans doubted me at first, and I didn't blame them. 'What hope have we got with you in charge?' asked one email.

But, credit to them, they stood back and gave me a chance. Here was a club in a capital city with plans for a new stadium drawn up on paper, and with every chance of establishing itself as a Premiership club if its finances were in order.

We had to have a clearout of players and spend a small proportion of the transfer fees received to rebuild the squad at a fraction of the cost, without weakening its ability to maintain Championship status. We sold Danny Gabbidon and James Collins to West Ham in a joint £3.1m deal, Jobi McAnuff to Crystal Palace for £600,000, and then Cameron Jerome to Birmingham City for £3m. When you start raising such fees at a club with a turnover of only £9m, it's incredible business, equivalent to Leeds raising £40m in transfers.

Another crucial component of turnings things around was the appointment of the right manager, and that's why we appointed former Southampton and Wolverhampton Wanderers manager Dave Jones, a man with a Premiership pedigree for a Championship team. He's a down-to-earth, brilliant guy who's as much at ease sat in my office as he is in the dug-out, and has superb man-management skills. In a strange way, because of the way both Southampton and Wolves dispensed with his services, we had a common objective – to prove our doubters wrong. He's also the first manager to allow me as chairman to sit in the dug-out! When we played away at Molineux in January 2007, Wolves had persuaded the Football League to ban all of our supporters because they feared crowd trouble. In protest, I refused to take my place in the directors' box or accept any hospitality. Instead, I remained in the dressing room throughout Dave's team-talk and joined him on the bench for the match.

'There's only one condition for you being here – and that is that you keep your mouth shut!' said Dave. He'd obviously become well-used to Sam Hammam's presence on the bench. But for me, it was a memorable experience, and I left with a bump on my head as a result of an overexcited jump as Jason Byrne scored our winner on his debut, and I clattered the top of the dug-out shelter.

Being with Cardiff meant an inevitable return to Elland Road. The first time was in December 2005, two and a half years after my departure, but it was clear feelings were still running high.

A few days before the game, I received an anxious phone call from the Leeds chief executive, Shaun Harvey, who was clearly hoping beyond hope that I wouldn't be turning up.

'I've been asked by the police and safety advisory group to ask whether you intend to come to the game . . . We're very nervous about it, Peter,' he said.

I hadn't even thought about not going. 'Yes, I'm coming. You're not going to try and stop me, are you?'

'No, we just want to make sure that, if you are coming, the proper security is in place and you're protected, and we wanted you to know how hostile it's going to be.'

I wasn't naive. Memories linger long in the football fan. But I wanted to go for Cardiff, and I *needed* to go for myself because it allowed me to break the taboo of not going back, a bit like confronting a phobia.

In public, Leeds insisted there would be no extra security measures but they ensured I didn't drive to the ground, and asked that I enter and exit the stadium on the team coach. We brought our own security guards on the bus and, as we arrived at our hotel on the city outskirts, there were about ten police outriders shepherding the bus.

'This is way over the top,' I overheard one officer say. 'What on earth do they think is going to happen?' I wasn't nervous. Once you've driven through a baying mob of Galatasaray supporters, nothing can faze you.

I sat beside manager Dave Jones. He looked at me as if I had the plague. 'Why are you sitting next to me?' he said, in mock horror, 'Why should I be at risk if anything comes through that bloody window?!' Inside the ground, he made me disembark first. 'Go on, you get off. If there's anything being thrown, it's hitting you first!' and the entire team burst into laughter behind him.

There was a tiny pocket of a protest – about twelve fans – but I really did feel that the majority of Leeds fans were more concerned about the result that day than the ex-chairman. I felt the club had been whipped into a mini-panic by a media coverage that had Leeds boss Kevin Blackwell speaking under headlines such as 'Blackwell's Peace Plea'.

Inside Elland Road, everything felt surreal. This stadium which had once meant so much to me had lost its magic, and felt like any other away ground. I felt nothing.

The Kop spent about five minutes ridiculing my name but it had been a lot worse when I'd been chairman. In fact, on this occasion, some corporate supporters shook my hand, and wished me luck. There was something else starkly different – the ground seemed half empty; less than 21,000 fans turned up that day, a far cry from the near 40,000 capacity we used to pull in every other week. Then I noticed the directors' box had been moved. When I was chairman, we sat to one side of the halfway line, just off-centre. But under Ken Bates, the enclosure had been moved directly in line with the halfway line. It was like I'd returned to my old house, found some stranger living there, and all the furniture had been moved around. And the atmosphere didn't feel the same. It just didn't feel like home any more.

We won the game 1–0 thanks to a Jason Koumas goal. I was wise enough to sit down and stay still as the rest of the Cardiff fans celebrated. Maybe the Bluebird blood hadn't yet been infused into my veins. Or maybe it was just common sense in the circumstances. Either way, I got through the afternoon without incident and felt that, whenever our sides met again, I could return with a semblance of normality. But I was mistaken.

Come the 2006–07 season, Leeds were still suffering the hang-over from losing the previous season's Championship play-off final, and after soaking up some early pressure, Willo Flood gave us a 1–0 victory, and three points stolen again from Elland Road.

After the match, I walked down the steps of the directors' box to return inside the stadium, and into the chairman's suite, where everyone was gathered. As I entered, Ken Bates shouted across the room, 'You can fuck off – get out of here now, and don't come back!'

I thought it was a boisterous joke at first because, before the match, Ken had made comments blaming my reign as chairman for the club's ongoing financial troubles. But the silence that followed his outburst confirmed it was no joke.

I didn't know what to say other than, 'What have I done, Ken?' and I walked over to him, stood there in the far corner of the room.

'You know exactly what you've done . . . Your behaviour in the directors' box was unacceptable,' he said.

I wasn't going to stick around and be made to feel unwel-come again at Elland Road. So I wished him well for the rest of the season, left the suite and went to the dressing room to join Dave Jones. I've not spoken to Ken since. I thought about his accusation – 'your behaviour in the directors' box was unacceptable'.

When Flood scored, I stayed in my seat. One year on, I was perhaps a little more passionate than on my first visit, but it was no more than a double clench of my fists, and a loudly whispered 'YES!' The way Ken was carrying on, you'd think I'd jumped up and down. He surprised me that day. What doesn't surprise me is his continual focus on my 'legacy' that he's continuing to fight. And the events at the end of the 2006–07 season would give him even greater reason to shift the focus from his record in office at Elland Road to mine.

In one of those twists that football's natural sense of drama always throws up, Leeds United's survival in the Championship partly hinged on our result at Ninian Park on the penultimate weekend of the season. Our opponents were Hull City, and both sides were scrambling over one another to get clear of the trapdoor into League One (the old Third Division). If Hull and Leeds achieved the same result, the relegation issue would go to the final game of the season, and that was the outcome I was praying for. I didn't want to even think about the result of our game being a determining factor in Leeds' relegation. But the fact was that, if Hull won and Leeds lost or drew, Leeds were down.

With two minutes of normal time remaining in both games, it looked like a stalemate that would be settled on the final day of the season. Hull were beating us 1–0. Leeds were ahead of Ipswich by the same score. Then, in another unbearable twist, Alan Lee equalized for Ipswich with a flick-on header. Alan was the player I'd transferred from Cardiff just twelve months earlier. Hull's directors, ears stuck to their mini-radios, let out a cheer.

I shut my eyes, and cupped my face in my hands.

The final whistle blew at Ninian Park, and Hull had won. But in Leeds, the fans had invaded the pitch, causing the referee to halt play. It took police and stewards another thirty minutes to restore order before the ref could bring the teams back out to complete the final ninety seconds. I was in the boardroom as Hull's chairman, Adam Pearson, the former commercial director at Leeds, paced outside, waiting on the result. His cheers, and the domino cheers that rang out from the boardroom, confirmed their survival, and Leeds' demise, dropping into the third tier for the first time in the club's history; set to play at places like Cheltenham and Gillingham, a world away from the not so distant memories of the Nou Camp and the San Siro. I was gutted for them but I was also pleased for Adam. He's done a great job at Hull, turned things around and worked tirelessly. So I was torn between not wanting to see either my old club or an old friend go down.

It was because I was with Adam that in the spirit of the occasion I decided to be hospitable, and mark our visitors' survival by opening a bottle of champagne. I'd have offered it to any other visiting chairman in the same circumstances. Adam was stood at the top of the steps leading from the boardroom to the directors' box, looking down on the pitch, his nerves still frayed. 'I needed some fresh air!' he said.

'Here, take this,' I said, handing him a glass of champagne, 'congratulations!'

It was just my luck that a stray journalist, no doubt still tapping his match report into his laptop, spotted this gesture. Next thing I know, it's being reported on BBC Radio Five Live that the two former Leeds directors are cracking open the champagne to celebrate Leeds' demise. It led to a volley of outrage on the radio phone-in, and a bombardment of emails to Cardiff City over the next few days. I appreciate how it must have *appeared* in the twisted perspective of an observant journalist, but neither Adam nor I was pleased about Leeds' relegation. Nothing saddens me more than to see their plight. The club – and especially the fans – don't deserve it.

Ironically, on Friday 4 May 2007, I found myself in the offices of Cardiff City Council, preparing to sign the final contracts to gain 'unconditional' status for the new stadium, and place £58m into the council bank accounts to fund the project. As soon as I'd put my signature to paper, my mobile telephone rang. It was a friend telling me Leeds United had gone into administration, and faced an uncertain future as Ken Bates sought to revive the club again. The timing of those two events on the same day struck me as an odd synchronicity. In two years at Cardiff, we'd saved the club and taken it from a basket-case going bust to signing off on approval for a stadium project that had appeared dead in the water.

In that same two years, Leeds had gone from Premiership contenders in the play-off finals of the Championship to relegation into League One. That day, the contrasting worlds and fortunes of football could not have been starker. It was a bittersweet moment. I've only ever wanted success for Leeds United – as a fan, as chairman, now as a former chairman. More than anything, I want Leeds – now out of administration – to prosper and climb back to its rightful position as a top club, but that all depends on the right management decisions being taken, and the right manager being found. I couldn't be sorrier for what has happened to that great club, and for my part in that tragedy. But, as the stories of both Barnsley and Cardiff prove, there is a way back, and nothing would make me happier than to see Leeds United rediscover a winning attitude, using the lessons learned from the past. The baton has now passed to Ken Bates. It's down to him and the next manager, and I wish them good luck.

EPILOGUE

My history is Leeds United. My future is Cardiff City. I'm not going to be forgiven in Leeds, regardless of the mitigation I've now written. My job now is to move on and look ahead. I can't wind the clock back and handle things differently.

The DTI inquiry into the running of Leeds United during my chairmanship concluded in December 2005, and was publicly announced in the New Year. All members of the plc were cleared of any wrong-doing. The DTI accepted that mistakes had been made but that we'd acted properly at all times, and followed appropriate corporate practice. It was both a relief and vindication after what had seemed like a constant besmirching of all our business capabilities. If I couldn't be cleared in the eyes of the fans, then exoneration by the government powers was good enough for me. After all, they had scrutinized the minutiae of every document and transaction, and not relied on newspaper headlines, and the deflections of subsequent regimes at Leeds.

If I had my time again at Leeds, I'd more be stringent and cautious. You don't learn lessons in football when you're flying high; you learn lessons in times of crisis. I learned more in my last six months than I did in the previous four and a half years. The strategy we went for was a bold one and we came pretty damn close to succeeding. However, there is no escaping the reality that, despite an exciting journey, we failed. For that, I'm sorry. In future, I would not place so much faith in one manager's ability, and I would build the possibility of under-performance into the budgeting equation.

It went both brilliantly and terribly wrong in my time, but it's equally gone just as wrong in the years since I left.

Leeds were good enough to make the play-offs in the 2005–06 season, knocking on the door of the Premiership and, back then, Ken Bates was spoken about as the man who had 'performed a mini miracle'. Leeds were firmly back on track, putting the past behind them. But then they squandered that chance, and suddenly it was my fault again! It seems that a lot of the financial issues of the past have become convenient excuses for present-day failures. Sooner or later the likes of Ken Bates will need to accept that he – and only he – is currently responsible for the fortunes of Leeds United; that he and only he is responsible for appointing Dennis Wise as manager. Sooner or later, he'll stop looking over his shoulder looking for others to blame, and start looking ahead. By the way the club handled its emergence from administration, it has meant Leeds going into the 2007–8 season with a fifteen-point deduction. So before a ball is even kicked, the mountain Leeds has to climb is that bit steeper. It was a sanction imposed by the Football League because it decided that the process through which Leeds came out of administration was not the normal route followed by other clubs. It was another irony that I found myself as one of the seventy league chairmen who convened in London on 9 August to vote on that sanction following Leeds' appeal. Once more, I grappled with the fan within me, but I've learned my lessons about being led by emotion and I had to act as a chairman, in the interests of football as a whole; my vote was not against the fans of Leeds but decisions taken by its management. It is why I was one of sixty-four out of seventy chairmen who voted in favour of a sanction, and one of the fifty-four who voted in favour of the fifteen-point deduction. I saw Ken Bates in the hotel lobby, and we didn't exchange words. There was nothing more to be said. He must now get down to the serious business of reviving a great club.

I think that the rest of football – and especially those clubs in the Premiership – should perhaps look at the story of Leeds United and realize that the finances, fortunes and gambles inherent within this volatile market don't make 'the Mighty Whites' a unique and pitiable exception. The Leeds story might well provide the template of how not to chase glory but it also acts as a warning that such a precipitous descent is a possibility stalking clubs with blind ambition, just waiting for them to fail. Its danger lies in the voice of supporters crying out for team investment, shouting for those multimillion-pound stars to be bought; it lies in the manager's talents that will one day stumble and fall; it lies on that road to riches that the days of Sky TV has laid out before us all, tempting us to keep up with the Joneses, tempting us to live beyond our means. These days, my feet are firmly on the ground and yet my sights remain set on a life back in the Premiership.

The future at Cardiff looks exciting and secure. In Dave Jones' first season in charge, we achieved mid-table respectability but the rebuilding was still going on. Then, in the 2006–07 season, things started to click, as Dave forged a talented team that led the Championship for three months, assisted by the goal-machine that is Michael Chopra, signed from Newcastle for £500,000, and now at Sunderland after a £5m transfer. We were vying for the play-offs with about ten games to go but our form fell away towards the end of the season and we finished a disappointing thirteenth after we were hit with a series of suspensions and injuries. But Cardiff have made their presence felt, and proved they are capable of competing in the top six of the Championship, with a real potential to push for the Premiership for the first time in the club's history.

You can sense the expectations rising around Ninian Park. Already, that is beginning to show in the postbag and emails we receive. One season-ticket holder wrote to me at the end of last season, bemoaning how the team could drop from first to eleventh in a matter of months. Then he wrote this: 'You lot are clearly not serious about getting promotion, and that's why you've refused to invest in the team. If we are to believe your ambitions, when are you going to start matching them with proper investment worthy of a Premiership challenge?'

I know enough about the journey from hero-worship to demonization to treat such spending demands from fans with a wry smile. I felt like writing back to that supporter, and many more like him, to explain that I've been here before, and to trust me on this one. I'm a lot more risk-averse and prudent these days, without losing the ambition to move things forward, and I can cope with impatient fans, hungry for success.

But you only have to be around Cardiff to sense there is a buzz in the city about all that is possible for its football team. We've made seven exciting new signings for the 2007–8 season, including Robbie Fowler; the second time I've managed to tempt Robbie away from Anfield. His appetite for the game never ceases to impress me and he's bound to make an impression on the Championship. But he did make me laugh when our paths crossed for the first time since he'd penned his book about his transfer away from Leeds. He seemed wary of me and asked if everything was alright between us. 'Course it is!' I said. 'Why shouldn't it be?'

'Well, coz of all that stuff I wrote about you in my book,' he said, somewhat timidly.

'Robbie, don't worry – just wait till you see what I've written about you in mine!'

Another player from the Leeds past has also asked that we let bygones be bygones – Jimmy Floyd Hasselbaink. I was holidaying in Orlando, Florida, in July 2007, still in negotiations with Robbie's representatives, when he called me on the mobile, wondering if Cardiff would be interested in his services after his release from Charlton Athletic.

'Jimmy, you told me to fuck off and said you never wanted to speak to me again!' I reminded him.

'Yeah, I know . . . but that's history, and I've matured a lot since then,' he said, as friendly as you like.

'No,' I said, 'what you mean is that you're unemployed!' and we managed to bury the hatchet and have a laugh about it all.

With the team Dave Jones has now put together, Cardiff fans have every reason to feel excited.

The new stadium will be worthy of Premiership football, and the community seems to be getting more and more involved with the club. Just before the end of the 2006–07 season, I decided to open the doors and allow the fans to spend an afternoon with the players. The 'ambassadors' – the loyal season-ticket holders – queued in their hundreds to have shirts and balls signed, and pose and chat with their heroes. In my childhood, I'd have given anything to have had such an opportunity with the likes of Gary Sprake and Billy Bremner. And to see young fans – and their fathers for that matter! – grinning in awe to be in such close proximity to their heroes made it a special day.

As I stood against a pillar talking to some supporters, one little boy, dressed in bluebird blue, tapped me on the back and asked if I'd autograph his football. As I found space for my signature, he looked up and said: 'Mr Ridsdale? Who do you like better – Cardiff or Leeds?'

I looked at him, thinking of how to respond to an awkward question posed by a boy no older than ten.

'And be honest,' he added, cheekily.

His dad was stood right behind him, equally keen for the answer. So I told them the truth: 'I'm giving Cardiff City 100 per cent of everything I've got, and I'm enjoying the challenge of ensuring this club finds the success it deserves. I love Cardiff City, but there'll be a small part of me always looking out for Leeds United, too. You must remain loyal to your roots.'

The boy blushed, took back his ball and rolled it in his hands, taking in all the players' autographs he'd collected that afternoon.

'Thank you, Mr Ridsdale,' he said, 'I want to have your job when I'm older.'

His dad and I burst out laughing, and the boy blushed some more.

'If I were you,' I said, and I pointed across the room to striker Michael Chopra, 'I'd go for *his* job first. It's a much better life, believe me.'

'BLUEBIRDS FLYING HIGH'

Like most things in football, the script wasn't being followed. Not long into Act I of the 2007–08 season, someone inserted an ugly twist into the plot, and our league dreams were thrown into Cardiff Bay with lead weights tied around the base.

Robbie 'God' Fowler and Jimmy Floyd Hasselbaink had instilled fresh excitement into an expectant audience, and a big-thinking management team was keen to produce a blockbuster which transcended the previous season's form, in the push for promotion to the Premiership. It was a happy ending every Bluebird visualized over and over in their heads. What no one had foreseen was a bombshell from stage left, just three days into the new campaign.

A rambunctious creditor filed a lawsuit demanding immediate payment of a £24m debt – a potentially crippling action which came armed with the capability of placing the club into administration. For a minute (and it was one minute which lasted eight months) it felt like I'd been regressed to the bad old days, turned away from the land of hope and rehabilitation, and deported back to the hell of scandal and public condemnation.

Newspaper headlines of financial woe and incompetence returned to stalk me into Cardiff City's intended new era, casting a cloud over Ninian Park; the same cloud, some argued, that had dumped its monsoon of troubles on Leeds United.

Headline-writers were once again hyping talk of imminent 'financial disaster'. 'LEGAL GAFFE COULD BRING DOWN CARDIFF', yelled the *Daily Mail*. Even as far away as Thailand, one over-excited newspaper suggested: 'RIDSDALE UP TO HIS OLD TRICKS'. Then *The Times* declared in the autumn: 'BACKERS CALL FOR CARDIFF'S BOARD TO RESIGN', and the article read: 'Ridsdale admitted in his recent autobiography that when he discovered £30m debt, saving Cardiff would be like saving the *Titanic*. But the Cardiff ship is sinking much quicker than he thought.'

I remember reading such coverage with a rising sense of panic, like someone being confronted with an old phobia which the therapist had promised would never return. The future was conspiring against us, and returning me to the past. I could hear them laughing in Leeds, backed by a cackling chorus of 'We told you so . . .'

Our ship was taking in water not because of anything we had done. It was in danger because we were being torpedoed by one of our own creditors, Langston, over a debt agreement which predated my chairmanship. Yet, not surprisingly, it was perceived to be my fault, and one fan's irate email provided a distant, tiresome echo: 'It appears my beloved club is on the brink of administration. You are responsible for this. Where has the money gone? You are a disgrace Mr Ridsdale to the good name of Cardiff City. If you have any decency, you will tender your resignation asap . . .'

Here we go again, I thought. So much for 'pastures new'.

The dire reality was that Langston wanted us to pay back £24m, loaned to the club under the previous regime and chairman, Sam Hammam. It was he who had ultimately agreed to pay back it back in 2016 on terms which reduced the loan to £15m, and handed Langston the naming rights to the new stadium at a value of £9m. But, without warning, the creditors seized on a contractual technicality, thought they'd found a loophole, and served a writ. Suddenly, a club with an approximate annual turnover of £10m had a £24m gun to its head.

If the legal action went against us, administration was inevitable, with the inherent consequences of a ten-point deduction in

the league. I dread to think what downward spiral that would
have triggered. What exacerbated matters was that no one knew
exactly who was pulling the strings at Langston – a company
with origins shrouded in mystery after its previous dealings with
the ex-chairman. We didn't know who they were, they jjndidn't
want to meet, and certainly didn't want to talk. What also made
this odd set-up feel increasingly strange was that lawyers refused
to unmask their key brokers. Yet, according to a judge who
ultimately heard the case, our evidence promised a real prospect
of establishing our suspicions that the creditors' 'governing
mind and will' was steered by one man – none other than
Sam Hammam, the very man who had saddled the club with
the loan in the first place.

My own view was that no matter who was behind Langston,
their legal action was designed to put pressure on a Ridsdale-
led board to resign, allowing someone else to seize control of a
club which was suddenly back on its feet and looking forward
to renewed income streams derived from the new stadium. But
this would have still spelled administration and trouble for
the future, and that was a prospect I was determined to avoid,
for the club and our fans. We'd worked too damned hard to
carve out an exciting new future for it to be undone by a lawsuit which, in my opinion, was both mischief-making and
unjust. I could never understand how, by any stretch of the
imagination, such a lawsuit had the interests of the club at
heart. Besides, we were in the right to resist repayment until
2016, in line with the terms agreed. Yet it was clear we faced
an intransigent force, determined to drag us all the way to the
costly indignity of the Royal Courts of Justice in London to try
its luck. So the fate of Cardiff City would be left in the hands
of a judge and his interpretation of the specific complexities of
a loan contract.

We kicked off the new season with the Sword of Damocles
hanging over Ninian Park. I could have screamed with helpless
frustration because I recognized that legal defeat was a possi-

bility, and that would mean we'd lose everything. The fear of going bust would hang over us for the majority of the season and, consequently, would strangle our finances, debilitate our progress and leave me in a recurring nightmare.

•

Walking into the Municipal Club in City Road, Cardiff, was like entering the lion's den. Like most working men's clubs, it's not a place for the faint-hearted or thin-skinned. Or, for that matter, a besieged football club chairman. But one cold night in November 2007, I found myself pitched into the hot seat to face the wrath of angry fans. Results had not been going our way, and the team hovered just two places above the relegation zone. I walked into a spartan upstairs room, with a bar to the right, and the chatter died away, intimating that someone unpopular had just entered the fray. I call this group the 'lieutenants' of the fan base because Sam Hammam used to take them out, give them the inside track and involve them intimately with the decision-making process at the club. With his departure, their influence may have diminished but they are still a valuable sounding board, so their collective voice remains important.

I shook a few hands diplomatically, then looked around and noticed one chair stood empty in the middle of the floor. I took my seat, turning it around so that I sat with its back in front of my chest. A horseshoe formation of other chairs faced me, occupied by about twenty moody-looking 'lieutenants' of the Cardiff City fan-base, arms folded and scowling.

'He's the worst manager we've ever had, and he has to go!' barked one man.

'And if you're going to stick by him, you can go, too,' said another, defiantly.

The venom and antagonism levelled at Dave Jones was emphatically expressed in an atmosphere which can only be described as tense and highly emotional. This fiercely loyal band of supporters echoed the impatient sentiments that had poured into my email inbox, too. 'The man is taking us backwards, get a back bone and sack him!' was one, typical of the hundreds of missives that bombarded my computer.

We had won three out of fifteen Championship games, drawn six and lost six. When coupled with the back-end results of the previous season, that meant 49 points accrued from 50 games (so the statisticians informed me). But I was at the games, too, and was witnessing results which belied the truth of the football being played. We also drew matches in which we had pummelled the opposition, and suffered two back-to-back 1–0 defeats because in both games we had missed a penalty in the 90th minute. There was nothing fundamentally wrong. Not only that, but it seems too many supporters were forgetting that, just two years earlier, Cardiff had travelled to Gillingham on the penultimate game of the season, needing a point to avoid relegation to League One. Yet Dave Jones, steadily and effectively, had ensured his side had finished 11th and 13th – the best for some thirty years in the club's history. I therefore failed to see how he could be the 'the worst manager we've ever had'. On the contrary he was, to my mind, the best manager the club has had in years, and the architect behind the team's constructive, solid pass-and-move football.

It's not as if we were playing awful football and getting trounced; far from it. So I, for one, was not prepared to mimic the short-term haste shown by other clubs, in removing the manager at the first sign of trouble. I learned my lesson at Leeds not to pander to an emotional minority, and I was determined to stick to my guns with the long term in mind. Far too many clubs take the populist decision to sack a manager without giving thought to his replacement.

It's easy to sack someone, far harder to find an improvement. As chairman, I didn't think there was a better manager in our division than Dave Jones. Manchester United didn't build their empire with a short-term strategy. They spent years building solid foundations, and believing in Alex Ferguson long before he delivered success. Besides the financial argument, their story is a lesson in the value of keeping your belief and being patient, as long as the performances and potential remain consistent and lively. That's what I told the fans at the Municipal Club that night: Dave Jones is the man, we're backing him, so let's hold our nerve.

A day earlier, the club board had decided to back the manager as the clamour for his head grew in both the fan forums and the South Wales media. We stuck to a professional perspective as opposed to being swayed by a panicking, popular vote. When I had met Dave for a chat in his office at the training ground, he was unflustered by the fuss over his position. He's not a man who is easily affected by outside pressure, abuse or insults. He's a man who sits with a quiet belief in himself, and cracks on with the job. He's as cool as ice when the heat is on, a good man to have around in any crisis, and he instils an unemotional calm into his players, too.

I didn't have a moment's doubt in placing our faith in him. I remember explaining the events of the previous days, and the decision we'd reached as a board. We're not a chairman–manager partnership that indulges in analysis, so the short and brief conversation went something like this:

'Can you sort it?' I asked.

'Yes, of course I f****** can,' he said in his thick Scouse accent.

'In which case, you have the full support of the board. Go and do it,' I said.

Cardiff City went on to win ten out of their next sixteen games in all competitions, and Dave deservedly won the January 2008 Manager of the Month award.

•

Above the main entrance to the Cardiff City boardroom, there is a framed photo of legendary captain Fred Keenor trotting down the once-famous Wembley steps. He's cradling the FA Cup to his chest like a newborn, while being mobbed by fans wearing bowler hats and trilbies. I've often stared at those sepia-toned images from 1927, unable to associate the club I know with the distant glory of its history.

At the start of the 2007–08 season, as the hardback edition of *United We Fall* went to print, a friend joked about how fitting it would be if we could somehow recreate that Wembley dream. We stood there, looking at all the framed images in the club's Fred Keenor suite, like two schoolboys looking up at the moon and dreaming that one day they would set foot on it.

'I'd be happy if we got as far as the fifth round!' I laughed.

'I'd be happy if we got through the bloody third round for a change!' he replied.

Seventeen minutes into our third round tie in January 2008, his head must have been in his hands . . . because at that moment we went 1–0 down to British Gas Southern League Division One Midlands side Chasetown, through an own goal by Kevin McNaughton.

Dave Jones had been banned from the touchline so had to sit with me in the stands. 'If we get knocked out by this lot, we'll never live it down!' I said, leaning over to him.

'And if I get banned from the touchline again,' he replied, 'remind me never to sit next to you again. We've only played seventeen minutes, and you're already panicking!'

Goals from Whittingham, Ramsey and Parry eased my worries as we avoided a banana skin quite comfortably in the end, but I'll never forget the day for its carnival atmosphere. This, for a club with average crowds of two hundred, was *their* cup final, and the day captured the magic of what the FA Cup is all about.

I think I decided there and then that an FA Cup run is not good for the blood pressure.

Meanwhile Langston's £24m debt, and the looming court case, continued to strangle the club and deter would-be investors. Our budget for the year had received a further equity injection with more cash for club shares, and the flow of substantial joining fees from sales of seats in the new stadium. But no one wanted to inject money into a club with an uncertain future, or buy seats in a stadium that might become defunct. So both those income streams – totalling around £4m – were lost, and the legal bill to defend the club from such action was well on the way to its final total of £500,000. A club with an annual turnover of £10m cannot sustain financial blows on that scale, and it meant we were operating on a month by month basis.

Things became so bad that it even reached the point where we had to haggle for a bargain over Christmas decorations for the players' party. I was back to a life of waking at four o'clock in the morning, number crunching on the calculator, and yet this seemed far, far worse than the predicament at Leeds because the scale of the debt outweighed the value of the assets and the squad. This meant it was ten times more stressful than anything that occurred at Elland Road.

Two things happened that kept the club going: first, the decision to sell two players – Chris Gunter to Spurs and Steven McLean to Plymouth – during January's transfer window, and second, the revenues from a continuing good run in the FA Cup. By the end of February we'd conquered Hereford United and then Wolverhampton Wanderers, surprising many with our progress into the quarter-finals. But the cup run wasn't just keeping expectation levels on the boil, it was also helping keep the club alive. We needed to stay in the tournament because we desperately needed the revenues.

Dave Jones was effectively managing a team with both hands tied behind his back, unable to add to his squad at a time when the team needed strengthening. I felt his frustration because we needed to capitalize on a rich vein of form by building on the progress he'd made. But our backs could not have been tighter against the wall. We couldn't even afford to bring in a loan player. Langston's action had almost brought us to our knees and, as the court date loomed at the High Court in March 2008,

I couldn't with any confidence predict what would expire first –
the FA Cup run or the very existence of the club.

•

Mr Justice Briggs had already heard one case by the time the
matter of Langston v Cardiff City FC Ltd was called to the
Royal Courts of Justice on the morning of 12 March 2008 for
its two-day hearing. He'd just presided over Mr Graham Calvert
v William Hill, and thrown out a claim by the punter who
unsuccessfully argued that the bookmaker exploited his gambling addiction, and, therefore, he didn't owe them a £2m
account debt. It was ironic that a gambling case preceded us
because, as I walked through the Gothic entrance of the famous
courthouse with our legal team, it felt like we were gambling
with the future of the club, while backing our judgement, our
argument and our sense of fairness. All the newspapers preview-
ing the case spoke of us standing 'on the brink of financial
disaster'. For once, that was no exaggeration.

I sat in the courtroom with the same helplessness that grips
me on match days, unable to influence events taking place
before me, save for shaking the hands of the key players and
wishing them luck. We stated our case, and then had to wait
for a further seven days for the considered outcome. Thankfully, Mr Justice Briggs ruled in our favour, saying we had 'a
real prospect of a successful defence', and should not be sub-
jected to a summary judgement. That decision felt like a 90th
minute equalizer in a crunch match; there was no sense of
euphoria, just an overwhelming feeling of relief. It meant the
case could, technically, proceed to a full hearing but, according to Sam Hamman, Langston are now in the mood to negotiate by opening discussions about the way forward. If they are
truly interested in protecting the future of the Bluebirds, this
sensible option, which was always open to them in the first
place, will be explored by both parties. In the meantime, the

threat of administration had been lifted, and the future was secure.

Dave Jones always said it felt like we were 'thirty minutes away from administration' at every stage of the 2007–08 season, and I admired the way he, his staff and the players kept a professional focus throughout a campaign which was unavoidably distracted by off-the-field events. But when the darkness cleared that week, we were able to see a much brighter prospect on the horizon because, suddenly, we would find ourselves one game away from our first FA Cup final in eighty-one years.

The quarter-final at Middlesbrough (played three days before the court case) was a fixture many had signposted as the end of our adventure. But there was only one side who looked like a Premiership outfit that day, and it was the team in black and yellow. We soaked up the pressure for the frantic opening minutes but then Peter Whittingham curled home a beauty after ten minutes, followed thirteen minutes later by a power-header from Roger Johnson. The elation on Roger's face as he was mobbed by Gavin Rae and the rest of the lads summed up both the electric charge and the disbelief that consumed the city that afternoon. We defended like giants from that moment on, kept playing fine football and there was no way back for Boro.

It was a major result against all the odds and, somewhere in the back of our minds, we dared to entertain thoughts about making our own history, and superseding 1927 with the achievements of 2008.

I couldn't believe it when the draw took place for the semi-finals at Wembley, and we were paired with Barnsley. Here was the club I'd helped rescue from administration and, in my opinion, had received little thanks. In fact, the owner Patrick Cryne had reportedly told the *Yorkshire Post* that I'd left no legacy to the South Yorkshire club. I found that hard to swallow. As much as I've tried to be diplomatic about my parting of the ways from Oakwell, it left me with a sour taste in my mouth and so the semi-final became deeply personal. In football, whether you are a player or a manager, it is human nature that you'll always want to turn over your old club to prove a point or settle a score. As a chairman, I felt I was let down by the management at Barnsley. There was no way I could even contemplate defeat, especially on such a grand stage.

On the day I sat there, in the Royal Box, on the edge of my seat. I couldn't have felt more sick, or more pressure, if I'd put every asset in my name on a correct-score bet. Even my wife Sophie was kicking every ball, heading away every attack, and punching me on the arm with every ounce of her frustration. She had shared the Barnsley experience with me and so it was personal for her too.

Then, in the ninth minute from Tony Capaldi's long throw-in, Joe Ledley hit a superb left-foot volley that gave us a 1–0 lead, and ultimate victory, bang, into the top-right corner of the net. That moment, that day, I tasted football ecstasy, screaming until I was hoarse as the referee blew his whistle. I kept telling myself, 'We've done it, we've done it,' but it wasn't sinking in – Cardiff City in the FA Cup final at Wembley. Out of 731 teams in the tournament, we were one of two finalists, alongside Harry Redknapp's Portsmouth. Travelling back to Cardiff that night, we cracked open the champagne on the team coach and, suddenly, eight months of grief over the court case – plus the tidal wave of demands to sack Dave Jones – melted away into an irrelevance. We were miles away from such nightmares, and enjoying the surreal surroundings of a blue-and-white fantasyland, cutting our own FA Cup final single with singer-songwriter James Fox and belting out the lyrics, for all of England to hear, to 'Bluebirds Flying High'. Win or lose, Saturday, 17 May 2008 was going to be an unforgettable, unbelievable experience.

•

When the big day arrived, and as the invasion of England began, we bought the London air and filled it with Welsh passion. We pushed aside the tedious repetition of the 'Big Four' finalists and injected a new energy into the greatest tournament of them all; we added a renewed shine to the FA Cup. And, to add to the fervour, we turned the FA's domestic cup into a final which became national in character. Cardiff v Portsmouth might as well have been billed as Wales v England, the red dragon breathing its fire into the face of St George.

The hairs on the back of my neck stood up to respect the Welsh national anthem, 'Land Of My Fathers', as Katherine Jenkins led the 25,000-strong all-Welsh, man, woman and child choir which filled the West Stand behind the goal. It didn't matter that I'm a proud Yorkshireman, it didn't matter that few of the team were Welsh, because the rousing Welsh anthem is enough to send the chills through even the most disinterested observer. There was no better sound than hearing our fans belting their hearts out, and no better sight than the many thousands of yellow and black flags fluttering and rippling from within that condensed mass of Bluebird blue.

In that moment, standing with Sophie in the Royal Box, I wanted to press the pause button and soak up the occasion. Like a child on Christmas morning, I was both reluctant and eager to unwrap the present, torn between devouring and savouring the magic. England coach Fabio Capello was seated to the right of Sophie and I wondered if he, or any foreigner for that matter, could ever truly grasp the soul-soaring significance of making it to the FA Cup final. Could you ever associate with what I'm feeling right now, I thought. Could you ever know what this day truly means to our fans?

For that matter, could the likes of Chelsea, Manchester United, Arsenal and Liverpool know what it truly feels like to reach a final against the odds, for the first time in 81 years, and taste the fine flavour of prestige and history? The 2008 Cup final actually *meant* something to both unlikely occupants of the Wembley dressing room. Not even Portsmouth's Premiership status could diminish the size of their achievement – first-time finalists for 69 years. Two underdogs ran into the stadium that day, breathing a gust of fresh air into a final to blow away its cobwebs. The unorthodox fixture alone was a spectacle in itself and, as chairman of Cardiff, I felt a pride that made me stand as tall and as vast as the Welsh pride which greeted the national anthem.

I thought about the man who had brought me my flask and sandwiches to Elland Road in 1965, when I'd slept overnight in the queue for a ticket, just like Cardiff fans had done for semi-final tickets against Barnsley. I looked back down the road from excited chairman to excited schoolboy fan, and could hardly believe this final destination. Dad, Mum, I thought, I hope you're both up there, sharing all this with me.

In the tunnel before the game, a silver-haired man stopped me and shouted, 'Can't have had much better days, eh, Peter?' He was spot on.

I attended four Wembley finals as a Leeds United fan: 1965, 1970, 1972 and 1973. I experienced some exultant nights in Europe as chairman of Leeds, and felt the electric charge of matches played in the Bernabéu and San Siro; and progressed to within one step of the Champions League final until Valencia put paid to that dream. But nothing – *absolutely nothing* – could beat reaching the FA Cup final as chairman of Cardiff. It was the most memorable day, the most remarkable occasion, within all of my football memories. The man was right – days don't get any more momentous than this.

I'd been visiting the dressing room to shake the hand of every hero who'd reserved that day in history. The Arrows' hit 'I Love Rock n Roll' was belting out from a stereo in the corner, pumping everyone's adrenalin. Dave Jones sat on a physio table, swinging his legs, as chilled as I'd ever seen him. Neil Kinnock described him that day as 'the calmest, most relaxed person in the whole of South Wales'. He couldn't have said the same about me. My legs had started vibrating with nerves shortly after noon, and I must have chewed more gum than Alex Ferguson does in an entire season.

When three o'clock arrived, and 90,000 fans erupted as the referee's whistle signalled the start of the match, we took the game to Pompey. As Joe Lovejoy later reported in the *Sunday Times*, Cardiff 'played football that was a credit to the Championship' and 'they were the equal of their more celebrated opponents'. Roy Collins, in the *Sunday Telegraph*, said we contributed to a 'feast of football' when compared to the previous year's final, and his colleague Duncan White added that Cardiff 'at times, played like the Premier side . . . and competed with intelligence'.

We were undone in the end by a stroke of luck for Portsmouth and a stroke of misfortune for our keeper Peter Enckelman, who, in the 37th minute, spilled a low cross whipped in from the right, and Kanu was there to bundle home the rebound. That one soft goal decided it; the additions of Ramsey, Thompson and Sinclair failed to find the equalizer. There was the silence of understandable dejection in the dressing room afterwards, no doubt heightened by a sense that the reality of an upset had been within our grasp. OK, we might not have wrested the trophy from the English and brought it back to Wales as they had done 81 years ago, but we are now able to frame a photo of the FA Cup final XI 2008 to hang beside the sepia image of 1927, and recall in vivid colour the Herculean achievement and effort which made heroes of the team that day. They were unlucky, brave and proud in defeat. Each man, in every round of the tournament, did the club, the fans and the whole of Wales proud. Meanwhile, Leeds United took its 'Mighty White' following to Wembley for the League One Play-Off final but missed out on a deserved promotion to the Championship. The achievement in over-turning the fifteen point deficit and making it to the final cannot be under-estimated and, whilst the disappointment was evident in their fall at the last fence, the 2007–08 season

proved that they will soon be back where they belong. The story
of Hull City's rise into the Premiership is an inspiration to the
likes of both Cardiff City and Leeds United, as is the return of
Stoke City to the top flight.

•

Who knows what the script holds for the 2008–09 season?
I'm hoping we'll by vying for the Premiership, no longer handi-
capped by the Langston episode. I'm convinced we would have
been up there last season had it not been for outside interference
but, in the end, we were six points shy of a berth in the playoffs.

It is a testament to Dave Jones that he took us so close, and
to an FA Cup final, against such a tortuous financial backdrop.
For those fans who were quick to judge him, too keen to insult
the board's belief in him, I hope they'll realize the lesson of time
and patience, and that our faith in the right man was well placed.
He, like me, like the fans, passionately believes that the sleeping
giant within Cardiff City is awakening from its slumber. Its
potential started to stir that day at Wembley and, with a new
stadium now taking shape, there is an excitement about the
future that few in Cardiff's football world have known before.

At the end of the Cup final, as I and the rest of the Ridsdale
clan came down the the escalators from Wembley's second floor,
I spotted four fans, in their thirties and bedecked in blue, waiting
patiently at the bottom. I suppose recent experience had condi-
tioned me to steel myself. Then, one of them stepped forward,
reached out his hand and smiled.

'Shake my hand, Mr Ridsdale?' he said. 'I just wanted to say
thank you; thank you for all you've done, and for giving us such
a memorable day. We'll never forget it.'

People often ask me what pleasure there can possibly be in
the life of a football club chairman. The answer is this: there is
an impossible challenge in pursuing impossible dreams in this
beautiful game. And when you touch, hold and taste the impossible, by taking Leeds United on a European odyssey or Cardiff

City to an FA Cup final, the joy and immense satisfaction contained within those short-lived but unforgettable moments far outweighs the grief, insults and abuse. Sometimes, it just takes a handful of fans to wait at the bottom of an escalator to remind me of that addictive truth.

Acknowledgements

It requires teamwork to publish a book, and I'm indebted to the people involved in a process which began in earnest in the summer of 2006.

There were many who didn't have faith in this project, and some who advised against it, but I was lucky to find a first-class team who believed in the importance of telling this story. Sometimes, history isn't pretty but that shouldn't diminish the significance of the events that took place, providing a necessary insight while also highlighting lessons to be learned, in life and in football.

I'd like to thank everyone at the publishers, Macmillan, for backing me: David North and not forgetting Lorraine Baxter, Georgina Difford, Neil Lang and Wilf Dickie. But special thanks must go to Richard Milner, who steered this book from concept to reality, an expert urging me on from the touchline; and to John English for his careful copy-editing. I'd also like to offer sincere thanks to literary agent Ali Gunn for never failing to believe my story would make it into print; ghost-writer Steve Dennis for shaping my life into words and teaching me more about myself than I thought possible (whether I feel better for the experience is a moot point!); and commentator Ian Dennis for not only introducing me to his writer brother but for being such an ally at BBC Radio Leeds before his move to BBC Radio Five Live.

I also owe huge gratitude to sports journalist and one-time fellow Leeds United director David Walker for being a true friend throughout the highs and lows at Elland Road.

I would like to thank every Leeds United supporter. Whether

you're one of those who blame me, or one of the indifferent minority, we still shared some great times and your support in adversity and triumph was incredible. I also offer you my apologies for ultimately letting you down.

Stephen Harrison, the erstwhile finance director, deserves a big mention. It was his outstanding work and professionalism that came to the fore when the DTI investigated our decision-making. His painstaking attention to detail was instrumental in the board being cleared of any wrong-doing, and he was an ally, friend and invaluable professional to have at my side when the going got tough. Lindsey Culley, my PA at Leeds, also deserves a huge thank you.

In more recent months, I'm thankful to the staunch support I've been blessed with from everyone at Cardiff City FC – the supporters, the players, the management and fellow club employees. They all gave me a second chance to prove myself, and our exciting journey continues.

Finally I would like to thank the people who matter most – my incredible family. First, to my sister Judith, who was recently diagnosed with cancer. She's a battler and has been there for me since day one, and she remains the one Leeds United fan who has never criticized me, and has stuck with me through thick and thin. My boys, Simon, Paul, Matthew and Joe, who have had to carry the weight of the Ridsdale name through their schooldays and business careers, absorbing the flak and abuse, without wavering in their love and support. And my wife, Sophie, and our girls, Charlotte and Olivia – words fail me when it comes to expressing my gratitude to you three special ladies, and I send you my love, thanks and apologies. You bore the brunt of the pressure, fear and intimidation that my job brought to our doorstep. Despite all that, you understood my love for Leeds United, and why it was all so important to me; it was your love and support that gave me strength back then, and continues to keep me going to this day.

I accept that there will be many people who'll remain bitter about my time at Leeds, and will not greet the telling of this story with open arms. But this is an explanation I felt everyone deserved to hear, whether you agree with its content or not. I'm not seeking to profit from a decline that saddens me more than anyone knows, and I'm not putting this story out there to make money. That is why I've decided to donate all royalties from the sales of this book to St Gemma's Hospice in Leeds. While chairman at Elland Road, my fees for all television work, speeches and personal appearances were donated to the hospice and I feel it's only fitting that I make this gesture as a final contribution so that instead of continued rancour and ill-feeling, something good actually comes out of this book.

Whatever your opinions, and whether or not you ultimately agree with my explanation, thank you for taking the time to read my story.

Peter Ridsdale

Picture Credits

The author and publisher would like to thank the following for permission to reproduce images in the plate section:

Ross Parry Agency Ltd: page 2 – top; 4 – inset; 5 – all; 6 – top; 7 – both.

Getty Images: page 6 – bottom; 8 – both.

PA Photos: page 4 – bottom.

All other pictures are from the author's private collection.

Index